Walk East Midlands

Fifty Day Walks in
Derbyshire, Nottinghamshire, Lincolnshire,
Leicestershire & Rutland and Northamptonshire

**Ramblers' Association
East Midlands Region**

Edited by Chris Thompson

Copyright © Ramblers' Association East Midland Region, 2005

Published by Sigma Leisure – an imprint of
Sigma Press, 5 Alton Road, Wilmslow, Cheshire SK9 5DY, England.

British Library Cataloguing in Publication Data
A CIP record for this book is available from the British Library.

ISBN: 1 85058 824 4

Typesetting and Design by: Sigma Press, Wilmslow, Cheshire.

Cover photographs, clockwise from top-left: Linacre Reservoir, Derbyshire *(Alec Stainforth)*; Nassington, Northamptonshire *(Bob Coles)*; Southwell Minster, Nottinghamshire *(Gordon Gadsby)*; Brinsley Colliery headstocks, Nottinghamshire *(Alec Stainforth)*; the green at Grimston, Leicestershire *(A.J. Payne)*

Maps: Bob Peck and Jeff Nightingale

Printed by: Bell and Bain Ltd, Glasgow

Disclaimer: the information in this book is given in good faith and is believed to be correct at the time of publication. No responsibility is accepted by either the author or publisher for errors or omissions, or for any loss or injury howsoever caused. Only you can judge your own fitness, competence and experience. Do not rely solely on sketch maps for navigation: we strongly recommend the use of appropriate Ordnance Survey (or equivalent) maps.

Foreword

Wonderful! How pleased I am to review this new book of walks in the East Midlands. What an excellent way to celebrate the beginning of a new millennium.

At the time of writing this foreword, the Countryside and Rights of Way Act 2000 (the CRoW Act) is being implemented. This gives walkers the right to roam responsibly on mountain, moor, heath, down and registered common land. Access to these lands has long been a desire of the Ramblers' Association, which has continued the movement launched by the Kinder Trespass in the thirties where several walkers were arrested, with some going to prison. Many of those people, some sadly no longer alive today, continued to be involved in campaigning for the cause many years after the trespass. The implementation of the right to roam legislation throughout England and Wales in late 2004 and 2005 is a great achievement by the Ramblers' Association. It has secured us all a right to walk responsibly on the beautiful wild places in this country. These places are part of our national and natural heritage.

The CRoW Act will also, over time, ensure that our unique footpath network is fully opened up for people to walk on. This is another element of the cause that is the Ramblers' Association. Walking in the countryside is fantastic for your health, it is a key contributor to the rural economy, it connects the town with the country and is key to understanding the importance and relevance of the conservation and environmental protection of flora, fauna and landscape.

I must congratulate Chris Thompson from Nottinghamshire Ramblers, along with the many others from neighbouring counties of the East Midlands, for compiling this walking picture of our region. I particularly like the concept of long and short walks, which gives me an opportunity of doing some of them.

To everyone who buys this book, you are assured of many happy hours of walking. If you are not a member of the Ramblers please join. Whatever your age or ability you are assured of a warm welcome and we need your support to continue our work. We protect the rights and defend the interests of all those who love to walk in the countryside. We have a fabulous website (www.ramblers.org.uk) with a great deal of information for walkers on it and hundreds of walks every week all over the country. Please phone our main office on 020 7339 8500 for further information.

Nick Barrett
Chief Executive, Ramblers' Association

Preface

The East Midlands has somewhat of a recognition problem. Most people have heard or read of the area but many would have difficulty in identifying the counties that make up this particular geographical region of England. That factor may also contribute to the region, which has much to offer the walker, being undervalued and overlooked. The purpose of this walking guide is to put right this state of affairs and to show what the region can offer to those who are prepared to seek out new pastures.

The Peak District of Derbyshire needs no introduction for it comprises a large segment of the Peak District National Park that attracts millions of visitors, many of them walkers, each year. To a lesser extent, Sherwood Forest in Nottinghamshire, home to the legendary hero Robin Hood, is a well-visited area and attracts many from near and far. It also offers some good walking country. But what of the remainder of the counties that comprises the East Midlands? In addition to the two mentioned so far the region includes Leicestershire, Lincolnshire, Northamptonshire, and the smallest county in England, Rutland, which has recently regained its identity and independence once more. All of these counties have much to offer the discerning walker prepared to venture into places that are not immediately known but are well worth exploring.

The physical geography of the region varies enormously: from upland limestone plateaux to low-lying fenland; from ancient granite outcrops to fertile river valleys; undulating rolling hills to woodlands of infinite variety – this region has all of these and they are awaiting to be discovered. In addition to this there are many historical places and landmarks to be seen in an area that has played its fair share in the shaping of our country

When devising this guide it was decided from the outset that to take full advantage of visiting the wide range of areas, which might include an overnight stay, the walks should mainly be long day walks from 8 to 15 miles. This arrangement departs from the norm of walking guides where most of the walks are geared to half-day forays, but research has indicated a need for longer walks and we hope this guide goes some way to fulfilling this requirement. For those who perhaps might find the distances a little beyond their capacity, many of the walks have a shorter option yet still retain enough interest to make them meaningful and enjoyable.

It is hoped that this compendium of walks, all of which have been compiled by members of the Ramblers' Association in the East Midlands, will encourage both those within the region and those from outside to walk and discover what this unfairly overlooked bit of Britain has to reveal.

Walks of this type are available every week with your local Ramblers' Association group. If you have enjoyed the walks in this book and enjoy the countryside, why not join the Association? For contact details see 'About The Ramblers' at the end of this book.

Editors' Notes

Ramblers' Association members in the six counties that make up the region have pooled their local knowledge and put together a diverse selection of walks for the inquiring walker to enjoy. There are 50 walks in total: ten for each county – Rutland has been grouped with Leicestershire – many with a theme. Some are historical, for the region is rich in history. Places visited include Bosworth where Richard III met his end, and Ashby St Ledgers in Northamptonshire famously associated with The Gunpowder Plot: Remember, remember, the fifth of November …. Other walks will appeal to those that enjoy natural history – the area has its fair share of woodlands and forests: Charnwood Forest, Bourne Woods and Salcey Forest to name but a few. Other revelations are waiting to be discovered.

It was the intention from the outset to avoid the most popular and well trodden areas, which in the East Midlands is dominated by the Peak District Park in Derbyshire. Indeed this area is largely ignored by us, although two walks do come within its boundary; but there is more to Derbyshire and some very attractive scenery can be found outside the Park. Do not be misled that apart from the heights of the Peak District the remainder of the region is flat. This could not be further from the truth as some of the walks prove. Even Lincolnshire, which many consider completely flat, defies this notion where the long escarpment of the Wolds provides elevated walking with fine expansive views. Each County has its own distinctive make-up and surprises. One feature synonymous with the East Midlands is that it has one of the longest rivers in England: The River Trent. It rises in the Staffordshire Moorlands and flows 170 miles to empty in the mighty Humber. A walk has been included where this confluence meets. even though it is accepted it is outside the normal boundaries of the region. Nonetheless, it is well worth visiting as are the other 49 walks that make up this guide.

As Lead Editor, and on behalf of the editorial team, I would like to thank and acknowledge the contributions made by all those to the publication of this book. Without their hard work and dedication it could well have fallen by the wayside; those that devised the routes, those that walked (and re-walked) the route; and those that put together the narrative, the maps, and the photographs deserve the highest praise. We must particularly thank Dick and Marilyn Harrison for the many hours spent at the computer typing up the walks. It has been no mean task bringing the final article to publication. And it has been tinged with sadness. Our cartographer, Bob Peck sadly passed away on nearing the completion of the maps; he did a splendid job and will be greatly missed. Thanks Bob, and thanks to Jeff Nightingale who stepped in to finish the task

Now all that is left is for you to put on your walking boots and discover what the East Midlands have to offer. Do not, however, forget to check over your intended walk with an Ordnance Survey map before stepping out.

Editorial Team: Chris Thompson (Lead), Alex Staniforth, Geoff Rix; Comments can be sent to Chris Thompson via the publisher or by e-mail to ThompChris@aol.com.

Acknowledgements

This project would not have been achieved without the full support of the Ramblers' Association members from all the counties of the East Midlands involving the areas and groups in Derbyshire Dales, SYNED (South Yorkshire & North East Derbyshire), Lincolnshire, Nottinghamshire, Leicestershire & Rutland and Northamptonshire.

We list lead members of each area and give our heart felt thanks to all the members who gave their time to this project in the surveying of walks.

Derbyshire Dales: Charles Wildgoose

SYNED: Christine Deacon

Lincolnshire: Alan Hull & Ron White

Nottinghamshire: Geoff Rix and Chris Thompson

Leicestershire: Alan Loasby and Stan Warren

Northamptonshire: Maurice Tebbitt

Contents

Huddersfield

Barnsley

A1

Glossop

M1 M18 Doncaster

Rotherham

Sheffield

River Ouse

21

River Humber

Scunthorpe

Grimsby

M180

22

23

Louth

• 11
Worksop

• 5
• 2 Chesterfield

1
Buxton

• 3

• Matlock
4

• 6

Derbyshire

• 7

• 8

M1

• 12

Lincolnshire

24

25

Lincoln

• 13

Mansfield

• 16

15

Newark-on-Trent

Nottinghamshire

• 17

• 14

A1

Skegness

Gibralter
Point

Sleaford

Boston

Nottingham

• 18

• 26
Grantham

• 28

27

Fossdyke

Derby

M1

• 9

• 10

• 19

• 20

• 31

Melton Mowbray

Loughborough

• 33

• 35

Leicestershire

• 38

• 34

• 32

• 29

Spalding

Sutton
Bridge

Oakham

• 36

37
Rutland

Stamford

30

M69

M1

Leicester

A1

Peterborough

Nuneaton

• 39

Market
Harborough
• 40

• 41

• 42

Corby

M6

• 43

Birmingham

Rugby

Coventry

Kettering

Northamptonshire

• 44

• 48

• 45

Northampton

47

• 46

50

Bedford

• 49

M1

Milton
Keynes

East Midlands

The County of Derbyshire

Derbyshire is a Mecca for walkers. The wild moorlands in the north and the mill-stone grit edges on the eastern side of the county are usually alive with ramblers, climbers and, nowadays, mountain bikers throughout most parts of the year, whilst the softer limestone landscape of the "White Peak" attracts visitors at any time. However when walkers speak of Derbyshire what they normally mean, in reality, is the Peak District National Park. A careful consideration of the relevant maps soon reveals that this covers only around two-thirds of the county. For the most part, the remaining third remains undiscovered by many – except for the locals and those with a sense of adventure who wish to explore further afield.

Most of the walks in this section attempt to guide people to some of the areas and villages which receive less publicity yet, nevertheless, deserve some recognition for their intrinsic beauty. It would be unfair and unrealistic to compile a series of walks in Derbyshire without visiting some of the well-known honey-pots. However, where this is the case we have chosen lesser-used routes in the hope that ramblers will be able to escape the crowds that are attracted to this lovely part of the country. The district of North East Derbyshire, which has the town of Chesterfield at its centre, possesses some magnificent buildings – notably the Elizabethan Hardwick Hall and Bolsover Castle, perched on a limestone edge and dominating the surrounding countryside. The ruins of Wingfield

Walkers on Eyam Moor – Walk 1 *(Photograph: Gordon Gadsby)*

Manor and Sutton Scarcliffe Hall are still impressive and one needs to make little effort in order to imagine their former glories. The landscape here, although partly industrial and not as dramatic as other regions, has much to commend it. The area is heavily wooded, especially in the steep valleys, whilst the two reservoirs at Ogston and Linacre offer many opportunities for circular walks.

Moving south to the Amber Valley District, the River Derwent lies in the bottom of another deep valley and has woods on either bank. Shining Cliff Woods, now in the care of the National Trust, is renowned for its magnificent display of rhododendrons that should not be missed. On the high ground, to the east, is Crich Stand, a monument to the Sherwood Forest Regiment, whilst further up the valley lies the hamlet of Holloway, once the home of Florence Nightingale.

Close to the city of Derby lies the small village of Dale, which possesses many treasures, the most significant of which is surely the 40ft-high window archway which is all that remains of Dale Abbey. The abbey was destroyed during the reign of Henry VIII as he tried to reduce the influence of the Catholic Church. The Hermit's Cave, just outside the village and the church with a former public house built on the side are well worth making a detour.

South Derbyshire is perhaps the least known part of the county but is still worth exploring. One of the walks follows the route Bonnie Prince Charlie took when he marched from Ashbourne to Derby as he attempted to gain the throne of England in 1745. The pretty village of Osmaston with its thatched cottages will surprise many who are not familiar with the area. The two major rivers in the district are the Trent and Dove, which have Rights of Way on one bank thus enabling several miles of pleasant riverside walking to be undertaken by even the least energetic ramblers.

If you only manage to complete half of the walks in this section, I think you will agree that the County of Derbyshire has lots more to offer than just the National Park.

Highway Authorities

Derby City Council,
The Council House,
Corporation Street,
Derby DE1 2FS   01332 29311

Derbyshire County Council,
County Offices,
County Planning & Highways,
Matlock,
Derbys DE4 3AG   01629 580000

Tourist Information

Derby: 01332 255802

1: The Highs and Lows of The Derwent Valley

An exhilarating walk around the Derwent Valley starting from the historic plague village of Eyam and visiting the Riley Graves where some of the victims were buried. The river Derwent is crossed at Froggatt Bridge where the route ascends through Froggatt and Hay Woods to Nether Padley. After passing Padley Chapel, the Derwent is rejoined and followed to the picturesque Leadmill Bridge before climbing up over Eyam Moor to complete a memorable day's walk.

Distance: Long Walk18km (11½ miles); Short Walk 11.3km (7 Miles)

Duration: Long Walk 6 hours; Short Walk 4 hours

Maps required: OS Explorer OL1 – Dark Peak; OS Explorer OL24 – White Peak; OS Landranger 119 Buxton, Matlock and Dove Dale

Starting point: Pay & Display car park in Eyam (SK216767)

Terrain: Moorland tracks and woodland paths, can be muddy

Refreshments: Several public houses and cafés in Eyam, café at Grindleford Station, The Plough Inn at Leadmill Bridge

Bus/Train link: Sheffield/ Chesterfield

The Route

1. Turn left out of the car park and left again onto the main street. Pass St Lawrence's church, the plague cottages and Eyam C.E. Primary School to reach the Square. Follow road signposted to Hathersage past Miners Arms, climbing uphill past Wesleyan Reform Church and just past this reach a road on the left.

Short Walk

1. Turn left up Riley Back Lane, climb uphill, and pass Woodside Cottage to enter a wood. Climb uphill, ignore the first path to the left, but follow well-marked route uphill to reach road. Turn right and walk to road junction. Take road towards Grindleford, passing Mompesson's Well on the left. Continue along Edge Road to reach road junction (Sir William Road). Take right-hand path over wall and cross Eyam Moor to a minor road.

2a. Turn left, passing Leam Farm and follow road round sharp left-hand bend with Tor Wood on the left. Where road bends sharply right at the edge of Tor Wood turn left onto a track to rejoin Long Walk at point 6.

Long Walk

2. Just past the last house fork left signposted to the Riley Graves, to follow a track bearing right at a fork to the Graves. After viewing the site continue on the track to a footpath sign, right, for 200m through a wood then descend to the right through Stoke Wood to a gate. With the wall on your left, descend to a road, which you cross to the stile opposite. Descend straight ahead over two fields to the B6001.

3. Follow the lane opposite to Froggatt Bridge, turning left into Hollowgate and immediately right into The Green, then left into Malthouse Lane. At the T-junction, turn right, uphill. Just before the top of the slope, bear left into Froggatt Woods, through a narrow gate. Follow the narrow woodland path to reach an inscribed memorial rock. (See points of interest.) In 250m cross some stepping-stones and in 15m turn right up a faint path, eventually to emerge through a gate into a clearing. Cross this to a gate and follow the main track to a footbridge, with an iron handrail. In 150m, at a path junction, bear slightly left gently descending to emerge out of Hay Wood into Tedgness Road. Follow this pleasant road to the B6251 at Nether Padley.

4. Cross diagonally over the road to metalled footpath. At the foot of the slope, turn right – passing the café and crossing the railway bridge near Totley tunnel and the foot of Padley Gorge. Keep on this track, bearing left to pass Padley Chapel and over a cattle grid. In a few metres, turn left through a handgate to re-cross the railway. Keep the wall on your left to bear right at the footpath sign and follow the obvious path through two fields to cross the railway again. Turn left over the bridge and follow the path through Rough Wood to emerge in front of Kettle House.

5. Cross a track then veer left under a tunnel. At the far side, turn right, then left to meet a farm access road. Turn right on the track, which you follow to the B6001. Turn left over Leadmill Bridge, then right down the lane to Abney Gliding Club. In 250m bear left down a farm track, cross a cattle grid, then turn half-left to a footbridge. Continue ahead with a wall on left, to join the access road to Hoghall, and then ascend to a minor road. Turn right onto road and almost immediately turn right again onto a track.

Short Walk rejoins

6. Follow track and keep straight ahead over three fields to enter a wooded area, above Highlow Brook, to find a new stile close to the brook. Follow the signed path for 1km to Stoke Ford. **Do not cross the bridge**, but go forward for 10m, then ascend left on a clear path, to double back on your route to pass Gotherage Barn on your left. Follow the wall round to the left, then cross a stile on the edge of Eyam Moor. Take the middle of three paths over the Moor to emerge onto a stony track, to the left of a radio mast. Take the stile opposite and follow the wall, left, all the way to a minor road. Turn right and in 300m descend to a track opposite Highcliffe Farm. Continue down the track for

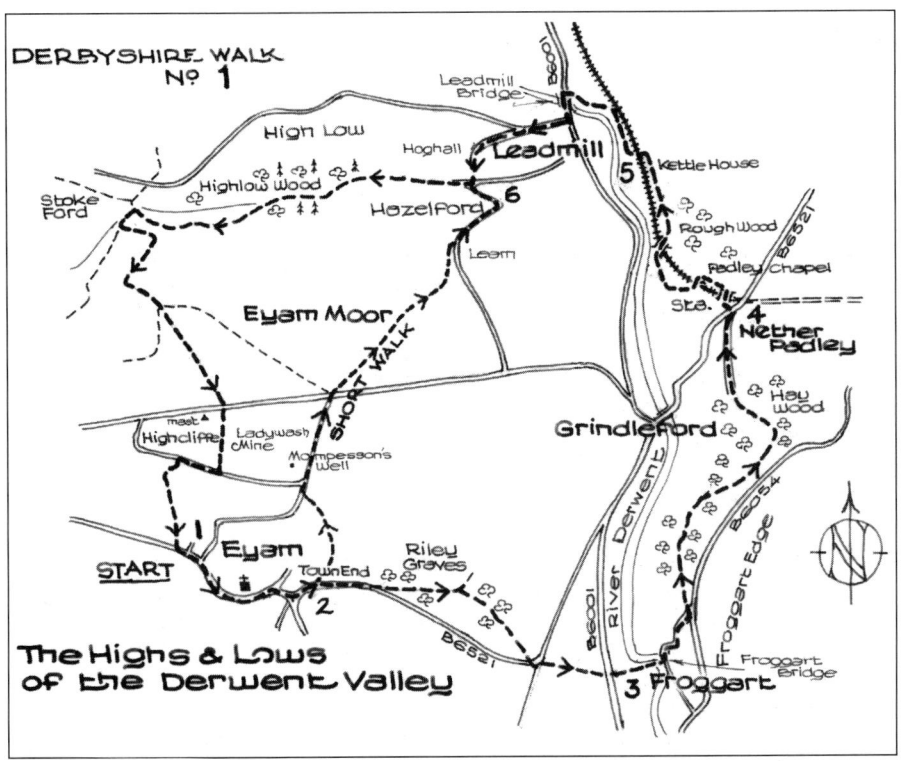

100m to a stile on right to follow a path through scrubland to cross a stream. Bear left and then in 150m turn left to follow the remains of a wall, left to a house. Turn right, then in 10m left into a fenced path, which leads round to the house front. Turn left (path between two walls). In 25m turn right and follow wall/hedge downhill to path between houses to main road. Turn left and in 250m, left again, back to the car park.

Points of Interest

Eyam – In 1665 a travelling tailor, one George Viccars, brought a consignment of clothes from London. This is alleged to have conveyed the deadly plague virus to the village. He died on 6th September 1665 and subsequently 80% of the population, around 250 people lost their lives. Today various reminders of this era can be found throughout the village, with hand painted signs explaining each site. In the churchyard are the remains of a Celtic cross and the grave of Catherine Mompesson, wife of the Rev. William Mompesson, who acted as leader of the village during the time of the plague. He later moved to Eakring in Nottinghamshire, where a cross marks the site of the 'Pulpit Ash', the scene of local church services.

The Riley Graves – Situated to the east of Eyam, close to the Top Riley Farm, lie the graves of six members of the Hancock family, who all died in the plague between 3rd and 10th January 1666. The site is now in the care of the National Trust.

Froggatt Wood – Another site now owned by the National Trust. An inscribed rock alongside the footpath states 'In memory of the parents, Charles and Josephine Bingham, Lady Riverdall presented 16 acres of Froggatt Wood to the N.T.'

Padley Gorge – The foot of the gorge lies adjacent to Grindleford Station and the mouth of Totley Tunnel. The Burbage Brook descends the gorge and after periods of heavy rain, the falling waters make an impressive sight.

Padley Chapel – Only the Chapel remains now, as part of Padley Hall in Upper Padley. This also has a grim history for in 1588 two Roman Catholic priests were captured nearby and taken to Derby, where they were hung, drawn and quartered.

Eyam Moor – An area of open moorland, above the village, which contains numerous Bronze Age tumuli and stone circles.

Ladywash Mine – Situated south-east of Sir William Hill, the mine now disused, was once an important source of iron ore.

2: Stone Edge and Linacre Reservoir

Discover some of the lesser known paths in a pretty area to the east of the Peak District National Park. From the ridge above Holymoorside the conurbation of Chesterfield, with its famous crooked spire can be seen, together with views of Bolsover Castle. In late April, the woodlands surrounding the Linacre Reservoir are carpeted with bluebells, whilst the hidden hamlet of Nether Loads, nestles in a delightful valley.

Distance: Long Walk 19km (12 miles); Short Walk 11km (6½ miles)

Duration: Long Walk 6 hours; Short Walk 3½ hours

Maps required: OS Explorer OL24 The White Peak; OS Landranger 119 Buxton, Matlock & Dove Dale

Terrain: Undulating, strenuous. Mostly good paths and tracks

Starting point: Linacre Reservoir Picnic Area. (SK336727)

Refreshments: Public houses at Wigley, Old Brampton and Holymoorside

Bus/Train link: Chesterfield

The Route

1. From the impressive information board in the car park, descend the wooden staircase to meet the main path. Turn right and follow this to the upper reservoir dam where you ascend some steps on the right to take first path on the left. Follow path until it meets footbridge, steps going down (ignore new bridge on the right), then go forward to the western end of the reservoir to meet Birley Brook. **Do not cross the footbridge** but continue forward on a faint path through the trees, keeping the brook on the left, to find a wooden stile crossing a stone wall.

2. Go forward between bushes then bear left, downhill, to cross a stream via stepping-stones. In 150m, take the wooden bridge and stile on the left to ascend a tree-lined gully into the hamlet of Wigley. Continue ahead then bear left to a crossroads. The Fox and Goose public house can be seen on the right, but go left along Bagthorpe Lane for 400m towards Old Brampton.

Long Walk

3. Opposite Riddings Farm Cottage (just before the Royal Oak) turn right through a stile. Go downhill, initially on a farm track, to veer slightly right to a stile. Over this, follow the wall on the right to another stile, cross the field to the right-hand corner and a third stile. Keeping the wall on your left, go forward to a stony lane, turn right and ascend into Wadshelf. When you join the road take the narrow alleyway on the left, next to the old chapel, opposite

School Lane, then cross two fields to the A619. Cross to the gateway opposite and follow the defined path over three fields to Hallcliff Farm.

Short Walk

3a. Walk past the Royal Oak public house and opposite the car park entrance turn right into a tarred lane. After 1km turn right, in front of "The Birches", then continue ahead passing through Frith Hall Farm to ascend to a T-junction near a bungalow named "Peakdale". Turn left along Westwick Lane, still on an enclosed track, for 1.5km to Ashgate (Go to point 11.)

Long Walk

4. Cross the small lane and ascend the steps to walk round the left side of the farm. Continue along an enclosed track and at its end take the second gate on the right to follow a fence on the left, to a stile underneath a power line. Descend through Hagg Wood to a footbridge and climb to a small stile to the left of Loads House Farm. Go forward, then contour around to the right to find a stile in front of the farmhouse, turn left over this to a road.

5. Turn left for 150m to where the road turns right, then keep ahead through a squeeze stile to enter a narrow enclosed path, turning right after 50m, then in a further 100m take the stile left into a field. After 10m go through a gap in the hedge on the right, then turn left to another stile. Over this turn right, then follow the hedge around to the left to pass through a stile by a gate. Go forward for 50m then, where the wall ends, turn right for 25m to a step-over stile and go forward to a second stile to emerge onto a farm access track. Descend, using the raised pathway on the left side of the track, to Nether Loads.

6. Just before the stream, take the squeeze stile on the left and in a few steps, a gate. Keeping the stream on your right, cross a small field to emerge onto another farm track. Go forward and where this turns right, keep ahead to cross an area of scrubland to an enclosed path on the left side of a plantation. This leads onto Loads Road, where you turn left and in 50m turn right up a track alongside a bungalow named 'Rivendell'.

7. Ascend gradually for 700m then bear right onto an edge path, overlooking the Hipper Valley. Continue for 400m, then step over a drainage gully and veer left, downhill, to the road. Turn right and in 30m turn left between two stone posts. Descend on the obvious path to a footbridge over the River Hipper then ascend, between stone walls, to Stonehay Farm. Bear left onto the access drive, then forward to a road.

8. Turn left and in 100m left again down the access road to Standedge Golf Club. In 300m, note the landscaped pond on the right with the unusual sign. If this is to be believed, you should start to walk 'snappily'. Continue uphill bearing right with the road to enjoy distant views of Sheffield. Pass the clubhouse and farm to a stile which leads onto the golf course – follow edge of

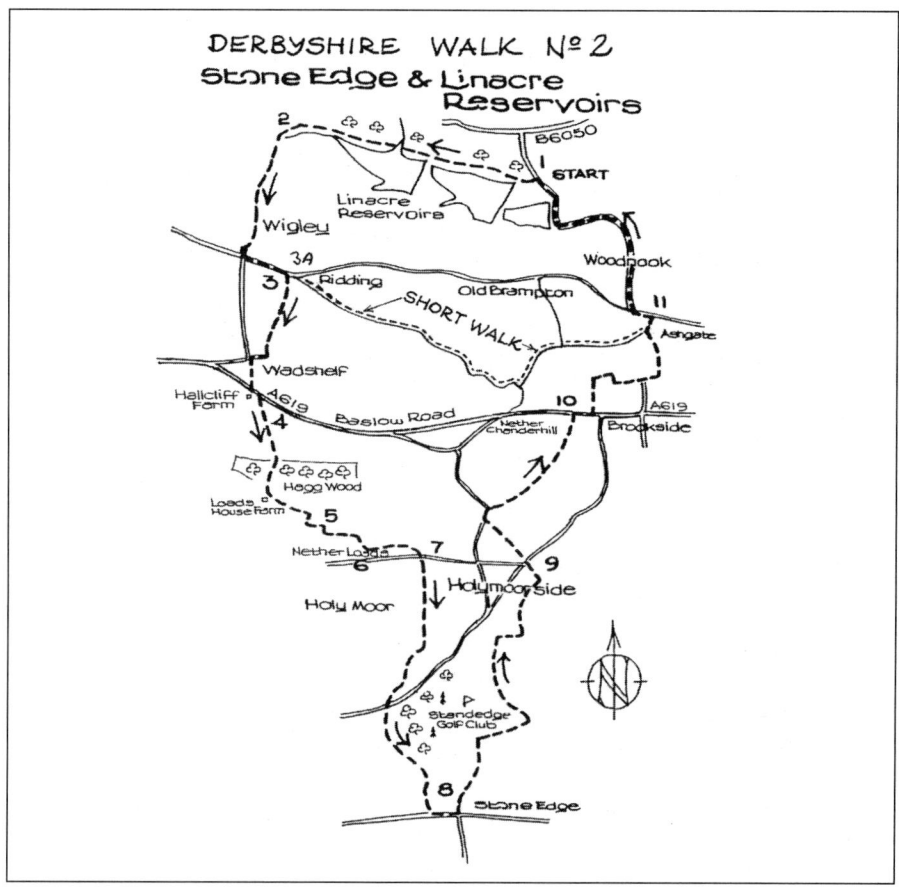

DERBYSHIRE WALK Nº 2
Stone Edge & Linacre Reservoirs

golf course path until just before gravel path turn right (sign just inside wood on left). Go forward for 150m to a path junction to turn left alongside a wall then along the wood edge to find a footpath sign pointing right. Follow this enclosed track downhill to a stile by a gate then ahead for 30m to a crossing track. Turn right, then left at Woodside Farm and in 100m enter woodland. Follow the perimeter path, passing the picturesque old millpond to emerge onto a minor road in Holymoorside.

9. Turn left to the Bulls Head inn and a crossroads. Go forward into Loads Road then turn right in front of the Lamb Inn. After 30m turn left up Windyfields Road and at the top, go forward between houses, to a field gate to cross three fields. At the fourth, veer slightly right to a stile onto a road, turn right and in 75m turn right again on the access road to Woodhead Farm. In 10m, take the stile on the left to cross an arable field, then turn half-right to another stile.

Turn half-left to descend to a muddy field entrance, go through this and ascend to a tree then a telegraph pole. Continue to find the stile in the field corner. Cross this then turn half-left to a footbridge then forward half-right to descend into an enclosed track. Turn left and climb up to the A619 road.

10. Cross the road and follow the paved path on the right for 100m to a stile on the left alongside Fairfield Farm. Follow the headland path to find a stile on the right; go over and continue in the same direction to a farm. At the multiple footpath sign, turn right, then go forward to a stile on the right of Leadhill Farm. Turn right over this and at the next stile turn left to follow hedges to a footbridge near some houses. Over this bear left to a stile, then forward up wooden steps to the field corner. Turn left, with the hedge on the right, to join a track; in 400m at a T-junction turn right to the main road in Ashgate.

Short Walk rejoins

11. Turn left then, just around the right-hand bend, keep ahead on a stony track which descends to Woodnook Farm. Continue ahead, descending into Duckside Wood and, just before an impressive stone bridge, turn left up a clear track to walk on the southern edge of the plantation. In some 300m descend to the right to walk on top of the lower reservoir dam to meet a flight steps which lead up to the toilet block and manager's office. Turn left on the road back to the car park.

Points of Interest

Linacre Reservoirs – The three reservoirs, now under the ownership of Severn Trent, were built to provide water for Chesterfield and the surrounding area. The lower one was built in 1855, the middle one in 1865 and the top one in 1904, all by the Chesterfield Gas and Water Board. Nowadays, visitors are allowed free access around the area and recently erected information boards provide plenty of opportunities to learn more about the flora and fauna.

Chesterfield – The distinctive Church of St Mary and All Saints, with its famous crooked spire, is never far from view on this walk. The spire, built in the late 14th century is around 70m high and twists outwards 2.6m on the southern side. The accepted explanation is that unseasoned timber was used in the construction and this distorted whilst drying out. George Stephenson died in Chesterfield in 1848 and is buried in Holy Trinity Church.

Holymoorside – Nowadays, almost a suburb of Chesterfield, it takes its name from Holy Moor just to the west of the village. Up to the early part of the 20th century, mining and quarrying were important local industries but these have now died out. The area around Stone Edge was particularly affected as can be seen just to the south of Standedge Golf Club. Hipper Hall, built in the 16th century, is the oldest building in the area.

3: On The Lead Miners' Tracks

The limestone area to the west of Matlock, is not as well known to walkers as the popular tourist areas further north up the Derwent Valley. The walk gives the discerning rambler an insight into this historic region once famous for lead mining, but nowadays farming is predominant. The Elizabethan Hall at Snitterton is a remote jewel, whilst the village of Bonsall, with its narrow roads is attractive at any time of the year. This walk will surprise the newcomer since the views over the Derwent Valley are breathtaking on the descent through Jughole Wood.

Distance: Long Walk 17.5km (11 miles); Short Walk 11km (7 miles)

Duration: Long Walk 5½ hours; Short Walk 3½ hours

Maps required: OS Explorer OL24 The White Peak; OS Landranger 119 Buxton, Matlock & Dove Dale

Starting point: Small car park on Oker Lane, Darley Bridge, just off the B5057 (SK271620)

Terrain: Field paths and woodland tracks, lots of ups and downs. Strenuous in places.

Refreshments: Square and Compass, Three Stags Heads, Darley Bridge; Kings Head, Bonsall and the Red Lion, Wensley (off route). Farm shop in Upper Town.

Bus/Train link: Derby/Matlock

The Route

1. From the car park walk up to the B5057 and turn left. In 150m turn right on the road signed 'Stanton Lees' (Oldfield Lane) and in 100m cross a small stream to find a hand gate on left, with a sign 'Courtesy Gate'. Through the gate and follow well defined path through wood past limestone outcrops and stream on left to where path meets a well defined route through wood. At this point, you carry straight on until you meet a footbridge on left. Turn left crossing over stream, walk up slope till it meets cross path turn left and continue ahead to the edge of the wood to take the stile, slightly hidden, to the right of the main track. Bear right across a meadow to a squeeze stile and then right, uphill, to a stile by a gate. Through this, turn left into a green lane, admiring the views to Riber Castle and Oker Hill. Eventually pass through a yard of Homelea House onto the road in Wensley.

2. Cross over to the entrance of Manor House, to find a stile leading to a narrow tarred path, which you follow uphill to a small lane. Turn left and in 50m

pass through a gate to descend into Wensley Dale. At the valley bottom bear left up the track to a footpath sign on the opposite side of the Dale. At the hilltop, go forward through a gate eventually to pass the ruined Dalesfields Barn on the right. Keeping straight on go through two gateways to follow a wall right to a stile. Now veer slightly right, crossing a track to a white footpath sign, seen in the distance. Turn right as signed and continue on to wall on left, by a signboard, to pass to the left of a large heap of rubble. Bear left on the path to a stile, then ascend the now clear path, which passes to the right of a small hillock, to a gap in a ruined wall. Here the path disappears, but continue ahead to the top of the rise, to find a stile in the wall ahead on the skyline. This is a path junction and the boundary of the Peak District National Park.

3.   The path is now obvious as you cross eight small meadows, which in summer contain buttercups, daisies and an assortment of other wild flowers, to a narrow enclosed path. Over this, cross one more meadow to a minor road. Take the stile opposite to cross four more meadows to a barn, bearing left to a stile, then ahead over a small field to another stile. Take the right-hand path crossing two fields to emerge onto Abel Lane. Turn right for 15m to a T-junction. **For the short walk** turn left into Upper Town to find Bell Lane at the main crossroads (Go to point 7.)

Long Walk

4.   Turn right at the T-junction and in 250m fork left. In a further 150m, take the stile left and veer right uphill, to cross four fields as way-marked, to enter a very short, narrow enclosed track. Take the stile at the end, then veer right to another stile and descend on a clear path to a further stile. Forward for 20m, then bear left to the grassy valley bottom, known as Horse Dale. (This was allegedly named after all the horses Oliver Cromwell had killed in the Dale.) A few metres ahead lies a ruined barn and the route veers uphill to the right of this to a way-mark post by a wall. Turn left uphill, with the wall on the right to a gap and another way-marker. Through the gap, go left uphill, in an enclosed lane to a stile on the right opposite a barn. Head towards the double footpath signs and cross a field to pass by Bottom Leys Farm, to another stile, then bear right as signed, to follow the way-markers to emerge through a stile alongside the farm access road, on to a road.

5.   Cross over to the unsurfaced track and in 500m take the stile left. Follow the wall through four fields to pass Leys Farm and a path crossroads. Continue downhill, passing a dried up dewpond, to a small copse and stile. Through this for 50m to another stile, then turn left uphill, as way-marked, with a wall on the left. Follow the path right, then left as signed, to a tall direction post at the end of a wall, bearing slightly left to a minor road.

6.   Cross to the stile opposite to turn half-right to two way-mark posts, the second by a wall. Keep ahead over several small fields to enter a narrow field

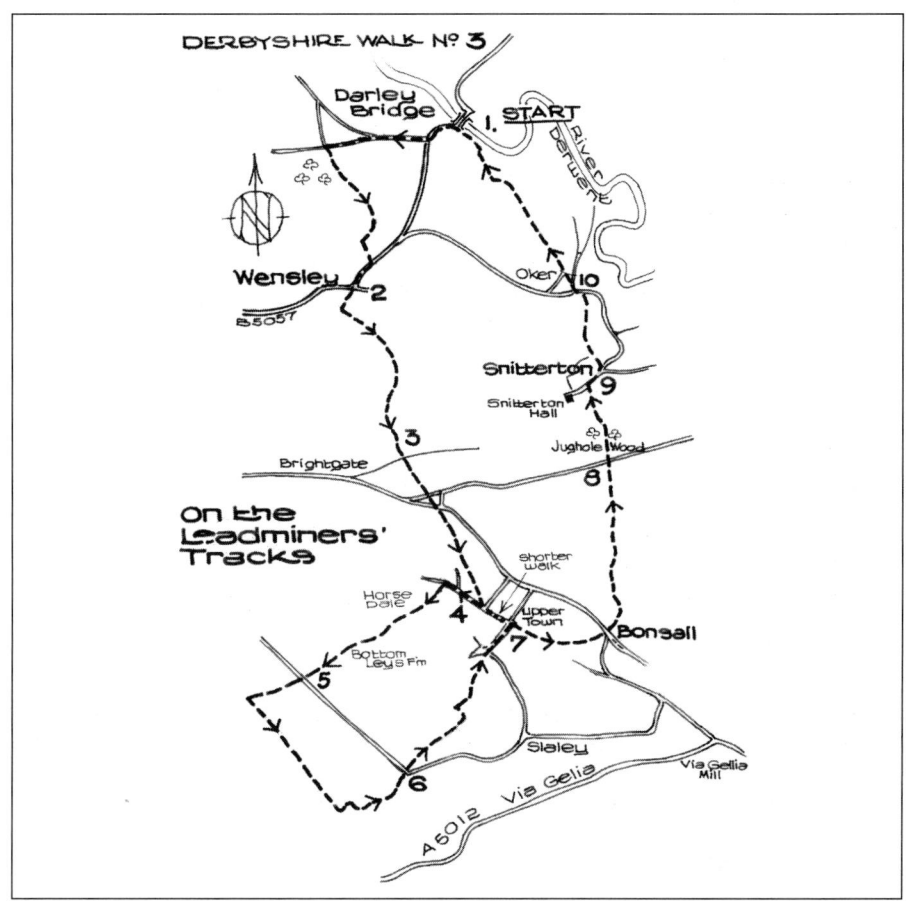

by a ruined barn. Turn left to a gate, then right into an enclosed track and in 150m find a stile on the left (under power lines). Bear slightly right to follow the obvious route across four fields to descend by a house into Horse Dale. Go ahead uphill and in 20m take the narrow tarred path, right. At the junction turn right up Bankside to Upper Town. At the road junction turn right into Bell Lane.

Short Walk rejoins

7. Continue ahead, ignoring all side paths, to meet a narrow walled path, which eventually descends into Bonsall. After admiring the Cross take the narrow path opposite, (behind the War Memorial) to ascend to a path junction. Turn left to follow a narrow path for 300m to a T-junction, to turn right,

uphill to a stile by a gate. Forward for 350m to another footpath junction and sign to take the stile left to cross two fields to a minor road.

8. Cross over, slightly right, to the stile then over a meadow to enter Jughole Wood. After crossing a small stream, ignore the stile ahead and turn right to follow initially the stream downhill and pass Jughole Cave. Continue downhill, ignoring all side paths, to cross a cattle grid, south of Leawood Farm and follow the farm access drive to a minor road. Turn right for 50m into Snitterton, noting the Bull Ring on the road corner.

9. Take the narrow path left, signed 'Wensley & Winster', to a small gate. Follow the wall, right to a farm bridge, over a steam and ahead to a stile and eventually out onto a road. Turn left, then right onto Aston Lane and after 25m left over a stile hidden in the hedge. Now aim uphill for the top right-hand corner of the meadow, to find a path into the trees. Follow this to find some steps and a stile.

10. Bear half-right as signed, passing to the right of a ruined barn, then forward for 300m to a path fork. Bear right as signed to cross three small meadows, to pass a farm on the right and onto its access road. Shortly after going through a gate, take the stile right to descend alongside the hedge, left to another stile and stepping-stones. Follow the clear path to a field corner then continue to a stile by a gate. Over this turn left and in 50m reach the car park.

Points of Interest

Darley Bridge – The beautiful stone bridge, which straddles the River Derwent, dates from the 15th century.

Wensley – Not to be confused with its more famous Yorkshire cousin of the same name. The Derbyshire Wensley was a lead mining centre and is unusual in that the village was built on a natural ledge high above the 'dry' Wensley Dale or Valley.

Bonsall – The historic Market Cross with its thirteen steps was once the centre of trade in the village when locals sold their home produced goods. The Kings Head Inn, opposite the Cross was built in 1677. The village itself was another lead mining centre, whilst the nearby Jughole Cave contains some evidence of that long gone industry. Nowadays you are more likely to come across potholers exploring its mysteries, than miners.

Snitterton – The village name was derived from 'Snytta's Tun' or farm. The old Bull Ring still remains on the small green and is one of the few remaining rings left in the county. The Elizabethan Snitterton Hall, tucked away to the west of the green, is believed to have been built in 1631, by John Millward. During the 19th century, the Hall became a farmhouse, but is now a Grade I listed building.

Oker – This tiny settlement's name, derived from old English, means 'One Tree Hill'. When one views the hamlet from Jughole Wood the reason is perhaps obvious, since one tree clearly stands out above the rest.

4: The Ups and Downs of Ashover

The countryside to the east of the Peak National Park offers the discerning walker much to admire. This walk starts with a short climb to gain a glorious viewpoint above the upper Amber valley. There follows an equally sharp descent past old lead mine workings to lead us by fields, tracks and woods, to the open expanse of Ogston Reservoir, noted for its bird life. Two ridge walks offer fine vistas over eastern Derbyshire; the highest point of the walk near the end, with its views over Ashover is truly outstanding.

Distance: Long Walk 16km (10 miles); Short Walk 11km (7 miles)

Duration: Long Walk 5 hours; Short Walk 3 hours

Maps required: OS Explorer 269 Chesterfield and Alfreton; OS Landranger 119 Buxton, Matlock and Dovedale

Terrain: Undulating countryside. Some steep ascents and descents. Mostly on footpaths, bridleways and country lanes. Can be muddy.

Starting point: Public car park, Ashover Village Hall (SK351632)

Refreshments: The Black Swan, The Crispin Inn, The Old Poets Corner in Ashover. The Miners Arms, Milltown. The New Napoleon, Ogston Reservoir.

Bus/Train link: Chesterfield and Matlock

The Route

1. From the car park, turn left down the main street, note the plaque outside The Crispin Inn, then pass Ashover church to turn right at The Old Poets Corner. Cross over to walk down the left-hand side of this road for 250m, go past the last house and continue until the wall finishes. Here turn left down a rough track to reach the River Amber. Cross this and ascend steeply ahead, keeping to field edge by side of wood till you reach path going right, to pass the ruins of the former Ashover Corn Mill on your right.

    As you climb you see, on the skyline, a boundary wall with an unusual pattern. The gritstone slabs are turned on their end to form a fence; this style is unique to the area. Before reaching this, a footpath is met contouring the hill, turn right along it for 50m. Then turn left up a path, skirting behind a large tree in a rock outcrop, to a stile in the 'fence' to enter a field. Keeping the wall to your right, go ahead to a stile to enter a hedged track, which leads to a minor road.

2. Turn right and after 50m go over a stone stile, to enter a field. The path

follows a wall passing an old farm building on the left to enter a gully, as it ascends to a wood. Turn right, climb the stile and follow the path up through the woods, eventually reaching Holestone Gate Road. Turn left and follow for 600m, to reach Old Engine Farm. Take footpath opposite leading to a walled enclosure of trees. Turning right, follow the wall for a quarter round to take a path which cuts right, across the field, to a boundary wall. Turn left alongside this wall and then follow path to a stile in the field corner. Cross the stile and continue along the path to the edge of Cocking Tor.

3.   **Take care at this point.** When the path comes abruptly to the edge, turn right. The path is undulating and needs care, especially when you have to descend at way-markers. Where the path bears sharply left, take this and descend to meet a rough track. Continue left along this track past the old quarry workings, aiming for the old mine chimney. When this has been reached take a steep path that descends to some cottages. Now follow the broad path down from the cottages and continue to where it turns sharply right. The route is straight, as indicated by a fingerpost; the path continues between fences and two squeeze stiles, to a wooded copse, with a quarry on the left. Descend some steps to a junction of paths to take a path on the right into Milltown village by The Miners Arms.

4.   Walk up to the road junction, noting the pinfold on the right and turn right along the road, soon veering left. After 100m take a minor road on the left, Brown Lane, and ascend for 150m. Near a dwelling (Fern House – garage), on the right go through squeeze stile just before gate. Follow path, with a wall on the left-hand side. Proceed past another dwelling, through a gate to a wall and hedge-lined path, follow it to a squeeze stile into a field. Aim half left – the path is sketchy in places – to a stile in a boundary wall. **Do not** pass through the stile, but turn left besides the wall, passing through two fields to a minor road. Turn left down the road and after 20m, at a road junction turn right along a footpath opposite Brown Lane.

The path at first is broad between a wall and a hedge. After the third field, pass through a squeeze stile on the left and continue for 50m to another squeeze stile by a gate. (Do not be tempted to take the broad entrance into an adjacent field). Take the squeeze stile into a field where the path continues, with a hedge on your right. Go forward in the same direction keeping to the high ground above the River Amber. Go through a series of fields, with stiles to a wood and follow the obvious path through the woods to exit by a stile. Continue to follow path through fields for 500m to a road by a cottage turning left here into the hamlet of Woolley Moor, passing Ogston Reservoir. (This is an ideal refreshment spot, either at the public house or the reservoir picnic site).

5.   Retrace your steps, to ascend Temperance Hill (quite ironic!) at the side of the public house, for some 100m, to take a stile on the right into a field. Bear

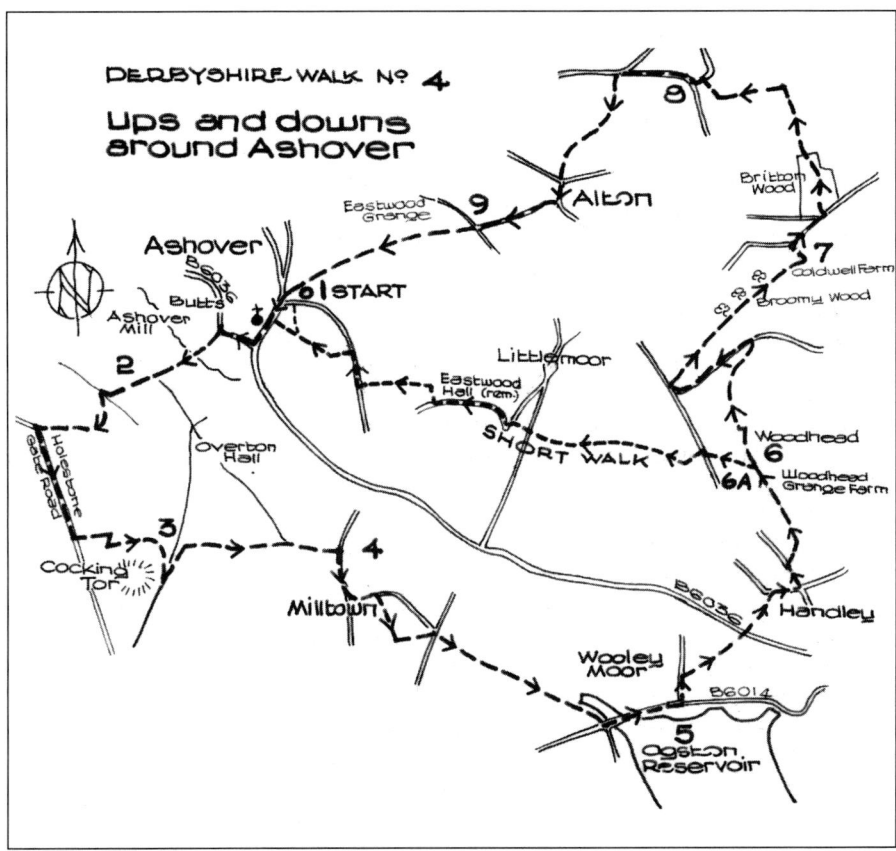

half-left, through two stiles into a large field and maintain the same direction to a stile in a holly hedge. Cross and then follow a farm track to reach the Ashover road (B6036). Cross this road to take the squeeze stile opposite, aiming half-left to another stile in a hedge, then head diagonally left up the field to the top left corner. Here you join a road, which leads into the hamlet of Handley. Turn right on the road and at a crossroads, turn left along Woodhead Lane. After 50m, turn right at a fingerpost into a field, to bear diagonally half-left to a stile in the field corner. In the next field keep the hedge on your right and when it 'dog legs' left, take a stile immediately in the corner into a small field. Then find a gap in a further hedge, to veer half-right and descend to a stone squeeze stile. Continue on the path to Woodhead Grange Farm, ignoring paths to the right and left.

Long Walk

6. On reaching the farm, follow path down steps to right. Follow path (keeping wall on left) till you see squeeze stile in wall; **do not go through** – take gate on right and follow path with hedge on right. Follow well marked path on ground through several fields till reaching stile and gate which leads onto a farm track. Follow this to a minor road. Turn left to a road junction and take a stile on the right at a fingerpost (fine views over eastern Derbyshire). The route is now way-marked as the South Chesterfield Way. Follow obvious path for 1.5km, passing Broomy Wood to reach Coldwell Farm.

Short Walk

6a. Take the minor road leading from the Farm to a road junction, Woodhead Lane. Turn right for 30m and at signpost on the left enter Woodhead Farm. (Not to be confused with Woodhead Grange Farm.) Walk up the main drive, passing between the farm buildings to a duck pond. Just past this, take a stile by a gate on the right, into a field and aim across field to a squeeze stile in the far corner. Continue in the same direction in the next field to a stile into a copse. Head uphill through the copse, leaving via a stile into a field. Ascend passing a power line pole to a stile in a wall and out onto a road. Cross this road a find a fingerpost opposite at a squeeze stile, to pass a large dwelling on the right. The path is now enclosed by wire fencing.

On reaching a stile and a minor road, turn left downhill on the road, which soon bears right, for some 350m to reach Eastwood Farm and the impressive ruin of the former Eastwood Hall. Turn right at the fingerpost into the farm entrance and immediately take a squeeze stile into an enclosure. Another stile opposite leads into a field where you turn left down by a hedge to follow the path through three fields to a road into Ashover. Turn right along the road for 200m, where a fingerpost on the left takes you into a small field. Cross to another stile and a path leading uphill, with a wall on your right. At the brow of the hill, turn right through a substantial gap to follow path, again with a wall on the right, for some 150m until you reach a sports pavilion. Here you can go across the sports ground and return to the car park. To visit Ashover, continue on the path between a wall and a hedge until you reach the road at the village church.

Long Walk

7. Follow way-marked path passing by farm buildings, through a gate eventually to leave the farm. Continue on a tarmac track to reach the road at a mobile home park. Turn right along the road for 120m to a road junction. Cross the road to a minor road on the left and take the stile on the right, leading into Britton Wood. Ascend a broad path through the wood to exit into a field with a wall and a hedge on the left. Go forward on the same path for 500m, ascending slightly to a small wood on the right. Look carefully for a stile in the left-hand wall, to find a path leading down through three fields, with a hedge on the right, to a stream. Cross this and follow the path through a copse to a stone clapper bridge, to a road by a stone road bridge.

8. Turn left on the road for 50m and at a road junction, turn right up Northedge Lane (signposted Ashover) and ascend for 300m to a further road junction. Continue uphill for a further 25m to find a fingerpost and a gate into a field. Almost immediately, bear left at the corner of a wall and follow the path up the field, keeping a wall on the right to find a gate. In the next field, turn left along the wall to another stile, then the path veers half-right uphill to cross three fields and stiles to enter a long narrow field. Leave this field by the top left-hand corner to gain a farm track. Here turn left to enter Alton village. On approaching the road, the track diverges; keep straight on to the road, then turn left for 30m then right by the telephone box. After 100m turn right up Brownhills Lane. Follow this for approximately 900m ascending to a road junction near Farhill.

9. Cross over the road, to take stile in the wall opposite to head for the highest point of the walk. After 20m the path diverges, take the right-hand spur to ascend and pass close to a walled enclosure. Ignore a path on right, but follow grass paths to the top of the escarpment. Here you are afforded magnificent views over Ashover. Continue now downhill and descend stone steps to a wide grass footpath. Keep a wall on the left to pass through two fields to a paved driveway, which leads to Eastwood Grange. The path turns left and, after 25m, you find an entrance in the wall on the right. Go down the steps to enter an enclosed walled path and an archway. Continue downhill to a second arch, which leads to a wicket gate and a field. Keeping the fence on your right, descend the field for 600m eventually to a gate by a house, to gain the main road in Ashover. Turn left for 100m to reach the starting point at the village hall.

Points of Interest

Ashover – set in the lovely valley of the Amber and surrounded by rocky hills. Ashover has a long and varied history; indeed the Romans worked the surrounding hills. The Babingtons of nearby Dethick are said to have built the tower and spire of Ashover church in the early 15th century. The historical Crispin Inn is associated with the Babingtons, when Thomas and his Ashover men returned from Agincourt. The inscription outside the inn gives an insight into a later period of our history, namely the English Civil War.

Eastwood Old Hall – the substantial ruins are a reminder of troubled times past. At the time of the English Civil War, Immanuel Bourne, the occupier, tried to keep out of the strife afflicting the country by not taking sides. However, through pressure he aligned himself alongside Parliament, but this did not prove any guarantee of safety. He was left with a ruined home – the damage being inflicted by the side he had allied himself too!

Ogston Reservoir – popular with sailing enthusiasts, this stretch of water, which contains the infant River Amber, is home on a permanent or temporary basis, for many types of wildlife. It attracts bird watchers from all parts of the country, on a year round basis.

Cocking Tor – a good point for the panoramic views of eastern Derbyshire. Nearby Ogston Reservoir is seen together with, on a clear day, the old and new Hardwick Halls and Bolsover Castle. A former quarry, now being returned to nature, has a substantial lead mining history, with its standing chimney still intact. Nearby is Overton Hall, which was the home of Sir Joseph Banks. He circumnavigated the globe with Captain Cook and encouraged Australia to become a nation.

5: Bess's Best Houses

A circular walk linking Bolsover Castle and Hardwick Hall, both homes of Bess of Hardwick. This is a lovely walk full of contrasts and complimented with two important historic houses to visit.

Distance: Long Walk 23km (14 miles); Short Walk 14km (9 miles)

Duration: Long Walk 7 hours; Short Walk 4½ hours

Maps required: OS Explorer 269 Chesterfield & Alfreton; OS Landranger 120 Mansfield & Worksop

Terrain: Undulating pleasant countryside, fields and parkland

Starting point: Cotton Street Car Park, Bolsover, near the Castle. (SK470707)

Refreshments: Public houses at Glapwell village and the Hardwick Inn

Bus/Train link: Mansfield/Chesterfield

The Route

1. Walk out of car park cross on to Castle Lane. Walk down and after 40m take opening on left (noting information board about The Conduit Houses). Follow tarmac path and, where path diverges, take left-hand path to reach steps ascending. Climb six flights of steps **(do not take top flight)** but follow path on right. At path exit, turn left up tarmac road to High Street opposite church. Turn right and walk to end of Main Street, which changes after the T-junction to Langwith Road. Continue across New Station Road to Darwood Lane in 100m. Follow this dirt track road for a few metres to take a footpath on the left. This takes you out of Bolsover into open countryside to a farm gate. Go through this and bear right with farm buildings soon reached on your left. The track goes into Palterton village on to Carr Lane. Continue to cross Main Street to a track and carry straight on through a stile at the side of a farm gate. Cross over stile and continue along track for 500m, leaving the track at a bend to continue forward, bearing slightly left on level ground. The route is not clear, but continue with a hedge on the right to a stile in the corner of the field. Cross over the stile to follow a headland path and cross a field along a clear track to reach the village of Glapwell at The Pinfold.

2. Turn left and walk to Back Lane. Turn right to reach the main Chesterfield to Mansfield Road (A617).

3. Cross the road with care to climb some steps on to Beech Crescent. Continue into Limetree Avenue to a footpath on the right in 100m, by a block of flats. This crosses open fields, going diagonally left to Ault Hucknall Lane. Take

the road opposite, Duke Drive, and walk several metres to reach footpaths on both sides of the road.

Long Walk

4.   Continue by turning right to cross two fields to Ault Hucknall and St John the Baptist Church.

Short Walk

4a. Turn left into a field, to follow a headland path to the far corner of the field. Cross over a stile and go forward across a large field to reach Rowthorne village. Turn left on the lane, then in 100m, turn right into Dale Lane. After 60m, take a footpath on the right to rejoin the Long Walk. (Go to point 10.)

Long Walk

5.   Take the bridleway opposite at the side of the new cemetery. This track leads into Hardwick Country Park, giving excellent views of the Hall. Continue in the same direction to a bridleway and The Grange. Pass through a bridlegate, then turn immediately left to walk across a field keeping close to the boundary fence to an access road and cattle grid. Cross a stile and turn right over an access road to descend to a kissing gate and continue to the ancient fishponds. The grass mound between the ponds is the Ice House. Continue downhill to the next kissing gate, to pass a quarry on the right, to a path junction. Turn right and walk along the path at the side of the Millers Pond. Turn left over the dam and then left again to reach the Visitor Centre and toilets.

6.   Continue to complete the circular route around the lake and walk uphill to the path junction. Turn right and walk to a further gate, **do not go through this**, but turn right to walk over the dam to its far end. You are now walking over the Great Pond. Looking back now, will afford you good views. Turn left, continuing around the Lake, into a plantation, passing over duckboards to a left turn out of the woods. Turn left to a kissing gate, then right to follow a metal fence to a cattle grid and the Hardwick Inn.

7.   Retrace you steps after visiting the Hardwick Inn to the cattle grid – pass through iron kissing gate and then walk in a north-east direction towards the old Hardwick Hall, crossing parkland, towards the stone steps seen ahead.

8.   After visiting the Hall, take the access road downhill, passing the stable yard and steam-driven joiner's workshop to a bend in the road. Go through a kissing gate on the left into a field and walk across parkland to a stile into Lady Spencer Wood. Continue through the wood on an undulating path to cross a stile and turning left to follow a track to a footpath on the left at Norwood Lodge. Take this path between houses into an open field and continue into woods along a clear track. Descend to a bridge over a stream. Continue over a field to a further stile onto Rowthorne Trail.

9.   Cross to a stile, to go straight ahead into an open field and then cross three

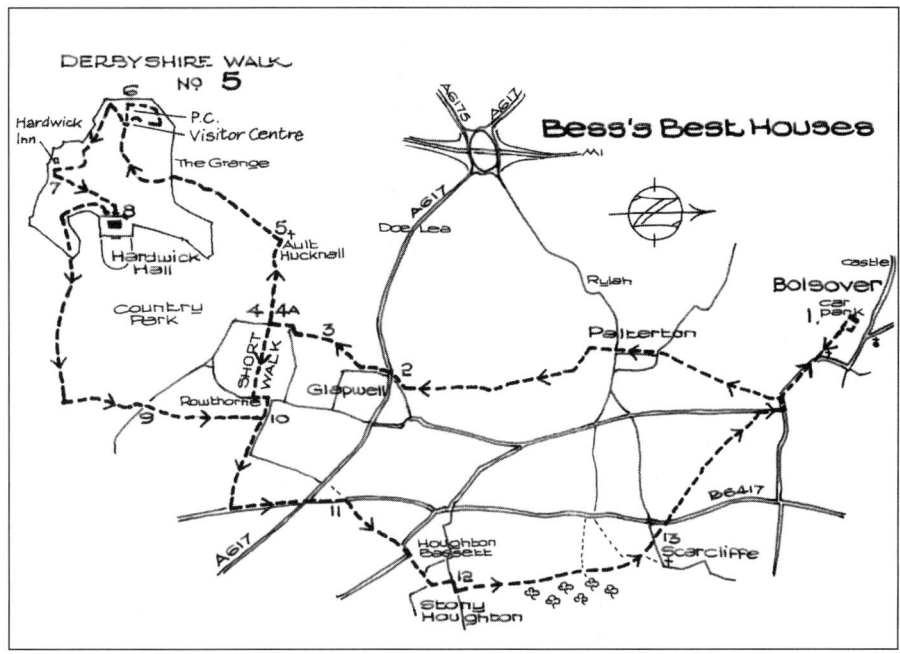

further fields to reach Field Lane. Cross again to the stile opposite and continue over fields to reach Dale Lane.

Short Walk rejoins

10. Turn right along Dale Lane to a bend. Keep ahead on a footpath to cross fields, follow headland to reach Long Hedge Lane, near the former Pleasley Colliery (now Country Park with concessionary footpaths). Turn left and walk along this lane to reach the A617. Cross with care into Green Lane straight ahead.

11. Go along this lane to the B6417 road and at the corner cross with care. Take the first road on the right towards Houghton Bassett, follow this round a series of bends (where road veers right take track on left to follow path between hedges). In 500m, where power lines cross the road, turn left and join the Archaeological Way.

12. Go through a metal gate and follow the headland path at the side of Roseland Wood. In 200m, ignoring the Archaeological Way to the right, continue straight ahead for 600m to a footbridge over a stream. Go through a coppice to join a further way-marked track into the village of Scarcliffe.

13. Turn left and after 20m, turn right along a narrow lane to reach the B6417 road again. Take the footpath opposite, cross two fields, and continue along a clear track into Hills Town, aiming for the water tower ahead. At Mansfield Road, turn right to rejoin Langwith Road, turn left to walk through Bolsover to the car park.

Points of Interest

Hardwick Hall – work began in 1590 and, by 1597, Bess of Hardwick, wife of the 6th Earl of Shrewsbury, took up residence, aged nearly 80 years. Her initials E S can be seen on each tower. The architect was Robert Smythson, whose family and descendants were involved with many Derbyshire houses, such as Bolsover Castle and Barlborough Hall. Given over to the National Trust in 1959 by the Duke of Devonshire in lieu of death duties, Hardwick Hall has a spectacular collection of tapestries. See also Walk 6.

Hardwick Old Hall – Bess was born in the Old Hall in 1520. Only the ruined shell remains, standing close by the "new" Hall. The site is managed by English Heritage.

Bolsover Castle – a castle has stood on this site for more than 800 years. The present keep dates from the early 17th century. It was once owned by Sir George Talbot, 6th Earl of Shrewsbury and husband of Bess of Hardwick. It was besieged and taken by the Parliamentarians in 1644, who maintained a small garrison there until it was sold as a private habitation in 1649. It is managed by English Heritage, who are carrying out extensive repairs.

Scarcliffe – a monument in the church tells the story of Lady Constantine de Frecheville, who left provision in her will for the church bells to be rung for 6 weeks each year in gratitude for her life having been saved. The sound of the curfew bell ringing enabled her to find her way out of the forest, escaping almost certain death. However, the bells have not been rung for more than 60 years.

Ault Hucknall – The Church of St John the Baptist, which has a fine window in the West end, dates from Saxon times, but was not mentioned in the Doomsday Book.

6: Three Notable Ladies of Derbyshire

A circular walk linking three notable Ladies of Derbyshire. Bess of Hardwick, who owned Wingfield Manor and played gaoler to Mary, Queen of Scots, during her sojourn there. We also visit Lea Hurst, near Holloway, a former home of Florence Nightingale, of nursing fame. In addition, we visit Crich Stand (Sherwood Foresters War Monument), the National Tramway Museum and High Peak Junction on the Cromford Canal. The walk has, along the way, many panoramic viewpoints.

Distance: Long Walk 20km (12½ miles); Short Walk 12.5km (8 miles)

Duration: Long Walk 7 hours; Short Walk 4½ hours

Maps required: OS Explorer 269 Chesterfield and Alfreton; OS Explorer OL24 White Peak; OS Landranger 119 Buxton, Matlock and Dovedale

Terrain: Hilly, surprisingly strenuous but excellent views on a clear day

Starting point: Lay-by side of the B5035 near entrance to Wingfield Manor (SK367548)

Refreshments: Public houses in Crich and South Wingfield. Café at High Peak Junction

Bus/Train link: Alfreton/Matlock

The Route

1. From the lay-by walk away from South Wingfield towards Crich along the B5035 for 100m to meet footpaths on the same side of the road as the lay-by. Take this path across one field to a path on the right (no footpath sign at time of survey). Turn right and walk parallel to B5035 towards Wingfield Manor, seen to the right. Mary Queen of Scots was held here. Cross four fields and at the footpath junction turn right and return to the B5035.

2. Through the stile, turn left and cross the road. Take the bridleway to Wingfield Park and continue along past Wingfield Hall to a footpath/bridleway junction close to Wingfield Manor. Take the footpath, climbing uphill towards the manor. The path goes past an entrance to the manor, then continues to a stile in the field. Through the stile and walk across two fields, ignoring path to right but continue straight on to a lane.

3. Take the path opposite (Park Mill) walking over a gravel drive, then across the lawn into an open field, aiming for a way-mark post and field gate seen ahead. The path crosses a further field as a mown path to another field gate. The route now passes a derelict cottage going over two further stiles. Aim then for two holly trees seen to the left to join a stream and farm track. Turn

left over the stream and walk up the track to reach two farm gates. Turn left (nearest gate) and walk uphill with a wall on the right, to the top of the field. Turn right through a gate then walk left up the next field (walk in the middle of the field). When you are near the top of the hill, aim for the field gate that comes into view. Go through a squeeze stile onto a track, turn right and walk to a path junction. (At this point, you can walk 80m to a seat to take in the view then return to path junction.) Walk uphill to a wood and follow a clear path through the wood to a stile. Go over the stile, turn left to follow wall on left and cross a field to a further wood. Go into this wood and follow a clear path, **(do not take private paths)** to a gate/squeeze stile. Turn left to walk downhill to farm gate at the side of the lane. (Entrance to Thorphill Farm.)

4. Turn right and walk down the lane (past path on right) to a road junction. Turn right, walking past Lady Bird Cottage, ignoring the path to Fritchley, to take the path on the right into a wood. Go through a squeeze stile at side of field gate for 30m, then go over a stile on the left into a field. Cross field on headland path, with a hedge on the right, to a squeeze stile in the right-hand corner of the field. Continue on the same line in the next field and, when the hedge ends, walk across the field still on the same line. Go under the power cables, with a disused quarry on your left. When you reach a further stile, turn right and walk across the field to a further stile at path junction. Turn left, head for field gate/squeeze stile and aim for the houses seen ahead, going across two fields to reach Crich village.

5. Turn left and walk uphill to take the footpath opposite Hill Crest next to Roe Court. Walk down the track to a field gate and enter the field to cross to a further entrance into the next field. Turn left and head towards the church going through a field gate/squeeze stile to follow the headland path to a kissing gate. Go through this gate to cross the cemetery to a further kissing gate, then cross three more fields to reach the road. (To visit the National Tramway Museum, turn left and walk to the next road junction seen ahead.) Turn right and walk along the road to reach the entrance to Crich Stand (Sherwood Foresters and Worcestershire Memorial). Walk up the tarmac track to Crich Stand. (Here there are excellent views of several counties.) The path then continues from the footpath sign contouring around the hillside to reach the boundary of quarry workings. Follow the boundary fence to a path junction at power lines.

Long Walk

6. Turn left, still following quarry fence, to descend to cross tramway lines and continue straight on to reach Cliff Farm. Turn left along farm drive to reach Wakebridge.

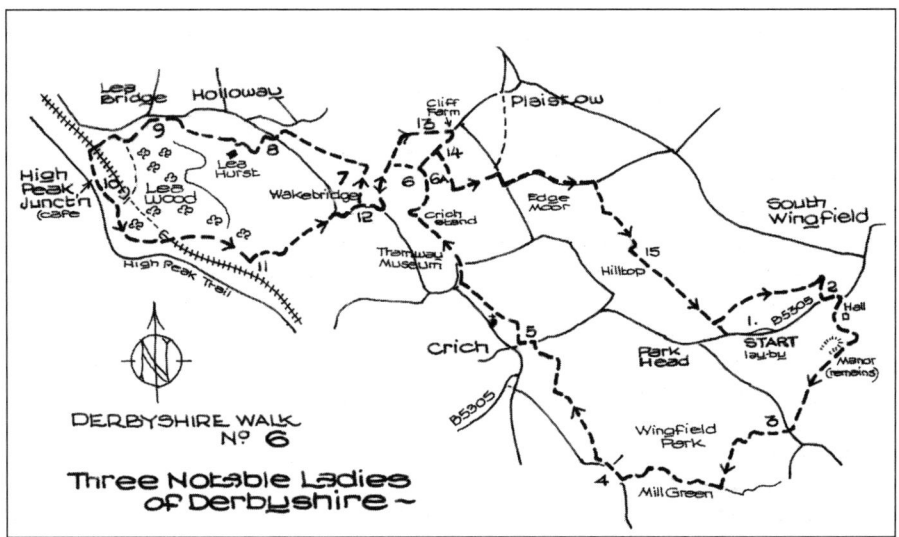

Short Walk

6a. Turn right, go over stile and walk down lane to a path on the right. (Go to point 14.)

Long Walk

7. Turn right along the road and take a footpath, on the right to Dethick. Cross the field to Wakebridge Farm, to take the path to the right of the farm. Continue uphill, ignoring the track on the right, to a footpath sign on your left. Take the path up the bank into a field. **Do not go through gate,** but follow the headland path to another field gate/squeeze stile. Through this, turn left and follow the land drain to reach the field edge, with excellent views of the River Derwent valley. Then follow the field edge across three more fields to take a path at top of the plantation, which eventually descends steeply to a road near Holloway (ignore path into Upper Holloway as you go downhill).

8. Cross the road to take the stone paved alleyway past Normanhurst Cottage to cul de sac (note old spring). Continue to a road junction, here turn left downhill to a footpath just past Bracken Cottage. Follow this path with a deer fence to left and walk to the path junction. **Do not turn left through gate** but continue straight on, noting the large house ahead. (This is Lea Hurst, the former home of Florence Nightingale.) Our path crosses the driveway to Lea Hurst to continue around the boundary of the house. You then reach a stile and the return of the deer fence. Follow this path to another stile into open parkland, then, with a wall on your right, descend to a road. Turn left and walk downhill to the road junction at Lea Bridge.

9. Take the footpath opposite the road junction, along track into Lea Wood, passing a lodge and then just past the gateposts take a path on the right. Follow this, with a high wall on the left, to a bridge over a stream. Turn right to a road, then turn left and walk up the road to footpath on the left. Walk down the path going over a bridge to the River Derwent, pass a sewage farm and railway line to reach the Cromford Canal. (High Peak Junction including visitor centre.)

10. Turn left to follow the canal towpath towards Ambergate, passing Leawood Pumping Station (often open to the public). Shortly after re-crossing the River Derwent, cross over the canal bridge to the towpath on the other side. Turn left and follow the towpath, passing Homesford Cottage path junction, to go into a tunnel. Continue along the towpath to another path junction and bridge over the canal (note O.S. bench mark 270).

11. Walk up the steps to reach Leashaw Farm. Turn left over the canal bridge and walk up a farm track to the road. Cross road and walk into Leashaw Wood, follow a well marked path uphill, ignoring all paths leading off, to reach stone stile at the end of the wood. Go over this stile into an open field to follow a clear track to reach the road. Turn right and walk back to Wakebridge.

12. Walk up the drive to Cliff Farm on the footpath signed to Plaistow Green. On reaching a footpath just before the farm, climb uphill to take newly diverted path on your left. Walk behind the farm, going across a field and contouring around to rejoin previous line of footpath. Head now for a field gate in a gap seen ahead. Go through the gate, contour right around remains of a wood and on reaching the ridge top head for gate at field corner ahead.

13. Walk into the field, cross towards another Cliff Farm and pass to the right of a green roofed barn. Go through a gate, along a farm track to reach the drive-way to Cliff Farm. Turn right past Cliff Farm to a footpath on left to Crich.

Short Walk rejoins

14. Cross three fields to a path junction. (Crich Stand seen above). **Turn left** and head down a farm track to Plaistow House, going through three farm gates to a road. Turn right, then left and walk down Hollin Lane. Ignore paths to Hollins Farm and West House Farm. Just past the farm entrance to Hilltop Farm, take a bridleway on the right.

15. Walk up the bridleway, steep-sided at first, then it goes into an open field to reach Hilltop Farm. At the farm, walk through the farmyard, to take a track on the left through a white farm gate. (Another excellent vista of Wingfield Manor comes into view.) Walk along the track across a field to a field gate. Then continue, turning left and following the track through several fields with hedge on your right to reach the B5035. Turn left and return to your car in the lay-by.

Points of Interest

Wingfield Manor – situated on the rise of a hill near the village of South Wingfield. The 15th-century manor house was built by Ralph, Lord Cromwell. Mary, Queen of Scots was imprisoned here on two separate occasions in 1569 and 1584 under the care of the Earl of Shrewsbury. The local squire, Anthony Babington, attempted to rescue her but leading her to safety, they were caught. Both of them were later beheaded. Take a look around the manor house, as the history and architecture provided by the ruins make it one of the most interesting properties to visit in this area.

Bess of Hardwick – Bess was born in 1520 at Hardwick Old Hall only a short distance from the present Hall. She was married at 12 and her young husband soon died leaving her a great deal of property. She later married Sir William Cavendish, who died in 1557 and left her his entire fortune. Her wealth was now so great that only Queen Elizabeth I was a richer woman in England. She married for a fourth time, another rich man, George Talbot, 6th Earl of Shrewsbury. It was after his death that Bess started the building of the new Hardwick Hall in 1590. Now, apart from its impressive architecture, it is also famous for its needlework and tapestries. The 6th Duke of Devonshire inherited the Hall in 1811 and was responsible for promoting the legend that Mary, Queen of Scots stayed there. The tomb of Bess of Hardwick is in Derby Cathedral.

Holloway – This small village is famous as Florence Nightingale lived here at Lea Hurst, a 17th-century gabled farmhouse. Florence's father (Edward William Shore, who later changed his name to Nightingale) enlarged the house in 1825. He left it to Florence in his Will and after her courageous work in the Crimea she retired to the house. She died in 1910 and the house was sold. Today is a home for the elderly, occasionally open to the public.

The Cromford Canal – completed in 1794, it ran for 14¾ miles from Cromford to Langley Mill where it joined the Erewash Canal. It was engineered by William Jessop and Benjamin Outram. Sir Richard Arkwright was a major shareholder as it gave an outlet for his mill at Cromford. The Butterley Tunnel collapse in 1900 caused the closure of the canal. It was officially abandoned in 1944. Today much of the lower end has been lost but the upper end remains in water and is still used. The restored steam driven Leawood Pump house built to lift water from the River Derwent to the canal and High Peak Junction, which joins the canal to the Cromford and High Peak Railway, are worth visiting.

Crich and Crich Stand – A large village with its hilltop church and lovely market cross. Today the village is famous for the National Tramway Museum, which offers a wonderful opportunity to enjoy a tram ride with Victorian street scenery. High above the village is the War Memorial and Regimental Tower to the Sherwood Foresters and Worcestershire Regiments. Erected in 1923, the tower stands 1000ft above sea level. On a clear day, this gives spectacular views of Leicestershire, Nottinghamshire, Derbyshire and just into South Yorkshire.

7: The Famous Wells of Tissington

A circular walk close to Dovedale, visiting the lovely village of Tissington, famous for its Well Dressing in May, and also the village of Fenny Bentley.

Distance: Long Walk 15km (9½ miles); Short Walk 12km (7½ miles)

Duration: Long Walk 5 hours; Short Walk 3½ hours

Maps required: OS Explorer OL24 White Peak/Explorer 259 Derby; OS Landranger 119 Buxton, Matlock and Dovedale

Terrain: Level ground along Tissington Trail but rest of walk undulating, steep in places

Starting point: Narlows car park near Fenny Bentley (SK164505)

Refreshments: Dog and Partridge public house, Thorpe. Coach and Horses public house, Fenny Bentley.

Bus/Train link: Ashbourne/Buxton

The Route

1. From the car park, turn left and walk in an easterly direction on to the road. Shortly where the road bends sharp left in a northerly direction, continue straight on to the Tissington Trail car park at Fenny Bentley. Turn right onto the trail and take the first path on the left at the finger post to Fenny Bentley (this is opposite the path to Thorpe and Dovedale).

2. Descend to a stream, climb uphill to a field and cross three fields to reach Fenny Bentley.

3. Turn left at road and in 100m take the path down to St Edmund's Church. Walk through the churchyard to main road (A515). Cross the road, turn right for a few metres and then take footpath left (NE). Bear slightly right and continue forward for 100m to the end of the cottages where the path divides. Take the left fork (N) under the power cables and ascend steeply for nearly 1 km parallel to the A515 to reach Bassett Wood Farm. (Refreshments are available here.)

4. Follow driveway out of the farm (E side) walking past the Tissington Trekking Centre. Two hundred metres further on take the path on the left through a gate, cross the field to a track on the far right corner and after turning left (NNW) the Tissington Trail is crossed. (Tissington Station, car park and toilets.) Immediately after, bear left on the road and walk past a pond on the left. Turn sharply right at road junction (NW) to pass the church on the right and Tissington Hall on the left. In 200m, at the post-box, turn right

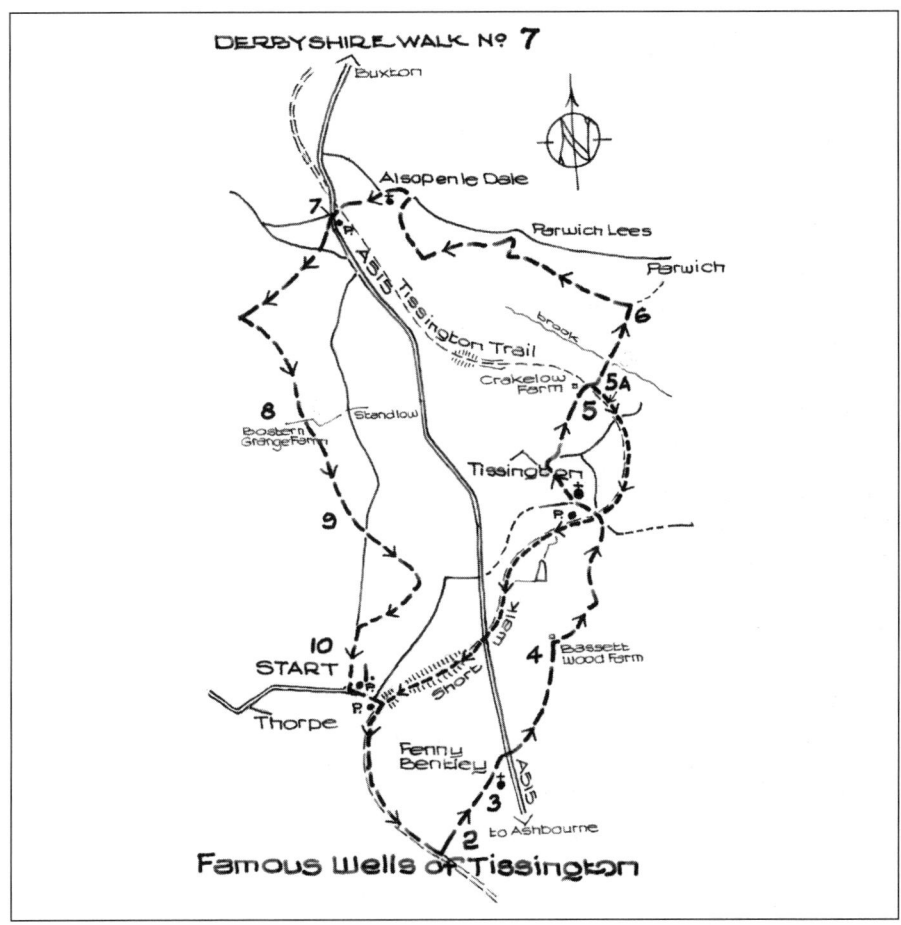

DERBYSHIRE WALK No 7

Famous Wells of Tissington

down Chapel Lane (note cottage built in 1846). Take footpath on the left (N) after last cottage and continue (N) to the crest. (The aerials of Alport Heights are visible to the ESE) and descend to Crakelow Farm again to cross the bridge over the Tissington Trail.

Long Walk

5. **Do not walk down to the Trail,** but turn right at the end of the railway bridge and immediately **descend** to the stile to continue downhill to Bletch Brook. Go over the stile and bridge to climb steeply for 500m. Continue uphill over the ditch board to go slightly right, then ascend to cross three further fields to a stile in the corner of the field. (If you want to visit Parwich, turn right here, over stile and walk into the village where there is a public house.)

Short Walk

5a. Turn right here onto the Trail and return via Tissington Railway Station and onto Fenny Bentley Railway Station. Continue to Narlows Car Park to return to end of the walk.

Long Walk

6. Turn left and follow the footpath with a hedge on the right. In the third field, take the path that goes straight on, **not half-left**. Walk across five fields and, in the sixth, enter the parkland of Parwich Lees. Continue straight across the field to pass a house to a track. Cross over this, then across a field to the far left-hand corner. Go through the squeeze stile, cross a field, go over a stile then across another field bearing left around a bank. Go uphill to the left of a plantation ahead, crossing a field to a stile.

(Option here to descend right to Alsop-en-le-Dale to turn left at road, then walk through the hamlet. Go 200m after the church to take the footpath on the left rising to Alsop-en-le-Dale car park on the Tissington Trail.)

Alternatively, *take a stile on the left of the field, then over a stile to walk half-way across the field, to a gate entrance and another stile. Cross over two fields to pass through gate before bridge and turn immediately left to cross stile leading to steps. Ascend steps, turn right and follow Tissington Trail to Alsop-en-le-Dale car park.*

7. From the car park go over the A515 road to take the footpath (SSW direction), to cross a second lane. Continue in the same direction up the track towards New Hanson Grange, to follow the track uphill to a path junction. Turn left (signed Tissington) and walk across four fields to reach Bostern Grange Farm.

8. Walk past the farm, through squeeze at side of metal gate to follow track with wall on the right, crossing four fields to a stile and track (note lime kiln on the right).

9. Cross track and continue in southerly direction following a clearly marked path to a wide track. Turn left and follow this track to reach the road.

10. Turn right and walk down the lane with care to a path junction at the Dog and Partridge Hotel and the car park.

Points of Interest

Fenny Bentley – A beautiful village with a manor house. Once the home of Thomas Beresford, Lord of the Manor, who fought alongside eight of his 16 sons at the Battle of Agincourt. The effigies of the Beresford family including his wife and 21 children are seen by their tombs. The manor house, which has a 15th-century square tower built into it, is known today as Cherry Orchard Farm. This was also the home of Charles Cotton.

Tissington – Famous for the well dressing held in the middle of May, a ceremony that dates from 1350 or even earlier. It is believed the event originated to commemorate those who survived the Black Death. The village has six wells that are dressed annually. The Norman church of St Mary overlooks the village. Tissington Hall, was the home of the Fitzherbert family for nearly 500 years, built by Francis Fitzherbert in 1609. The estate consists of 2400 acres comprising 13 farms, 40 cottages and associated lettings. The Hall and Gardens are well worth a visit being open 28 afternoons throughout the summer.

Tissington Trail – This is the old railway line from Ashbourne to Parsley Hay. Today it is a popular walk and cycle trail passing through some beautiful countryside. Along the route can be found many old railway buildings and memorabilia – in particular, Hartington Station. There are several picnic spots on the trail.

Parwich – a delightful village with stone houses and church around the village green, Parwich Hall, built around 1747, and the Sycamore Inn public house.

Alsop-en-le-Dale – a tranquil hamlet. The Norman Church of St Michael was substantially rebuilt during Victorian times. A visit inside the church reveals an extraordinary 19th-century square mock Gothic pulpit. Opposite the church is Alsop Hall, privately owned and built in the 1600s.

8: In the Footsteps of Bonnie Prince Charlie

The walk follows the Bonnie Prince Charlie Walk as far as the outskirts of Shirley before returning via Wyaston and Clifton.

Distance: Long Walk 19km (12 miles); Short Walk 12.8km (8 miles)

Duration: Long Walk 6 hours; Short Walk 4 hours

Maps required: OS Explorer 259 Derby; OS Landranger 128 Derby and Burton upon Trent

Terrain: Undulating at start, mostly on footpaths, bridleways and country lanes. Can be muddy

Starting point: Ashbourne (Market Cross) (SK180467)

Refreshments: Ashbourne (cafés and public houses), Osmaston (Shoulder of Mutton public house), Shirley (Saracen's Head public house)

Bus/Train link: Ashbourne/Derby

The Route

1. The walk starts at the Market Cross in Ashbourne, goes downhill to the right into St John's Street. Turn right through the traffic lights into Church Street and go towards the church. Before the church turn left down Station Road, past the Ashbourne Leisure Centre to the T-junction. Here turn left and, almost opposite house number 50 (North Leys), is a footpath leading to steps which you ascend. Follow path across field, past radio mast keeping hedge on left to stile concealed in far left-hand corner of field. Over stile and follow enclosed path to Old Hill, turn right continue into Wyaston Road.

Take the right fork towards Wyaston as far as Willow Meadow Road where you turn left into the housing estate down to Chestnut Drive. The path goes between nos. 23 and 25, over a bridge and up the field to the Ashbourne by-pass. Cross road with care ascend steps and follow path to Caravan Park, over stile walk ahead through tree lined track to stile to exit Caravan Park. Follow path to edge of wood. At the edge of the wood bear right over a stile and a stream, and follow the edge of the wood to another stile. Cross the track leading to Blake House and climb over a stile into the field. Keep the hedge on your left until you enter a small plantation. Once out of the wood, aim for the left edge of the wood ahead, then at the corner keep the wood on your right until you come to a stile. Turn right onto the road, and walk past Osmaston Church. **(For Long Walk go to point 2a)**

Short Walk

2. Turn right into the village hall car park (notice thatch) and go over a stile in the left-hand corner. Follow the footpath, at field edge, keeping the hedge on the left. At the bottom of the field, go through a gap in the hedge and follow the path keeping the hedge on the left. At the bottom of the field, turn right to continue following the hedge on the left. At the tree line, follow the path to a stile (approx. 8m from the corner of the field).

Go over stile and follow the path through trees to another stile. Cross this stile and go straight down the field to a footbridge over a brook. Go over footbridge and straight on to a stile in the hedge. Over the stile, then walk in the centre of a gully until reaching the remains of a hedge. Walk up the field keeping the remains of the hedge on your left-hand side until you reach a field boundary with stone gatepost. Go through gap in the hedge to the left of stone gatepost and follow hedge line on the right to the top of the field to stile next to an oak tree. Go over stile and walk up the field towards farm buildings to pass between buildings and barn through steel gate and onto metalled road (Wyaston Road). (Go to point 3a.)

Long Walk

2a. At the village pond (note the unusual horse-shoe bench), bear left and take the centre track marked "Bridle Path To Shirley". This is a delightful walk past the pool and the old sawmill to Shirley. In Shirley there is another public house, the Saracen's Head, opposite the church.

3. Follow the bridlepath to Shirley and turn right just before the junction of Park Lane with Hall Lane to follow a footpath until you reach a footbridge over a brook. Cross over the brook, turning right to follow the Centenary Way.

Follow the path at the edge of a wood until reaching a footbridge leading into Greaves Wood. Cross over the bridge and follow the track through the woods. Go through a gate and follow the path straight ahead (pond on right). Continue on the path through three more fields, keeping the hill on the left, until you reach a farm gate. Go through the gate and follow the track to a road (Orchard Lane). At the road turn right past Wyaston Grove on the right and take the second footpath on the right through a wooden gate opposite a large house wall and then follow a green lane, keeping the hedge on the left. (Ignore farmer's obstructions across path.) Carry straight on down until you reach a stile next to a gate. (Do not take the stile on the right.) Follow path up the field (with hedge/fence on left) and cross two fields to Quillow Lane. Go across the road and through the gate. Head towards edge of building and continue with buildings on left until reaching a metal gate. Go through gate and walk down between a Dutch barn and farm buildings until you reach a metalled road (Wyaston Road).

Short Walk rejoins

3*a* Turn right and walk down the road until you reach Dobinhorse Lane on the left. Go over stile/footbridge into a field, heading towards the left-hand side of a tumulus. Go over the stile next to tree and holly hedge and cross over farm track to a further stile in hedge corner of field. Turn left along the headland with hedge on left to bottom of field to squeeze stile. Head diagonally right across next field to right corner to reach a gate. Enter overgrown tree area and after 25 metres turn left to stile. In next field aim to left of farm building seen ahead and then continue straight ahead (pond on right) to gap in fence. In next field, aim for farmgate/squeeze stile. In next field walk to farm track and follow to a farmgate – **do not go through this** but go slightly forward right to a stile.(farm buildings on left). Straight across field to reach footbridge over brook.

Turn right and climb uphill passing left of small coppice aiming to right of field to reach a stile 20 metres from corner (next to holly bush). Enter golf course and turn right along waymarked path passing green and teeing off area to join obvious path with boundary on left. Continue along this and look carefully for a stile on left into a small plantation. Over stile and immediately right out of plantation – careful here: tree branches and fallen trees in way – to enter field. Follow fence with boundary of golf course on right to far side of field to reach stile. Follow a waymarked path with care through scrubland to a further stile at end of scrub (at time of survey, the bottom of scrub area was under construction as part of golf course). Over stile to follow obvious path to reach some steps which lead down to Ashbourne bypass. Turn left towards the roundabout and carefully cross the road to follow the A515 into Ashbourne.

Points of Interest

Ashbourne – A small market town whose main street, Church Street, is little changed from 1645 when Charles I attended St Oswald's Church after his defeat at the Battle of Naseby. The 11th-century church is often called "The Cathedral of the Peaks" and has a 215ft spire. On the outside west wall of the nave, near the figure of St Oswald, marks made by Parliamentary artillery in 1644 can still be seen. Many other buildings in Church Street are worth closer inspection. On Shrove Tuesday the annual football game takes place between the "Up'ards" and the "Down'ards" – the inhabitants of each side of the Henmore Brook. The goals are 3 miles apart at Clifton Mill and Sturston Mill, any number being allowed to play and there are very few rules! Ashbourne is also famous for its Gingerbread, the recipe for which came with French prisoners from the Napoleonic Wars.

Osmaston – is a sleepy, beautiful mid-19th-century village and part of the Walker-Okeover Estate with thatched cottages.

Shirley – our walk does not go into the village, but is worth a visit. Shirley Hall is

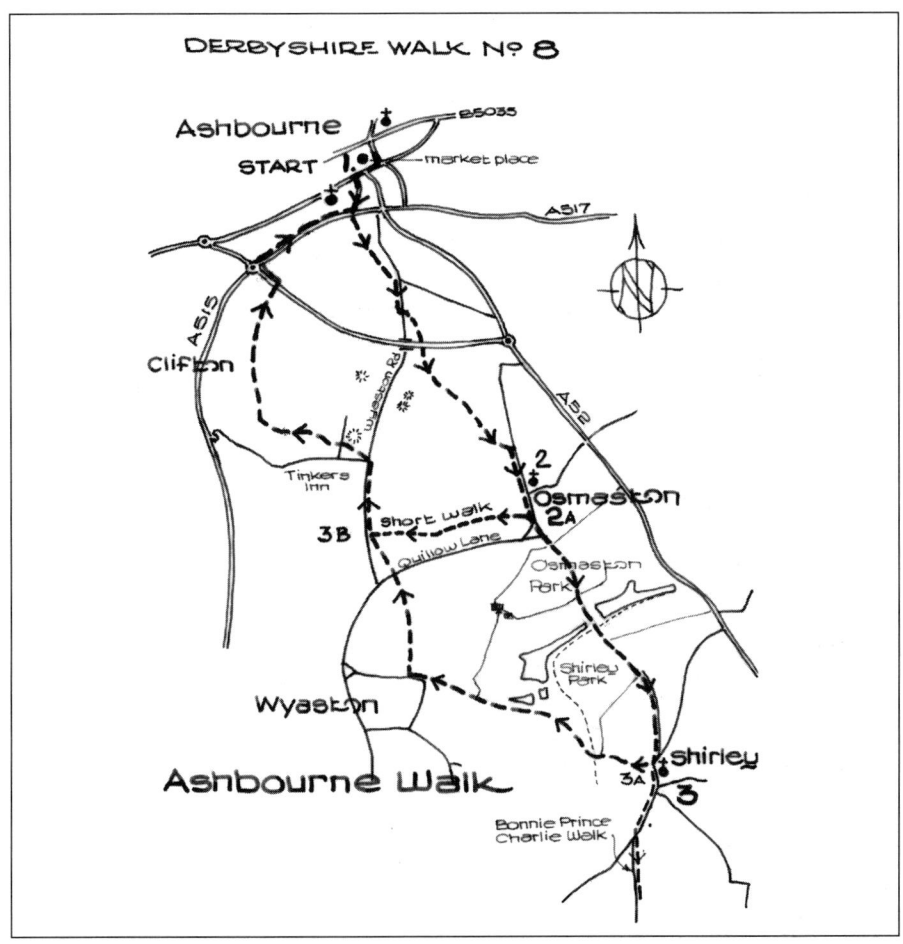

a 16th-century timber-framed house. Neo-Tudor Shirley House dates from 1939. The old rectory was the birthplace of John Cowper Powys in 1872.

Bonnie Prince Charlie Walk – A 28km (17 miles) walk in the general direction of Prince Charles Edward Stuart from Ashbourne to Derby in 1745. Also known as the Young Chevalier or the Young Pretender, he raised an army in the Highlands, and defeated Sir John Cope's army at Prestonpans, then crossed the border into England to march south to London. Discouraged by the lack of support from France and the English, when he reached Derby, his army officers forced him to retreat into Scotland. The Duke of Cumberland, William Augustus, defeated him at Culloden Moor on 16th April 1746. The Stuart prince escaped by ship to France with the aid of Flora Macdonald in September of that year.

9: The Hermit and Monk's Trail

Take a pleasant saunter to the Hermit's Cave and a ruined arch, the sole remnants of Dale Abbey. Then, across to Locko Park, to Stanley and a visit to the Cat and Fiddle Windmill, one of the best examples of a post mill in the East Midlands.

Distance: Long Walk 19km (12miles); Short Walk 8km (5 miles)

Duration: Long Walk 6 hours; Short Walk 2½ hours

Maps required: OS Explorer 260 Nottingham; OS Landranger 129 Nottingham and Loughborough

Terrain: Undulating parkland and field paths

Starting point: Park at Carpenter's Arms car park, Dale (ask for permission) (SK436389)

Refreshments: Carpenter's Arms, Dale Abbey and White Hart, Stanley

Bus/Train: Derby/Nottingham/Ilkeston

The Route

1. From the Carpenter's Arms car park take the road opposite called The Village. At end junction bear left (visit the ruined Dale Abbey and return to road). Continue past All Saints' Church and follow way-marked track uphill to a gate.
    Option – By taking a short walk ahead, going through farm gates and a farmyard, you reach the Hermit's Cave seen high on the bank on the right. Return to gate past farm.

2. Go through the gate and into a wood, the path eventually levels out and keeps to the edge of the wood. Pass through a further gate to more open land. Continue on the path (boundary on right) and soon see a farm on the right-hand side. Pass through wooden gate and go downhill to pass Columbine Farm and continue on obvious track, eventually going over a cattle grid. Climb uphill to reach the Ilkeston/Spondon road (A6096).

3. Cross the road, taking the path opposite and enter Locko Park. Continue along a clear track to a road going to Locko House just before the lake. Our path to Stanley goes right through kissing-gates and climbs uphill towards a wood. (We have fine views of Locko Park House.) Aim for the stile in a fence into the wood and leave the wood through a metal kissing-gate. Walk across the field to a small copse, cross a stile and footbridge, then continue straight ahead to the bottom right-hand corner of the field to a stile. Continue ahead with ditch on the left, to cross two further stiles and then to go straight across another field to a gravelled track.

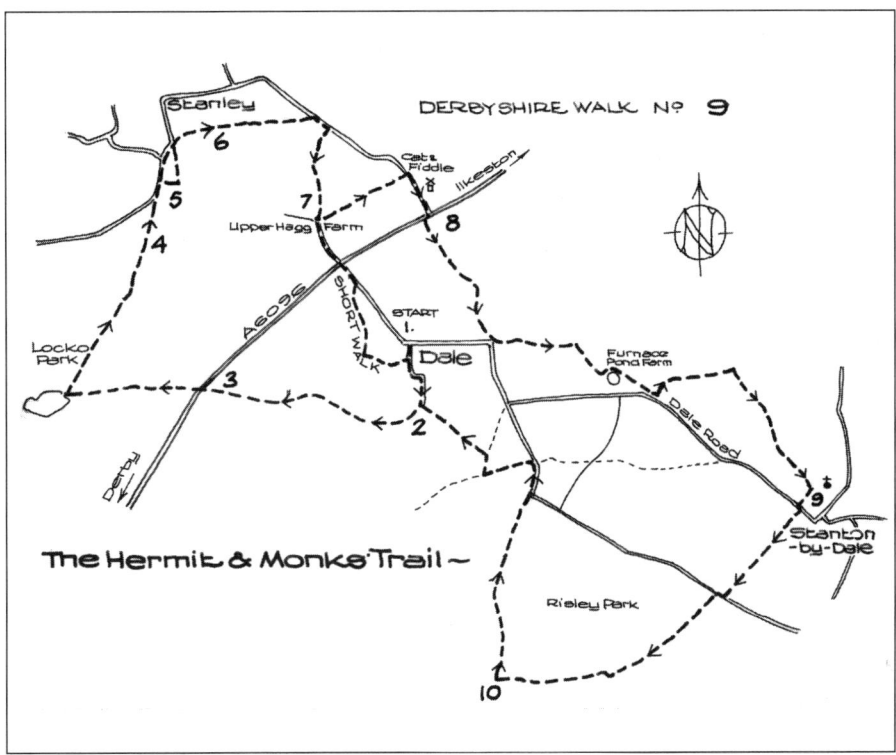

4. Turn left, go through a gate and immediately take a path on the right bearing north towards Stanley village which is seen ahead. At first follow wire fencing and hedge on the right, then after crossing a hedged boundary, you see houses and farm buildings ahead. Continue down field, through a gate with a bungalow on the left, to walk down a concrete track to a further gate. Carry on downhill to the road to reach Stanley village.

5. Turn right and walk up pavement to turn right onto Dale Road. Some 50m past last house cross a stile on the left towards a footbridge. Go straight across the fields towards the houses, passing underneath power cables. Walk up slight rise to wooden gate and stile to a road. Turn right for 45m and turn right again passing Abbey Cottage. Walk between houses, go over a further stile, walk down and cross a footbridge into a small wood, then climb out of the wood into a field.

6. Continue keeping boundary to the left, go over a further stile (boundary now on the right) and path bears left past electricity pylons and trees to cut across a farm track to a stile and bridge over Stanley Brook. Walk along the field (hedge on the right) on a small embankment to a stile near a house. Over the

stile turn right, walking diagonally right across the field towards a hedge and stile. Walk through a wooden gate onto a bridle track. At the junction, turn left through a wooden gate eventually to reach Upper Hagg Farm.

Long Walk

7. Take a path on the left through Upper Hagg Farm to a gate into a field (north-east direction). Continue on track, with hedge on both sides, to a stile. Go over this to a further stile in the right-hand corner of the field. Go straight on and walk across the field to Cat and Fiddle Lane. Turn right for 450m to a T-junction (note Cat and Fiddle Windmill on left).

Short Walk

7a. Turn left at the junction and walk down a tarmac road to the crossroads (A6096). Cross with care to take the road opposite (Arbor Hill), continue downhill and just after the entrance to Oakbridge Farm, take a path on the right. Go over stile to follow path and, just before field descends, take a stile in the left-hand corner of the field. Walk down field towards a large tree. With the tree at your back walk across the field with boundary on left to the corner and find a stile hidden from view. Continue on a delightful track turning sharp right to walk down a field into Dale Abbey village. Turn left at the junction to return to the car park.

Long Walk

8. Cross the road (A6096) with care to take stile opposite. Walk with hedge on the right (south-east direction), over a narrow footbridge in the corner of the field. Stay with the boundary for a while, then the path swings straight across to a wood and a stile next to a tree in the corner of the field. Follow edge of the wood, then swing right and go over stile into a field. Continue to another stile and footbridge straight ahead. Follow way-marked path slightly left to a hedge and further stile and footbridge onto the road. Walk towards a Ford sign seen on the left to take a way-marked path to the right between hedges. Pass through gate (collapsed on survey) and bear slightly right across a field to a stile. On the left, you will see Bassett Farm. Proceed with boundary on the right and, at the end of the track, turn right and follow way-marked route to Stanton by Dale, going over a stile (beside a wooden gate). Follow hedge-lined track over stile towards Furnace Pond Farm. Continue past farm skirting the pond on the left-hand side. As you pass the pond you will see a slag heap not too far away! The path continues in the general direction of this. Cross over a stile and walk by the side of the slag heap then, after a short distance, the path goes right towards a stile away from the slag heap. Climb the stile and continue straight across field on a clear path. Cross a small dyke and climb up to a stile to follow a well-trodden path overlooking the Stanton Ironworks. Continue on path and the end of the field turn right and walk with the boundary on the left up to a stile. Go

over this and walk with the boundary on the right (south-east direction, Stanton Ironworks on left). Soon the Stanton by Dale Church comes into view in front of you. On reaching a stile, go over this with a children's play area on the left. Continue into Stanton by Dale village towards the church. Just before reaching the church wall, there are three paths, one on the left to the church, one straight on to the village through a wooden kissing gate and one on your right. This last one goes through a metal kissing-gate in the hedge. (Take the opportunity to visit the village, return to the kissing-gate.)

9. Leave the field through the metal kissing-gate and go down the steps to the road. (The Chequers public house is adjacent for refreshments.) Cross the road and take the way-marked path through a metal kissing-gate. Cross over three stiles, keeping the boundary on the left, go over a further stile onto No Man's Lane. Turn right after approximately 45m, cross the road and turn left, the way-mark is high up on a tree. (Note the trig point in the hedge on the right.) Walk across a field to a lone tree in the middle and then go straight across to a gap in the hedge. This leads onto a golf course, and straight across there is a stile marked 'FOOTPATH' in white. Cross the field on a well-trodden path to the boundary on the right, crossing a wooden stile, through a paddock to a further stile. On the right is Risley Lodge Farm. Cross the stile with the outbuildings on the right and look for a wall and way-mark in front of you in a hedge. Cross a stile and go over tarmac track to a footpath opposite. Go over stile and bear left walking with boundary on the right-hand side. In the corner of the field cross footpath (signed Midshires Way) and walk on well-trodden path across the field towards the opposite hedge (mobile phone aerial on left), cross a stile and continue on designated path across the field. Cross a stile and there is a fenced wood on the right with a farmhouse and buildings to the left of the path. Cross the stile to the left of the wood and then go left (this area is known as Constitution Hill).

10. Walk with the boundary on the left, cross a stile and turn right onto a track. Cross the cattle grid with a plant nursery on the left. Pass the house on the right and, where paths cross, continue straight ahead with hedge on the right. Cross two stiles by metal gates and walk straight across the field to a metal gate opposite. Cross the stile and continue on track between hedge boundaries, eventually climbing two stiles. On reaching a road, turn right and then left onto Potato Pit Lane. It is approximately 250m to a way-mark and stile on the left. Cross stile and walk across the field towards the farm buildings, when by the side of the buildings turn sharp right and walk towards two trees. On the left are a gate and a stile. Cross field past a telegraph pole in the middle to a stile on the left of the wood. Cross stile and follow the path to a stile into Hermits Wood, taking the steps which soon change to a path, keeping the boundary hedge on the left. Below is Dale Abbey with the windmill on the horizon. Take more steps down and at the bottom go through a wooden gate on the left. Follow a gravel path passing the church on the right to join a tarmac road into Dale Abbey.

Points of Interest

Dale Abbey (including Hermit's Cave) – Legend has it that a Derby baker saw a vision of the Virgin Mary after which he renounced the world and lived as a hermit in the sandstone cliffs of Deepdale. Dale Abbey was founded on this site but all that remains is the arch of the east window. The hermitage can still be seen in the rocks. The present church in the village, All Saints' Church, is one of the smallest and strangest in England as the whole church is under the same roof as a farmhouse.

Locko Park – The landscaped park and lake were laid out by William Emes. The formal gardens to the west and north of the house were part of the alterations designed by William Stevens of Derby and carried out by William Drury-Lowe who lived at Locko from 1849-77.

Stanley – A priest's doorway, now in a wall, is all that is left of the Norman chapel, some of the buttresses and a small lancet window date from the 11th century. The font dates from the 14th century and the pulpit from the 17th. There is a brass tablet on the floor by the pulpit dedicated to Sir John Bentley of Breadsall, buried here 20 years before the Civil War.

Cat and Fiddle Windmill – To the north of village of Dale is the Cat and Fiddle Windmill. This 'post mill' was built in the 18th century and is an example of the oldest type of windmill. The stone roundhouse is capped with a wooden structure which houses the machinery; this is fitted onto an upright post, round which it can rotate to catch the wind.

Stanton by Dale – Stanton Iron Works in Iron Dale to the north takes its name from this village. The 13th-century Church of St Michael and All Saints is well preserved and a line of 18th-century almshouses stand nearby. Local buildings are of brick and stone construction, some of which were taken from the ruined abbey at Dale. The workers' cottages in Stanhope Street were amongst the first built in the country. The main street has a village cross, dated 1632 and a pump that was erected in 1897.

10: No Need To Be Cross In Repton

The village of Repton in South Derbyshire is perhaps best known for its Public School, however the remains of the old Market Cross, mounted on top of circular steps, makes an interesting feature at the main cross-roads. The attractive surrounding countryside, together with the pictur-esque hamlet of Bretby with its church and hall, combine to make this an interesting walk, in an area not renowned for walking.

Distance: Long Walk 18km (11½ miles); Short Walk 10km (6½ miles)

Duration: Long Walk 6 hours; Short Walk 3 hours

Maps required: OS Explorer 245 National Forest; OS Landranger 128 Derby & Burton upon Trent

Terrain: Undulating countryside, field paths and tracks

Starting point: St Wystan's Church, Repton (SK330272)

Refreshments: Public houses at Newton Solney, Lepton and Winshill

Bus/Train: Burton upon Trent

The Route

1. From St Wystan's Church, walk up Willington Road, past a row of delightful thatched cottages and just past a right-hand bend, turn left alongside the school sports ground. After passing the tennis courts, cross over the lane to find a stile in the hedge on the left, in front of the house. Over the stile, turn right, then forward bearing slightly left to pass on the left-hand side of a hedge to find another stile in the field corner. Continue along the top of the bank, with views across the Trent Valley on your right, for 300m, to cross a stile into a field. Walk up the right-hand headland path, **ignoring the stile on the right** at the start of a wood overlooking the River Trent. In a further 250m cross a stile in the field corner, turn left and continue on the bank top, which now leaves the river. In 250m go through a gate and in a few metres go over a stile into another field. Go forward onto the headland path, veering left with the hedge to find a small earth bridge and a stile on the right. Cross two grass fields, then bear half-right in the third, aiming for a stile in front of some large barns. Keep approximately 50m to the right of the barns to a stile and footpath sign between some bungalows.

2. The narrow path leads into Cricket Close at Newton Solney. At its end cross over into Blacksmiths Lane, then forward to ascend a flight of steps to join a tarmac path into the churchyard. Leave the church via the kissing-gate at the far end, turning left down Church Lane to emerge onto Main Street. Turn right and in 75m, left up a lane between the Lodge and the Newton Park

Hotel. After 400m, take the stile on the right to cross a large field to a stile between trees. Continue ahead in the next field, with a wood on the left, to a stile by a gate, then follow the hedge on the right to join a farm track, which leads to Bladon Farm.

3. Turn left through the farm buildings to join Wheatley Lane, which descends into Winshill. At the houses, turn left into Hollow Lane and, in 50m, bear left over a footbridge by a ford on the access road to a residential home. In 15m, take the footpath on the right.

Short Walk

3a. Continue to the right of the fence, parallel to the road, to go through a gate and follow an obvious path over four stiles for approximately 800m. Now follow it between a fence and stream until it goes left. Continue along and to the right of a hedge for approximately 800m as far as a stile adjacent to a gate. Go over the stile to follow a track to the road. Cross the road to take the path opposite, then continue alongside the hedge keeping to its right for approximately 800m. Here a track crosses a stream just before a small copse, cross track and stream to head uphill across a field. On meeting a stile, go over and through two small fields onto a track. Follow the track for about 700m, here another track forms a T-junction. Continue ahead past a derelict barn to go over two stiles. Now cross a field to a stile opposite and go down the path between houses onto the road (Chestnut Way). Cross the road to take the path opposite, then go over the stile into a field. Follow the path to the right of the hedge to another road (Mitre Way). Cross this road to the path opposite and continue on a tarmac path, which soon veers left to meet Burton Road adjacent to the Red Lion public house. Go right to the traffic island and then return to the church.

Long Walk

4. Follow a path to the rear of the houses for some 200m, to a broken stile leading onto an enclosed path by the houses, which eventually leads to Sales Lane. Turn left and in 200m go forward onto a gravel track for 500m to a bungalow on the right. Turn right as indicated, passing to the left of the dwelling, to join a sunken path, which becomes a headland path to a field. Cross a stile below the power lines, then go forward across another field to a stile by a gate. Follow the grassy track to locate a stile 30m to the left of a gate, which leads onto Bretby Lane.

5. Turn left and in 200m turn right opposite a nursery, down Mount Road. After 50m, cross the stile on the left, bearing half-right and aiming for the tower of Bretby church. Find the path and stile to the left of the church and descend onto Bretby Green. Turn right for a few metres to the stile opposite. Cross a small field to a footbridge, then go forward to walk to the right of a fence to emerge ono the access road to Bretby Hall. Turn left up to the hall

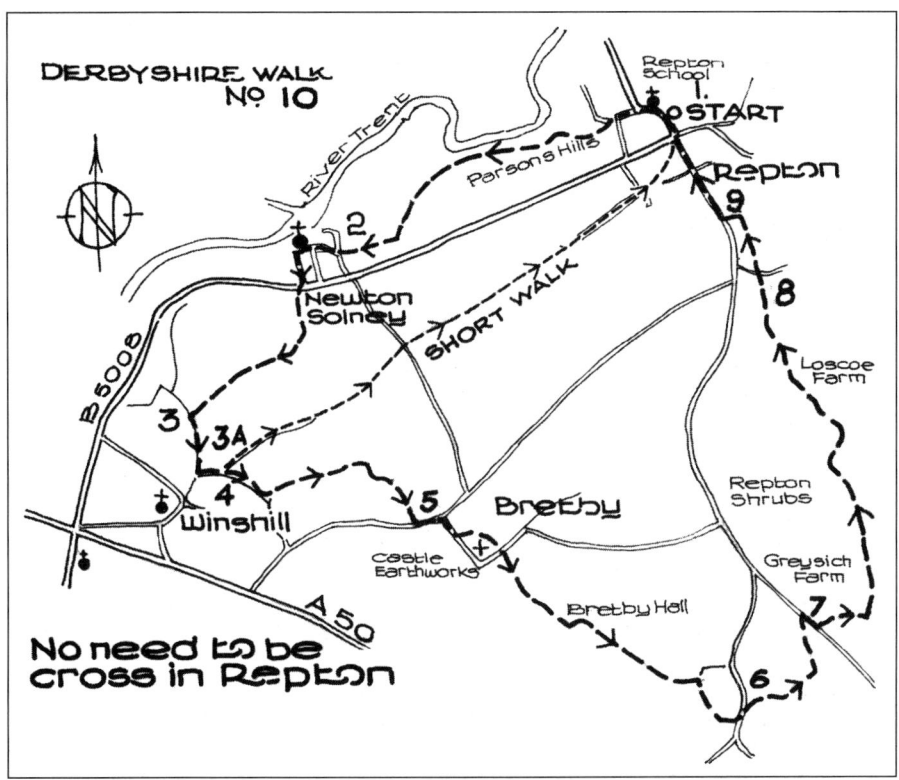

then left at the T-junction and, in 50m, bear right onto a sandy track by a wood. This descends to a series of fishing lakes then climbs to cross training tracks for horses before descending again into Hoofies Wood. At the bottom, turn right, passing a farm on the left to a stile by a gate. Turn left to a second stile, then bear left to follow a fence on the left for 150m, to meet a track which climbs up to a minor road.

6.   Turn left and in 100m take the footpath on the right, up the right-hand side of the field to a gap in the crossing hedge. Turn right for 25m, then left as way-marked, with a wood on the right. In 250m turn right again, as way-marked, to enter a narrow wood. Where the path forks in the wood, bear left, cross a clearing to enter a narrow field and follow the fence/hedge on the right for 300m. At its end bear left with the hedge to a stile, then forward through a gate onto Greysich Lane.

7.   Turn right for 150m to a 'hidden' stile on left. Bear half-right across a pasture to another stile, then go forward over a field to a tarmac access road. Turn left and follow this until it bears right to Fair View Farm. **Do not go to the farm,**

instead go forward on a rough track to the right of Repton Shrubs. At the wood end veer right then left up a hedged track to Loscoe Farm. Go forward on the now metalled lane and descend to a minor road.

8.   Cross the road to a stile opposite, noting Park Pond on the left. Proceed down the valley with a stream on the left for 1km to a stile in front of a house named Mount Pleasant on the right. Take the left fork through scrub grass to cross the stream and ascend between houses onto Main Street.

9.   Turn right for 400m to a crossroads. Turn left along Well Lane and in 30m turn right (past No 16) up a narrow alleyway to an estate road. Continue forward, through a cycle barrier, into another alleyway and in 130m turn right alongside a house named Souter Point. After 100m, bear left to emerge alongside the Red Lion public house on Burton Road. Turn right to Repton Cross, then left back to the church.

Points of Interest

Repton – This village, lying by the tranquil waters of the River Trent, is a place full of history. The first mention of Repton was in the 7th century when it was established as the capital of the Saxon Kingdom of Mercia. A monastery was founded here around AD653 housing both monks and nuns. The building was raided by the Danes in AD874. On display in the local school museum is a battleaxe excavated close to St Wystan's Church. It had been buried undisturbed for well over 1000 years.

St Wystan's Church – An interesting church famous for its Anglo-Saxon chancel and crypt. Although much enlarged in the 13th–15th centuries the church you can see today was built circa AD975. The chancel and part of the nave were enlarged in 1854 with the original Anglo-Saxon columns being moved to the 14th-century porch. The tiny crypt is claimed to be one of the few remaining examples of Anglo-Saxon architecture. This was discovered in 1779 by a workman digging a hole for a grave in the chancel floor.

Repton Cross – The ancient market cross at the central crossroads has been a focal point for centuries.

Repton College – This is a part of an Augustinian Priory founded in 1170. The Repton College was founded in 1556, by Sir John Port, as a grammar school for the local poor children of Etwall, Repton and Burnaston. Today, however, it is one of the foremost public schools in the country.

Bretby – this quiet village once had a castle but this was demolished and the stones used to build a mansion house. In the 18th century, this was also demolished and, in 1813, Bretby Hall was built by the designer, Sir Jeffery Wyatville. He was also the designer of the 19th-century extension at Chatsworth House.

The County of Nottinghamshire

Mention Nottinghamshire, and the first thing that springs to many people's minds is its association with the legendary character, Robin Hood. His exploits are well known and certainly his operational base of Sherwood Forest is famed throughout the world and is obviously included in this section. But that is not the only feature in the county and the walks included recall other people and places that have made their mark in this county of middle England.

The county is surrounded on all sides by larger neighbours, each distinct in their own way. While there are no outstanding areas of mountain and moorland as in Derbyshire, nor vast vistas of open countryside as in Lincolnshire, it does have its own attractions, which may be sought by the discerning walker. Its shape is roughly oval with the highest land in the west and the lowest in the east where the River Trent winds its way to meet the mighty Humber. Indeed, the River Trent travels one third of its entire length within the county. A typical cross-section reveals a series of north-south ridges decreasing in height as they progress eastward. The countryside of Nottinghamshire can thus be best summed up as undulating.

The coal measures in the west had a profound effect on the landscape for nearly two centuries. This is reflected in the writings of D.H. Lawrence who, being born at Eastwood into a mining family, had first-hand knowledge of their dominance in those parts. It may seem a little ironic but the highest point (now official) in Nottinghamshire is in fact a former colliery spoil heap standing at the giddy height of 205 metres (640 feet).

In the more arable farmlands of the east, a

Walking near Southwell, Walk 14
(Photograph: Gordon Gadsby)

unique remnant of medieval times is still practised today. At the village of Laxton, the retention of the three-field system of crop rotation continues whereby large fields are divided into narrow strips; these being allocated each year to local farmers by a special 'Court Leet'. Laxton is the last Open Field Village in England.

According to Niklaus Pevsner in his 'The Buildings of England', Nottinghamshire has very little in the way of outstanding architecture but recognises that the Minister at Southwell is an 'overpowering presence' and was raised to cathedral status in 1884. Its Norman, and later English architecture make it a 'must see' for walkers and visitors alike. It is also interesting to note that King Charles I surrendered to the Parliamentarians close by at the Saracens Head and thus ended the First Civil War. Even more interesting is the fact that he raised his Standard four years earlier at Nottingham thus setting into train the English Civil Wars. One further item worthy of mention is that Southwell is the home of the famous Bramley apple; the original tree is still in existence and can be viewed on special occasions. Another claim to fame is that Nottinghamshire was the origin of the Pilgrim Fathers and one of the walks takes in Babworth, near Retford, instrumental in the founding of this historic group.

The pretty villages near the Trent Hills and the panorama westwards from the ridge are well worth seeking out as are those in the south of the county known as The Wolds.

If you complete the walks in this section, you will get a better insight into what is often an overlooked county.

Highway Authorities

Nottingham City Council,
Neighbourhood Services (Rights of Way),
Lawrence House,
Talbot Street,
Nottingham NGl 5NT   0115 915 6078

Nottinghamshire County Council
Countryside Access Group,
Trent Bridge House,
Fox Road,
West Bridgford,
Nottingham NG2 6BJ   0115 977 2166

Tourist Information

Nottingham: 0115 915 5330

11: Snowdrops of Hodsock Priory

In February, the snowdrops in the woods surrounding Hodsock Priory form a splendid spectacle in a picturesque setting. Our walk also takes in Langold Country Park and Lake. Wallingwells, with the site of a former Benedictine Priory and Carlton in Lindrick, has a Norman church, with a tower, possibly the oldest in the County.

Distance: Long Walk 19km (12 miles); Short Walk 12km (7½ miles)

Duration: Long Walk 6 hours; Short Walk 4 hours

Maps required: OS Explorer 279 Doncaster, OS Landranger 120 Mansfield and Worksop

Terrain: Agricultural, Parkland and tracks

Starting point: Blyth Village Green. (SK 625869)

Refreshments: Public Houses in Blyth and Carlton in Lindrick. Café in Langold Country Park (limited opening hours)

Bus/Train link: Retford, Worksop and Doncaster

The Route

1. From The Green on High Street, cross the road, then turn right and walk towards St Peter's Church. Turn left along Sheffield Road (A634) and walk 200m to Park Lodge.

2. Turn left onto a track and walk to path junction just before the electricity pylons. Take path on right, walk downhill passing through two gates to footpath over the River Ryton. Go through a coppice and carry on passing through a gap in hedge to bear half-left near fingerpost and boundary stone. Cross two fields to a track.

3. Turn sharp right on track for a few metres then continue ahead with hedge on left to end of field. Here go through gap in hedge and continue roughly on the same line through a row of conifers to a stile at a metalled road, with radio mast and wood. Turn left and follow road past Hodsock Cottage, and a large barn, continue a further 1km to reach coppice on left, with a dwelling.

Short Walk

3a. Turn left, going past cottage into open field to cross over stream and continue uphill to stile. Turn right along Woodhouse Lane, passing Lilac Lodge on left and continue to Hodsock Lane. Go left for a few metres and then take a path on the right, across paddocks to a footpath junction and turn left (go to point 13).

Long Walk

4. Continue along the road to reach Worksop/Langold (Doncaster Road) A60.

5. Cross the A60 road, to enter Langold Country Park. Cross the car park to enter a wood at its right-hand end. Follow on path in a generally westward direction, through the wood to reach Church Street entrance road, with lake kiosk, toilets and car park.

6. Walk with the lake on your left, along a clear track eventually crossing a bridge over the head of lake. Just after this take a permissive indistinct path on the right, now following a feeder brook that is on your right. We follow the track for 400m into an open field to join a cross-field path at bridge. **Do not cross the bridge.**

7. Turn left before the bridge and walk diagonally left ascending, towards a hill, to reach the far side of the field and a stile. Turn right on a clear track to reach Buckwood Farm and road (Rotherham Baulk).

8. Turn left and then immediate right, along a bridleway track to a path junction at the edge of a wood. Turn right along another bridleway for 400m to a further bridle path on the left.

9. Turn left and walk along the bridleway for 800m with the hamlet of Wallingwells on the left for 800m, to cross a track, then continue for a further 250m. Note county boundary stone and stone gatepost in wooded area. At the end of the wood turn right and ascend a gentle slope after 250m turn left onto a footpath.

10. Turn left through a kissing gate crossing fields to reach Home House Farm on the left. (Footpath is indistinct.) Go forward for 200m and where the track bears right continue ahead on a poorly defined field path, aiming to the right of the church to reach South Carlton and to emerge at The Mill.

11. Turn left along Church Lane, crossing the mill race, and walk past St John the Evangelist Church to reach the A60 road. (Take time to visit this lovely church.) Cross the A60 road, turn left for 250m to reach Chapel Lane on the right.

12. Walk down Chapel Lane, turn left into Low Street and continue ahead past The Cross to reach Greenway. Turn left, then immediate right at footpath sign.

Short Walk rejoins

13. Continue straight on and walk across three fields with hedge on left to a stile. Go over the stile and continue along a track to reach Hodsock Priory at path junction.

14. Turn left going past the gate house on the left and then continue along access drive to the main road (B6045 Worksop to Blyth road) at Briber Hill.

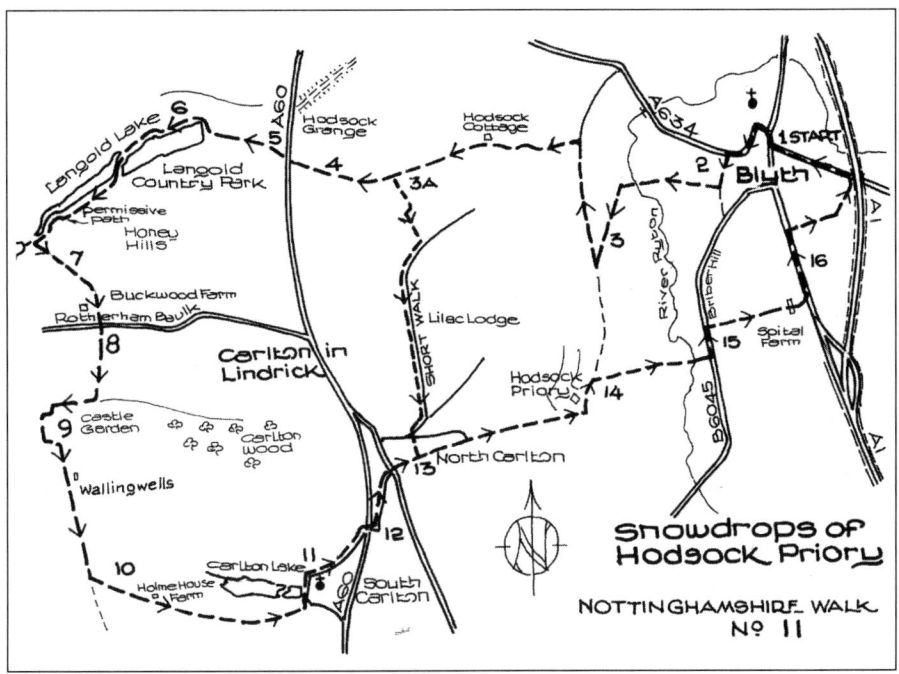

Snowdrops of
Hodsock Priory

NOTTINGHAMSHIRE WALK
N⁰ 11

15. Turn left **and walk with great care along the road for 200m.** (Briber Hill) to take an access road on the right to Spittle Farm. Continue past the farm to Spittle Road, Blyth.

16. Turn left and take footpath on right after 400m to follow the path passing a playground and school to a road beneath the A1 road bridge. Turn left along Retford Road to locate the main crossroads in Blyth and return to start of walk.

Points of Interest

Blyth – The Priory Church dominates the village. The Priory was founded in 1088 by Roger de Busli as a cell of the Abbey of St Cuthbert at Rouen. Take a visit to this church as it is steeped in history. At the other end of the village is St John's Hospital founded as a Leper hospital, rebuilt and later used as a school.

Blyth Hall – Built by Edward Mellish next to the Priory Church standing to its west, it was a distinguished late 17th-century house standing high and commanding an excellent view of the countryside around.

Hodsock Priory – Standing deep in parkland and wooded meadows, descended from the Cressy family to the Cliftons of Clifton. There is a wonderful 16th-century brick gatehouse leading to an early 16th-century Tudor house that was added to in the 1870s. Beautiful gardens within an ancient moat. Now the home of the present Lord Lieutenant of Nottinghamshire, Sir Andrew Buchanan and Lady Buchanan, the hall is famous for the snowdrops in February and March.

Carlton-in-Lindrick – Visit the church (St John the Evangelist) said to be the oldest in Nottinghamshire. The Mill on the edge of the park near the church is powered by the stream that feeds the lake of Carlton Hall (former home of the Ramsdens). The Mill is now a museum.

Wallingwells – This was a very small Benedictine nunnery built during King Stephen's reign (1135-1154). It was never rich or powerful having only nine nuns and a prioress up to the Dissolution in 1539. In the reign of Richard I, Dame Margaret Dourant, the second prioress died and was buried at Wallingwells. During excavations in 1829, her coffin was discovered and her remains were reinterred. A cross in a stone forming part of the garden wall marks the reinterment place.

12: The Retford Round

A pleasant walk skirting the market town of East Retford. The town is quartered by rail and water. The East Coast Main Line and River Idle run north and south, the Sheffield – Lincoln line and Chesterfield Canal east and west. Each of these four obstructions has to be crossed twice; unfortunately this incurs some road walking but it is still a worthwhile walk.

Distance: Long Walk 22.5 km (14 miles); Short Walk 9.5 km (6 miles)

Duration: Long Walk 6½ hours; Short Walk 2½ hours

Maps required: OS Explorer 270 Sherwood Forest, OS Explorer 271 Newark-on-Trent, OS Explorer 279 Doncaster, OS Landranger 120 Mansfield & Worksop

Terrain: No steep climbs, canal towpath can be muddy

Starting point: On by-road off A620, not in Hop Pole Hotel car park. (SK718818)

Refreshments: The Hop Pole; The King & Miller (North Road); Plough Inn, Ordsall; Packet Inn, Canal side; White House Inn, Whitehouses; many others easily accessible in Retford town.

Bus/Train link: Retford

The Route

1. From the Hop Pole Hotel cross the road and immediately over the canal bridge (No.59) turn right down steps to the canal towpath. Turn left along the towpath for approximately 220m then go over a stile (hidden in a hedge) on the left along overgrown footpath to Longholme Road. Here turn right and go over two stiles between houses Nos. 28 & 30. Cross the field towards the left-hand corner where a stile and plank bridge leads onto a path between two hedges. Follow this left and continue ahead on the road from Longholme Farm to reach Bigsby Road. Go along Bigsby Road; take second right into Cornwall Road and walk to the end. Turn left into Palmer Road and at the end left again, then almost immediately right into Carr Hill Way. Shortly bear left into River Close, and at the end descend steps between properties numbered 20 & 22 and turn right along Bolham Lane.

2. Cross the river at the bridge and bear right through a kissing gate and along the footpath to a track round the fishing lakes. Follow this track, (this is a permissive path not shown on current OS maps) keeping the river to your right until a kissing gate in the boundary fence near the line of metal electricity pylons (numbered HV32) is reached. Through the kissing gate, turn left onto a path along the boundary fence and continue to a metalled road. Here turn left, then shortly right onto Randall Way. At the end, turn left onto North Road. In approximately 220m cross the road at the crossing island, turn left and in a few metres cross onto a service road which runs alongside North Road. On reaching Fulford Avenue, bear left back onto North Road and continue for approximately 220m to the cemetery gate. Turn right into the cemetery taking the left fork to a gate onto the canal towpath at bridge (No.54b). (Note: the path through cemetery is not a public right of way and could be closed without notice. Please act with respect if a funeral is taking place.)

Short Walk

3a. Turn left here and walk along the canal back to the start.

Long Walk

3. Turn right and continue to bridge No.54. (Known as Lady Bridge, note deep rope cuts in stonework caused by horses dragging towropes along the wall.) Go under the bridge and turn right through the trees to reach the road. Turn right and go over the bridge and along the road for just over 480m. Just past 'Home Farm' house on the right, turn left at footpath signed 'Babworth Church ¼ mile', pass through two kissing gates and follow well-defined footpath to a third kissing gate. Continue ahead on a pleasant path and cross a stile on the left just before the church. Follow the footpath signs through the trees, over another stile on the right to a kissing gate.

4. Continue along the field boundary to the A620. Turn right and continue to a crossroads. Here cross over into the road signposted 'Clumber' and after approximately 220m turn left at a bridleway sign onto a metalled drive leading to Great Morton Farm. Pass the farm and continue straight ahead, passing under railway bridge with the hedge on your left, to a gate. Through the gate bear diagonally right to footpaths in the right-hand corner of the field, then left and continue with the hedge on the right to footpath signpost. Here turn left and continue to the trees of Whisker Hills and Retford Golf Course.

5. At the end of the field, go through the hedge on the left to gain footpath across the golf course. Bear right, then almost immediately left and ascend through the trees. Where the path forks, bear slightly right and continue to the top of the hill. Here turn right and pass through an opening in the barbed wire fence into a field. Follow the footpath left around the edge of the courses, until reaching a kissing gate. Turn right on track at rear of houses. After approximately 110m turn left by an oak tree into a housing estate. Bear right then left onto Gleneagles Way, Ordsall and follow this to the end.

6. Turn right and after approximately 220m go left down a grassy track. Where the track crosses a stream, turn left and follow the edge of the field to just

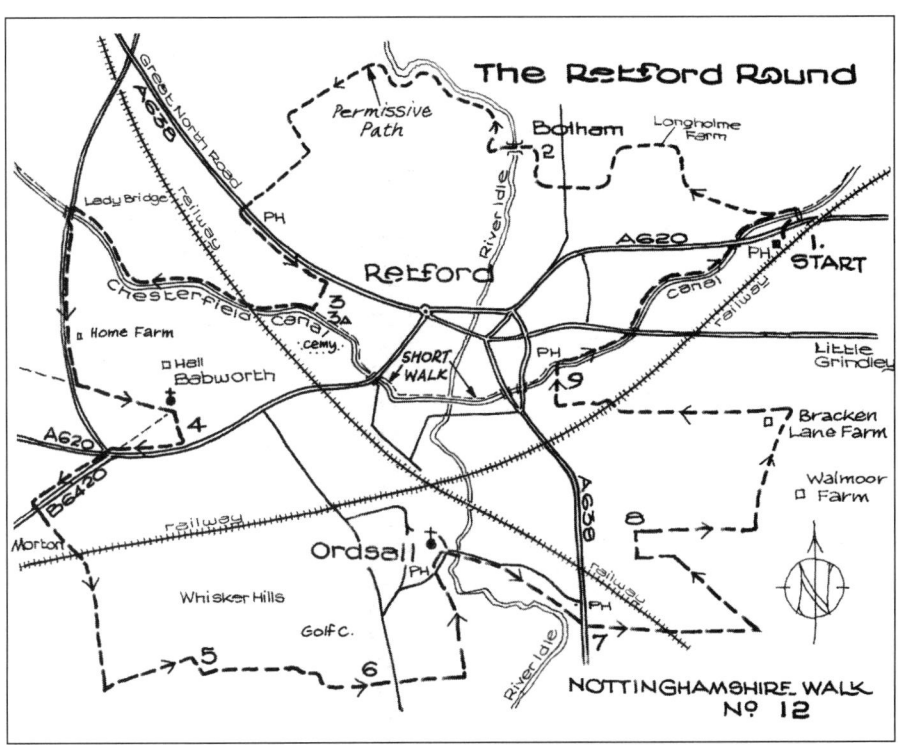

The Retford Round

NOTTINGHAMSHIRE WALK
Nº 12

before the boundary of private gardens. Here, the path bears left to a footpath sign to turn right into the private gardens. You then follow signs to a gate by the river. Turn left and follow the path by the river to High Street. Turn right and right again into Goosemoor Lane. Over the bridge after approximately 360m, go over the stile at the footpath sign on the right, crossing the field to another stile, continuing to a kissing gate and following the alleyway up to the A638.

7. Turn right, then immediately left into Grove Road. Continue along this road past the houses and over the railway crossing to a footpath sign on the left, just before the road turns right. The path goes diagonally across the field to the left-hand corner. Here cross two wooden plank bridges, follow the edge of the dyke, over a cross dyke, to an access path into the next field. Continue bearing left to a rusty green gate in the left corner of the field. Follow the path with the fence on your right to join the metalled road of Five Fields Lane.

8. At the end of the lane, turn right into Grove Coach Road. Continue straight on past the houses to a T-junction. Turn left, follow the lane past another road junction, and continue straight on to Bracken Lane Farm. Go over the stile on the left, then over another into a field. Continue ahead over another

stile, with a plank bridge into another field. Cross another stile continuing ahead to a final stile, leading into an alleyway emerging on to the road by a bungalow. Turn left, then immediately right and go over the railway bridge into Pennington Walk.

9.   Pass the school and continue along Pennington Walk, now a footpath, to the end. At the road, turn left over canal bridge (No.57) then right to reach the towpath. Turn left onto the towpath and continue to bridge (No.59). Under the bridge, turn left up the steps to the A620 and the Hop Pole Hotel.

Points of Interest

Retford – An ancient market town on the Great North Road, an important stopping-off point for coaches. The Chesterfield canal and the coming of the railway in the middle of the 19th century brought new industry and resulted in much Victorian building. The River Idle divides the town as east and west, both being ancient parishes. A lovely market town with much to see and enjoy.

Babworth – Famous for the Pilgrim Fathers, Babworth has close links with America through Richard Clayton (Rector 1586-1604) who became the pastor of the Separatist Church at Scrooby. The Whitaker family came to Babworth in 1898 living in Babworth Hall, which stands in a commanding position.

Chesterfield Canal – Engineered by James Brindley who died in 1772 during its construction, it was completed by his brother-in-law Hugh Henshall and opened through out in 1777. It runs for 46½ miles between the River Trent at West Stockwith and Chesterfield, it has broad locks (15ft wide) as far as Retford and narrow locks (7ft) thereafter. The Norwood Tunnel collapse in 1907 severed the Chesterfield end and the canal above Worksop deteriorated until it was closed in the 1960s. After a long campaign by the Chesterfield Canal Trust the section up to the tunnel and the Staveley to Chesterfield section are being restored.

Ordsall – An old village now incorporated as part of Retford, with Ordsall church a conspicuous landmark from the railway line. The church was restored in 1876 by T.C. Hine.

Randall Way – named after the famous Nottinghamshire and England cricketer, Derek Randall who was born in Retford.

13: The Great Fields of Laxton

Discover the medieval open fields of Laxton, the historical church at Egmanton together with the chapel at Moorhouses and for the more energetic walker, the site of Ossington Hall.

Distance: Long Walk 19km (12 miles); Short Walk 12km (8 miles)

Duration: Long Walk 6 hours; Short Walk 4 hours

Maps required: OS Explorer 271 Newark on Trent, OS Landranger 120 Mansfield & Worksop

Terrain: Field paths and tracks, can be muddy after rain

Starting point: Laxton Visitors Centre car park behind Dovecote Inn (SK723671)

Refreshments: Dovecote Inn, Laxton. The Old Plough, Egmanton

Bus/Train link: Newark or Retford

The Route

1. Leaving the car park cross over the tiny green towards the church and in 100m take the footpath right alongside the farm. Follow the hedge left to a gate, which you pass through, then veer left for 50m to a bridle gate and information board which gives details of the old Motte and Bailey castle. After exploring the site, return to the board and head westwards along the track to a stile by the side of another gate. Cross this, turn right over another stile and in 100m cross a third stile on the left. Angle right across the arable field to a footbridge and a fourth stile.

2. Forward up the right-hand side of the field and where the hedge ends turn left to a wide gap in the hedge opposite. Turn right on a track for 100m then bear half-left to a waymark at the hedge, continue left to a solitary tree with a stile and fingerpost nearby. Forward for 65m then turn right along the right-hand side of a line of trees to a stile at Kirton Wood.

3. Turn right through the line of trees, cross over a sleeper stile, then follow the dyke left for just over 1.5km on a headland path, passing the hollows of the ancient fish ponds. At the end of this field, turn left, through a gate to a minor road. Turn right and in 1km enter Egmanton. Take the road, left, to the church, then the footpath opposite to a footbridge and the village high street. Cross over to the lane which you follow for 500m until it bears right, then cross the arable field diagonally left, as way-marked to the perimeter of Egmanton Wood. Follow this along three sides to a footbridge. Do not cross this, instead turn left for 400m to find a stile, right, by a lone tree. Cross the

stile, heading half-left to a pylon to another stile/footbridge. Over this turn right to follow the hedge line as it curves left to a minor road just outside the hamlet of Moorhouse. Turn right for 50m to a stile, left, and cross the field to the old chapel. Leave the field along the access road to Chapel Farm.

Short Walk

4.   Turn right and go to point 6.

Long Walk

4.   Turn left and in a few metres left along the access drive to Thorpe Farm. Where the road turns right, keep ahead over a stile into a grass field, over a second stile then across field to short hedged track, at the end head slightly left and follow left side of ditch. Over bridge then follow a clearly defined path through Wadnal Plantation, then the field edge to Cocked Hat Plantation. Turn right at the path crossroads along a hedged track for 1km to a road.

5.   Turn right and in 25m left, through a copse, along a path which soon turns right and eventually emerges onto the road again passing to right of kennels. Cross over to enter the woods surrounding the site of the now demolished Ossington Hall. Follow the path for 250m to meet a main track, turn right and keep on this for 600m to meet the outflow from the lake. Keep ahead for 25m then right. At field edge, head towards a farm, joining the road to the left of the farm through a gap in the hedge. Turn right and head back into Moorhouse.

Short Walk rejoins

6.   Turn left along the Laxton road and in 250m left over the stile, forward to a footbridge then right across an arable field to another stile. Now keep the beck to your right as you follow it to Copthorne Farm. On entering the farm cross the stile on the right of the barn (on the bank of the brook), then through a hand gate to leave the farmyard, still close to the stream. After 350m you join a wide hedged lane which you follow as it eventually bears right over the brook and under the power lines to meet the road.

7.   Turn left to enter Laxton but at the T-junction turn left again, now going away from the village. After 150m take the stile right and cross the arable field, half-right, to a footbridge. Now keep straight ahead, aiming just to the left of the church. Once in the churchyard turn right along a paved path past the church to pass through a gap in the wall then along a narrow alleyway to emerge onto the main road opposite the old pinfold and the Dovecote Inn.

Points of Interest

The Motte and Bailey castle – The best preserved and largest in the county, dating back to Norman times. Originally belonged to the Birkin family but later passed to the Everinghams. Several kings visited the castle, including John and Edward I.

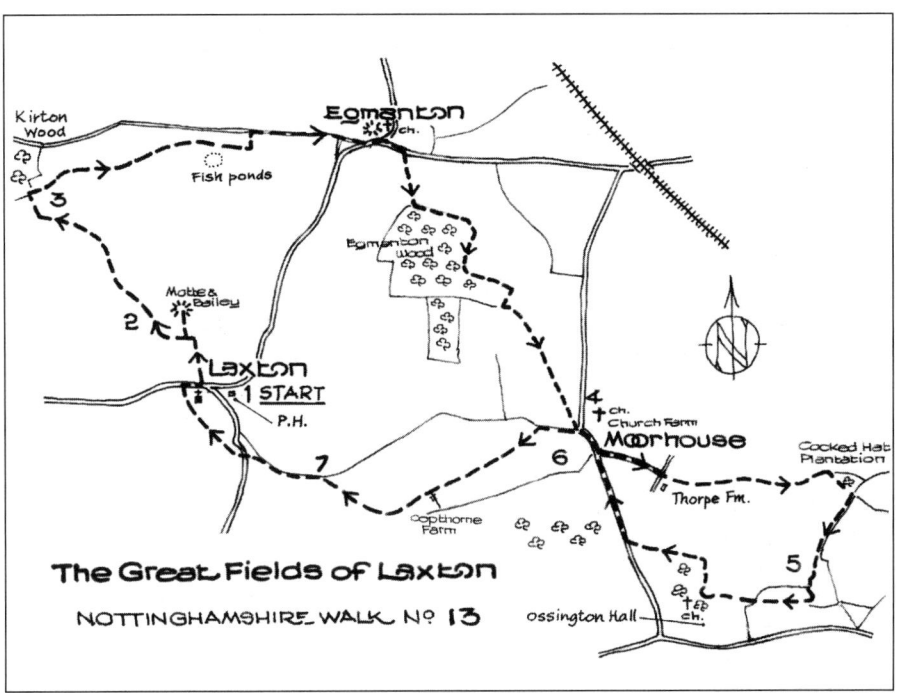

The Great Fields of Laxton

NOTTINGHAMSHIRE WALK № 13

Egmanton Church – Nottinghamshire's Shrine of Our Lady, highly decorative and well worth a visit. Pilgrimages are held here every summer to see the restoration work which was carried out by Sir Niniam Comper in 1896. Behind the church is a mound, the only remnant of another motte and bailey castle.

Moorhouse Church – Built by Henry Clutton in 1860 looks lost and forlorn in the field, surrounded by local cows. The keys can be obtained from the adjacent farm.

Ossington Hall – This was situated next to the church. The Cartwright family built a Tudor house but this was replaced in 1729 with a Georgian style one. This was enlarged in 1790 but after being used for military purposes between 1939-45, it was demolished in 1963. In springtime the churchyard is full of snowdrops and primroses and is well worth a visit.

Laxton – Famous for retaining the medieval open field system of farming. Full details of this can be found in the Visitors Centre next to the Dovecote Inn. The old pinfold was built in 1897 opposite the public house on the other side of the road. It was moved in 1969 by Nottinghamshire County Council and rebuilt in its present position.

14: The Bomber and Bramley Walk

A rewarding walk in Central Nottinghamshire around the Minster city of Southwell, the home of the Bramley apple, combined with a visit to the Halifax Bomber Monument, just outside Farnsfield.

Distance: Long Walk 18km (11 miles); Short Walk 14km (8½ miles)

Duration: Long Walk 5 hours; Short Walk 4 hours

Maps required: OS Explorer 270 Sherwood Forest, OS Explorer 271 Newark on Trent, OS Landranger 120 Mansfield and Worksop

Terrain: Rolling countryside, all paths in good condition

Starting point: Southwell Trail car park on Station Road, Southwell (SK706544)

Refreshments: The Reindeer, Edingley. The Waggon and Horses, Halam, numerous in Farnsfield.

Bus/Train link: Newark/Southwell

The Route

1. From the car park turn left down Station Road and, just past Cauldwell's Mill, turn left again to meet the banks of the River Greet. After 100m cross the footbridge, right then angle left across the field to a stile and large gate. This is the boundary fence for Reg Taylor's Nature Reserve. Bear right around the pond to another stile and gate to leave the reserve to cross a field, aiming just to the left of buildings, to find three stiles to emerge onto a minor road.

2. Turn left for 500m and where the road turns right go forward along a hedged lane. In 300m, turn right, going over a footbridge to cross a second footbridge at Maythorne Mill. Go right past the gentrified mill buildings until you reach the disused railway line, now called the Southwell Trail. Turn right on this for 2.5km to Kirklington Station picnic area. 150m past the car park descend the steps left to follow the Edingley Beck for 1km to meet the main road in Edingley.

Short Walk

3a. Turn left and, opposite the end of Station Road, take the footpath between houses to bear left to a paddock and arable field to Greaves Lane. Turn right, and then in 100m turn left to a T-junction and right again at next T-junction onto Newhall Lane for 1.5km to meet Cutlersforth Lane at T-junction. Ignore all crossing paths. Now go to point 5a to rejoin the long walk.

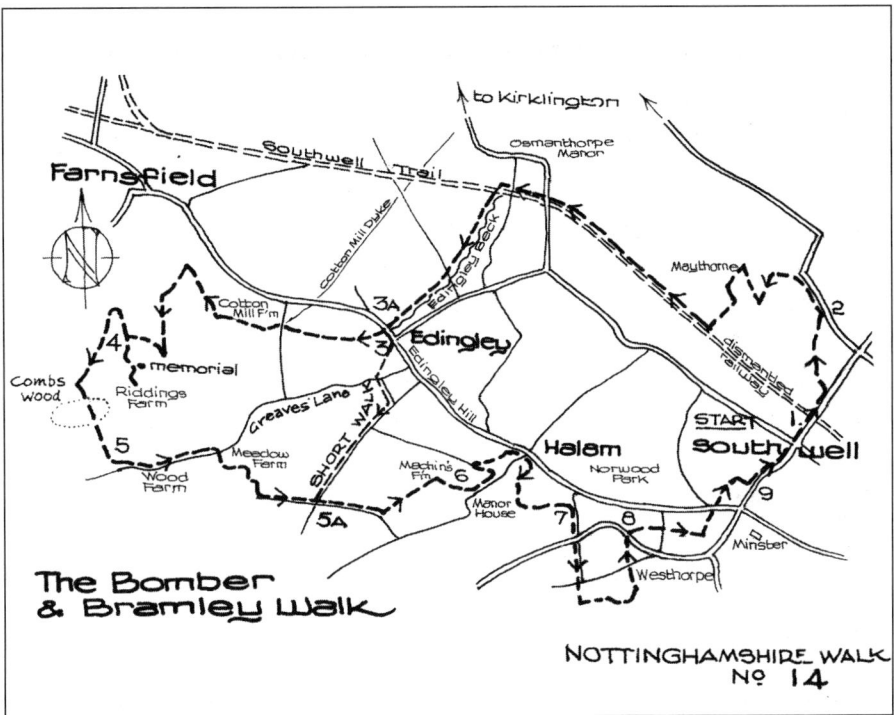

to Kirklington

Osmanthorpe Manor

Farnsfield

Southwell Trail

Cotton Mill Dyke

Maythorne

Farnsfield Beck

Cotton Mill F'm

3A

Edingley

dismantled railway

2

memorial

4

Combs Wood

Riddings Farm

Greaves Lane

Edingley Hill

START

SOUTHWELL

5

Meadow Farm

Wood Farm

Halam

Norwood Park

9

Machins F'm

6

5A

SHORT WALK

Manor House

7

8

Minster

Westhorpe

The Bomber & Bramley Walk

NOTTINGHAMSHIRE WALK
No 14

Long Walk

3. Turn right and in 50m left down the entrance to Manor Farm on right of church. After 40m take the footpath, right, crossing several small fields to join a farm access drive. Continue in the same direction crossing an arable field to a minor road. Cross over to a footbridge opposite and follow the headland path, by the dyke, to come to a track by Cotton Mill Farm. Turn right and, in 100m, left through a gate to follow a hedge, right, for 350m which leads to the Farnsfield Football Club ground. Just past the children's play area ,turn left, passing the changing rooms, right, to a small gate which leads to a small plantation. Keep to left-hand track. Follow the clear path over an arable field to meet a hedged lane, right. Take this and, in 350m, you come to a T-junction.

4. Our way is right, but 250m up the road towards Riddings Farm is the Halifax Bomber Monument. After 200m turn left along Combs Lane and in 600m left again on a headland path which lead into Combs Wood. Go forward, ignoring all side paths, to descend Robb Lane to meet Greaves Lane opposite Wood Farm.

5. Turn left and just past Meadow Farm, right, going uphill then bearing left to join a sunken path. At the top turn right and in 100m fork left along a hedged track. Bear right, then left for 700m to a crossing road. Keep straight ahead.

Short Walk rejoins

5a. After 600m take the footpath left on apex of bend, along a hedge, right, crossing a footbridge and two fields and two stiles to find a stile in the hedge right. Cross this, turn left and in 200m pass Machins Farm to meet a crossing path. Turn right, downhill, and take the stile left by the stream. In 100m cross a footbridge, then forward alongside Manor Farm to the road at Halam.

6. Turn left and opposite the Post Office, left again. In 250m, turn right, just before the stream, to cross the house lawn into a meadow. Follow the hedge, right, for 250m to a stile then bear right to the car park of the Waggon and Horses Inn. Forward up the main road to a stile on right, which brings you to the rear of the churchyard. At the cemetery veer left uphill to a stile in a narrow copse. Through the trees turn right and in 100m left, keeping a hedge on your right. Follow the clear path straight ahead, over a stile in corner, into the garden of Halam Gate house and onto the minor road.

7. Turn right, in 350m cross the B6386, onto a minor road. After 250m, the road turns left but continue forward and uphill to a stile, left. Cross the field to another road, turn right, then left and forward down an access drive to a fenced path, which leads to a gate into a meadow. Veer left to a footbridge and narrow path into Westhorpe. Cross the road to a narrow alleyway and up this to meet the B6386 again.

8. Cross the road to take the headland path on right, behind the houses. Follow this for 750m to turn left around the far side of the school playing field, to descend onto Queen Street, Southwell. Turn right and in 50m sharp left, along a narrow alleyway to a supermarket car park. Follow the road round to the right to cross the square and onto King Street.

9. Turn left to go downhill across Burgage Green to crossroads. Continue ahead down Station Road to your starting point.

Points of Interest

Southwell – The picturesque town is dominated by its 12th-century Minster, known as 'The Cathedral of Nottinghamshire'. To the east of the Minster lie the ruins of the Bishop's Palace and the remains of a Roman villa.

The Saracen's Head Inn – This is situated on King Street. It has a black-and-white timbered front and was visited by Charles I in 1642 and again in 1645.

On Burgage Green – The Georgian Burgage Manor was once the home of Lord Byron's mother. Further down the hill, only the gates remain of the old House of Correction.

The Bramley Apple – This was discovered in Southwell by a Mr Bramley in

1805. A descendant of the original tree is situated in the garden of a private house in Church Street.

Cauldwell's Mill and Maythorne Mill – Both were once working mills powered by water from the nearby River Greet. Nowadays they have been converted for commercial and residential usage.

The Southwell Trail – Now owned by Nottinghamshire County Council, it was formerly part of the Midland railway from Mansfield to Rolleston. The Trail stretches from Southwell to Bilsthorpe, a distance of 12km (7½ miles).

The Halifax Bomber Monument – Situated to the north-east of Riddings Farm, it marks the spot where the aircraft crashed in July 1945, killing all of its crew. The monument was erected by the people of Farnsfield in 1995 to commemorate its 50th anniversary.

Halam – Beautifully situated below the orchards of Norwood Park. Manor Farm was built in the 18th century on the site of an ancient manor house.

Westhorpe – Just to the south of the main street lies the site of Saint Catherine's Well (SK685534), one of the ancient wells of Southwell.

15: A Birdwatcher's Bonanza

This walk will be of particular interest to ornithologists since the route takes in a long stretch of the River Trent towpath and numerous lagoons. It also passes remnants of the gravel extraction industry. These have been restored and they provide a perfect habitat for swans, herons and Canada geese.

Distance: Long Walk 22km (13½ miles); Short Walk 16km (10 miles)

Duration: Long Walk 6½ hours; Short Walk 5 hours

Maps required: OS Explorer 271 Newark on Trent, OS Landranger 121 Lincoln

Terrain: Flat, riverside path and some arable fields

Starting point: Grass verge, Tinkers Lane, Girton (SK826656)

Refreshments: The Grey Horse, Royal Oak, and King's Arms – all in Collingham. The Lord Nelson, Besthorpe

Bus/Train link: Collingham

The Route

1. From alongside the River Fleet head north towards Girton to follow the main street. At the third bend, note the flood levels on the house wall, right, then ahead to the church. Take the lane opposite then veer right on a track. In 30m cross the stile, left, then forward over three fields to a short lane.

2. Turn left, cross the Fleet, and go ahead through a gate to follow a grassy track for 750m, ignoring two tracks on right, to a stile and steps up an embankment. Continue ahead, passing the remains of a lagoon on your left, for 500m to where the track bends left before reaching grid lines. Look out for a footpath on the right and follow it round the south side of a nature reserve to reach the River Trent just north of Besthorpe Wharf. Turn left along the floodbank and follow this meandering riverside path.

Long Walk

3. After 6km, pass a bungalow, to a fisherman's car park at the end of Westfield Lane. Take the stile left through the car park and in 150m turn right over a second stile. Follow this path for almost 2km to a footbridge in front of a small copse. On reaching the far side of the copse, turn left for 300m to cross the Fleet over an earth bridge. Continue ahead alongside the stream for 500m to a path T-junction at the south end of Collingham.

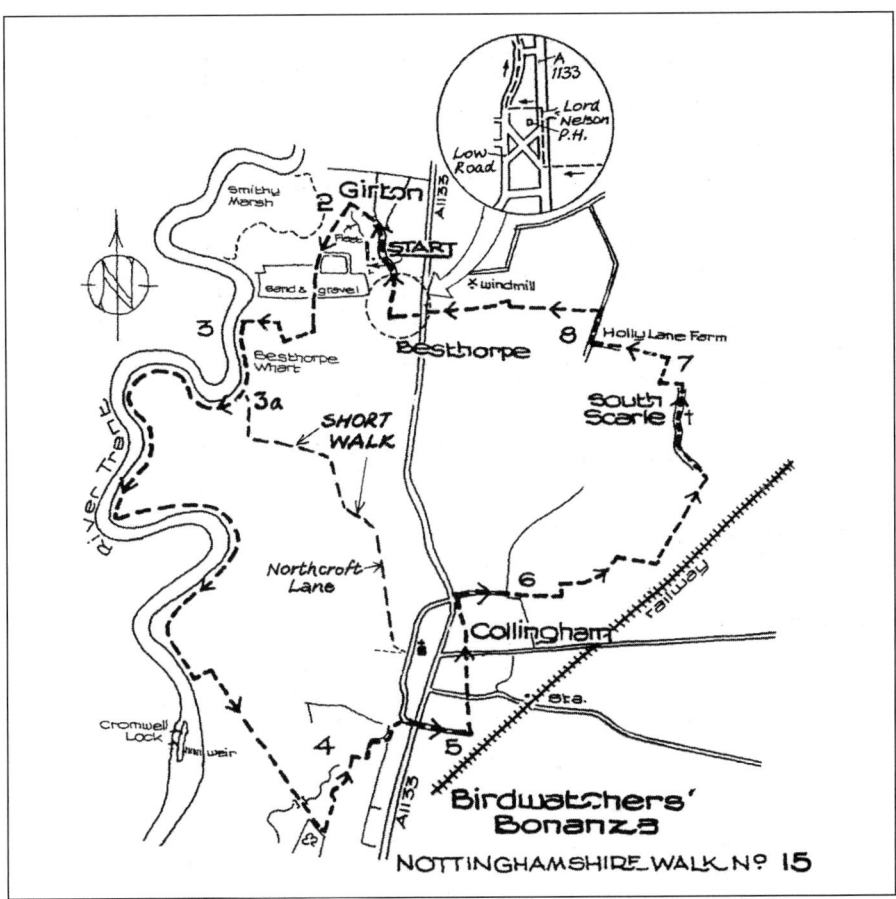

NOTTINGHAMSHIRE WALK Nº 15

Short Walk

3a. After 1km turn left onto a footpath just before the second clapper gate opposite a green marker cone in the river. In 300m, turn left to follow Northcroft
Lane to its junction with Carlton Ferry Lane. Turn left to North Collingham
church, then left again onto Low Street for 400m to the Grey Horse public
house. Cross over the A1133 and walk along Woodhill Road. Go to point 6.

Long Walk

4. Turn right into a fenced path and at the end cross the stile left into a small
lane. After 20m take the alleyway, right, cross over Cottage Lane to enter the
local cricket ground. Forward, keeping to the hedge left to cross the main
road (A1133). Go through a kissing gate and follow the hedge, right, up to a
railway line.

5. **Do not cross this,** but instead turn left on a clear path and left again across the field to emerge onto Dyke's End. Cross over to the estate road opposite, then forward across some waste ground to meet Station Road. Keep ahead, alongside the football pitch, to Swinderby Road. Go forward again, along an alleyway, to emerge by the side of a garage on High Street, opposite the remnants of the old cross. Turn right and right again onto Woodhill Road.

Short Walk rejoins

6. When the road bears right keep ahead on a track. In 250m turn left where the track forks and shortly right to follow a dyke for 400m. At the footpath sign turn right for 300m and cross a ditch board to a main track. Here turn left and in 1km left again into Amos Lane. Follow the lane into South Scarle, passing the church on your right.

7. When the road turns right, keep ahead on a headland path. After 150m turn left and in 200m turn right, for another 250m. Turn left at the way-mark and follow the hedge left until it ends. Continue forward over the field to enter the yard of Holly House Farm (now a home for cats and dogs) and over a stile to reach Moor Lane.

8. Turn right and in 150m left, to follow a good headland path to the main road in Besthorpe (note the remains of an old post windmill at Mill Farm, right). Turn right, pass the Lord Nelson public house, to a footpath sign, left. Follow the short path into Besthorpe village then turn right for 50m to a right-hand bend in the road. Keep ahead through a gate and follow the fenced path, to a small hand gate on top of the flood bank. Through this turn right and follow the River Fleet again, back to Tinkers Lane.

Points of Interest

Girton – A secluded hamlet once subjected to severe flooding as can be seen by the water level marks on one of the houses. Here the River Fleet follows the old course of the River Trent and adjacent to Tinkers Lane it becomes a lake, a very pleasant picnic spot.

Collingham – Now one very long village but with two parish churches when the village was split into North and South Collingham. The Old Cross rumoured, incorrectly, to be an Eleanor Cross, has been moved in recent years to accommo-date the demands of the motorcar. The original site was next to the garage oppo-site. Collingham is today surrounded by gravel workings, some of which are now being turned into nature reserves under the guidance of the RSPB.

Besthorpe – The remains of the post mill are the best surviving example of its type in the county. The original building had a brick base with a wooden upper structure. Nowadays only the base, the main post, quarter boss and cross trees remain but at least these will be preserved for the future due to its 'listed build-ing' status.

16: In The Heart of Sherwood Forest

A beautiful walk on well-drained paths featuring many things connected with the legend of Robin Hood. These include the Major Oak, Centre Tree, Archway House and the Cistercian Abbey at Rufford. This is an excellent winter walk.

Distance: Long Walk 19km (11½ miles); Short Walk 9km (6 miles)

Duration: Long Walk 5½ hours; Short Walk 3 hours

Maps required: OS Explorer 270 Sherwood Forest, OS Landranger 120 Mansfield & Worksop

Terrain: Forest bridleways and field footpaths

Starting point: Sherwood Forest Visitors Centre car park, Edwinstowe (SK627676). Note: There is a parking fee during summer weekends.

Refreshments: Numerous public houses in Edwinstowe, also a café at Rufford Abbey.

Bus/Train link: Mansfield

The Route

1. From the car park walk towards the Visitor Centre entrance, then bear left following the red way-marked posts for the 'Birklands Ramble'. At a major path junction, where the red route bears right, continue straight ahead to follow the edge of the forest. After 1km turn left at the footpath sign to come out onto the A6075. Turn left, then opposite Villa Real Farm right down a track to a path junction. **For the long walk** turn right and in 10m left to cross two footbridges. Keep the River Maun on your left to emerge on Mill Lane. Here bear left to meet the main street in Edwinstowe.

Short Walk

1a. Turn right walking parallel to the River Maun on the left to Forge Bridge. Go to point 5.

Long Walk

2. Turn right, then left just after going underneath a railway bridge. Follow this headland path for 2km to come out onto the A614. Cross over, with care and take the signpost track to the right. In just over 1km you arrive at the minor road from Wellow.

3. Cross over into Rufford Country Park following either of the lakeside paths to the Abbey ruins. Leave the park along the old main drive to find a narrow path left, just before the old main gates, which leads to the main entrance

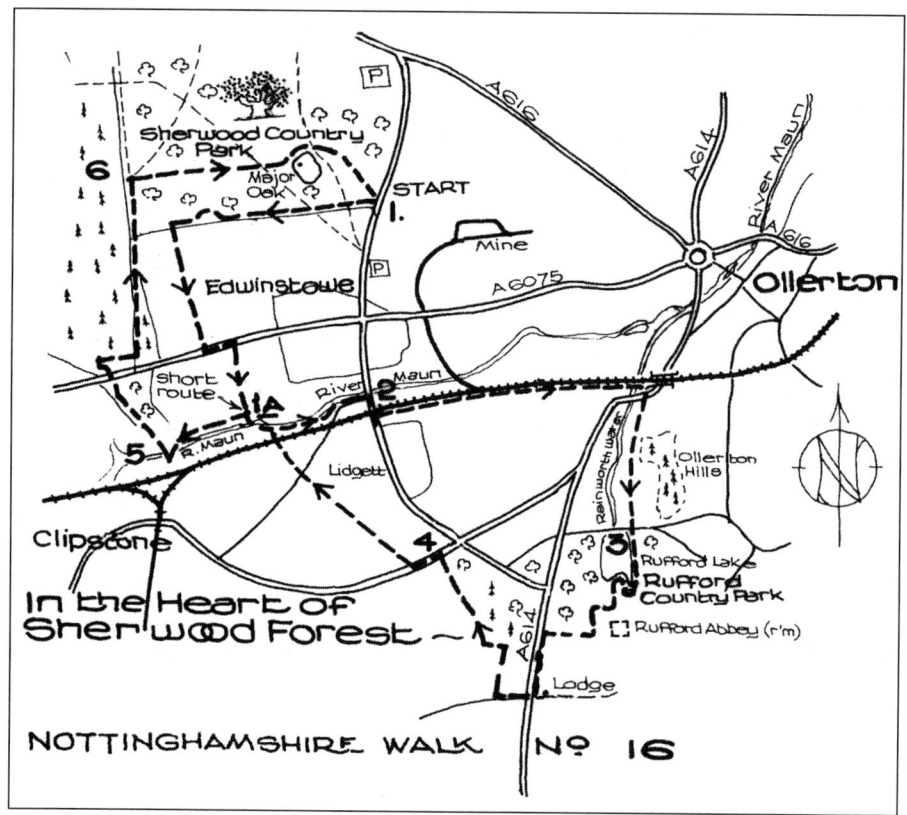

and the A614. Turn left and in 500m right, opposite Manor Farm, to join the Robin Hood Way. Cross over the drive leading to Center Parcs holiday village and, after 200m, bear right along a field-edge path. Bear left at the end of the field, then right through Broadoak Brake to follow another headland path to meet a minor road.

4. Turn left and in 350m right alongside Holly Farm. Forward to cross another road and a railway line to meet up again with the River Maun. Turn and cross the two footbridges (again) to another path junction. Turn left to follow the Maun to Forge Bridge.

Short Walk rejoins

5. Turn right along a wide track, passing Archway House, to the A6075 and cross over to a junction of tracks. Turn right and follow this winding path, which runs parallel to the main road, to cross over a wide track, and then bear left to join a clear path, which runs northwards. Ignore the bridleway right after 1km, then forward to a major junction at Centre Tree.

6.   Turn right, ignore all side paths for 1.5km, to arrive at the Major Oak. Turn left, to follow the blue way-marked posts, to the Visitors Centre and car park.

Points of Interest

Rufford Abbey – Founded in 1148 by Gilbert de Gaunt, the Earl of Lincoln. The present house, built in Elizabethan times, was allowed to decay but it has been tastefully restored by Nottinghamshire County Council. The country park contains two icehouses, animal graves, an exhibition centre at the old mill, gardens and orangery.

Archway House – Built by the Duke of Portland in 1842 as a copy of the Gateway to Worksop Priory. The facade has sculptures of several of the characters from the Robin Hood legend i.e. Maid Marion, Richard I, Friar Tuck and Will Scarlet. Nowadays the building is a private residence for two families.

Centre Tree – The site is supposed to be the centre of the old Sherwood Forest that stretched from Nottingham to Worksop.

The Major Oak – Claimed to be the largest oak tree in England. The diameter is over two metres and legend has it that Robin Hood and some of his men hid inside the tree.

Railway – The railway was part of a grandiose scheme to construct a line from Manchester to Sutton-on-Sea and there to build a Dover-style harbour. Due to financial difficulties, only the section from Chesterfield to Lincoln was built.

Thoresby Colliery – Scene of many a skirmish during the 1984 miners' strike. Now one of the county's few working mines.

17: Headstocks and Headstones

A walk full of surprises, all of them pleasant, in an area where mining is fast becoming a memory. Most of the footpaths here are over grass, a contrast with the arable land to the east of the county.

Distance: Long Walk 13km (8 miles); Short Walk 10km (6 miles)

Duration: Long Walk 4 hours; Short Walk 3 hours

Maps required: OS Explorer 260 Nottingham and Vale of Belvoir, OS Explorer 269 Chesterfield and Alfreton, OS Landranger 129 Nottingham and Loughborough, OS Landranger 120 Mansfield and Worksop

Terrain: A few, not too steep, climbs

Starting point: Car park on A608, south of Brinsley. (SK464485)

Refreshments: Brinsley: Robin Hood, White Lion, Yew Tree, Bagthorpe: Shepherds Rest; Underwood: Hole in the Wall.

Bus/Train link: Eastwood

The Route

1. Next to the car park is an old mineral railway; follow this route through pleasant woodland until a path veers left to Cordy Lane and the Yew Tree public house. (At present, the path has a fence at the end of it, due to a landowner dispute. If still blocked, return to a path that leaves the railway and goes onto Cordy Lane. Turn right and walk to Yew Tree Inn.) Cross road and turn right to walk up Cordy Lane to footpath on left. Take footpath at side of house to a stile, cross pasture to far corner then over stile, along alleyway between industrial units to a lane. Turn right and walk to footpath seen on left.

2. Cross a boggy field walking in a straight line to next boundary fence/hedge, enter next field and turn immediately right. Cross field to reach two stiles, at second stile join metalled road. Carry straight on and follow clear route to reach road at the side of the Hole in the Wall public house. Opposite the public house is a small path leading to a terraced street, turn left.

3. At the bottom of the street, cross the stile, descend to a gate and continue to the left-hand corner of the next field. Continue down, still on grassland, to enter the yard of Brookside Farm. After passing by the farm, bear right to a road. Turn left through the tiny hamlet of Bagthorpe as far as the Shepherd's Rest public house.

Short Walk

4. Continue to the stile on the left and go to point 6.

Long Walk

4. After the public house, turn right, pass left of the public house and keep straight ahead on a well-trodden path. Ignore all path junctions to a road. Go straight ahead along the road as far as a fenced path on the left. Follow this to a street, cross it and go up the unsurfaced road to join the B600 at Selston. Turn left, then first left again into Lea Lane, ignoring the first avenue on the left, but take the second which leads down to Home Farm.

5. The path passes right of the farm to a gap beside a farm gate. Continue downhill beside the hedge and cross a footbridge. Bear slightly right in the first grass field, keep left in the next and cross the Bagthorpe Brook and the stile just beyond it. Turn left here and follow the brook and left-hand hedge, cross a stile and go onto the road again in Bagthorpe. The Shepherds Rest public house is just to your left or you could go right to visit the Dixies public house and return. Cross the road to a stile.

Short Walk rejoins

6. Follow the hedge uphill, then keep to the left of two more pasture fields. (Crich Stand is visible from this point.) Turn left up a road and right along Plainspot Road. **Follow this road in a left turn** and look out for the former Primitive Methodist church on the right near the foot of the hill. Turn right along the back lane and continue across a meadow to another road.

7. Cross straight over and take the right-hand path down to a stream, cross a causeway and then left down a field edge. Continue across the next field and ahead to a fenced path by-passing Gin Farm to a metalled road. Turn left and take middle track, which continues as a green lane, to a gate. Go through gate and across field to a bridge over the River Erewash, which you cross for a brief visit into Derbyshire.

8.   Go forward 50m, turn left by a double stile, then go forward to another. Angle slightly left to cross another bridge and follow the clear path, ignoring a stile on your left. Keep ahead to a stile, then to another and turn left up the field to the corner. In the next field aim slightly right to a stile and follow a clear uphill path to join Stoney Lane.

9.   If suffering from thirst, turn left up the lane then right to the White Lion or Robin Hood public houses. Continue then to your starting point.

Note: To use the new bridleway, cross Stoney Lane, go onto a path opposite to walk between houses to a field. Turn right following the right-hand hedge to a further stile at the top of the field where you join the new bridleway. Turn left and walk along bridleway to the road and your starting point.

Points of Interest

Brinsley – In the 12th century, the Duke of Devonshire built the hall and manor house, both of which still survive as farms. Pollington Colliery closed in 1919 and Bodtod Colliery some time later. Before the headstocks were removed, it was used in the filming of D.H. Lawrence's 'Sons and Lovers' in which many Brinsley residents were used as extras.

The church was originally called St Saviours but the name was later changed to St James. The village did have ten public houses at one time, but only five now remain, the oldest being the Robin Hood coach house.

Underwood and Bagthorpe – Both villages are part of the Parish of Selston. Underwood was a former colliery village, with rows of terraced houses. The headstock now stands in the churchyard of St Michael and All Saints.

Selston – St Helen's Church has a Norman font with a mobile history. Two hundred years ago it was removed from the church and taken to Blackwell. It was then returned, not to the church, but to the Bull & Butcher Inn, where it was fixed to the pump. Later it was used as a flowerpot in a private garden, then it was rescued in 1906 by Rev Charles Harrison who restored it to its proper place.

The churchyard houses the grave of Dan Boswell, King of the Gypsies. For many years, the gypsies would return to Selston to pay their respects and their new-born babies were brought to the church to be baptised. The epitaph of **Dan Boswell** reads:

> *I've lodged in many a town*
> *I've travelled many a year*
> *But death at length has brought me down*
> *To my last lodging here.*

18: Astride The Roman Road

A varied and interesting walk featuring the picturesque Trent Valley villages of East Bridgford and Kneeton and the Belvoir Vale hamlets of Flintham, Screveton and Car Colston, which has the largest village green in the county.

Distance: Long Walk 20km (12 miles); Short Walk 11km (7 miles)

Duration: Long Walk 6 hours; Short Walk 3½ hours

Maps required: OS Explorer 260 Nottingham & Vale of Belvoir, OS Landranger 129 Nottingham and Loughborough

Terrain: Field paths across pasture and arable land. Riverside path can be very muddy after heavy winter rain.

Starting point: Free public car park, Main Street, East Bridgford (SK695430)

Refreshments: The Royal Oak, Car Colston; The Royal Oak, Screveton; Boot & Shoe, Flintham and several pubs/shops in East Bridgford

Bus/Train link: Trent/Barton Rushcliffe Line 3 Nottm. / E Bridgford / Bingham

---

The Route

1. From the car park turn left for 50m, then left again into Walnut Tree Lane. On the double bend, take the alleyway, right, between some houses. Go straight ahead past the converted windmill to a junction of paths. Turn left, then follow the headland path, left, for 300m, then angle right to a gate, which leads to a minor road. Turn right onto the minor road to a right-hand bend to turn left on a path, which initially runs parallel to the A6097 then joins the sewerage works access drive to Trent Lane.

2. At the junction cross the stile right to follow the defined path across two fields to rejoin Trent Lane opposite the Marina entrance. Cross over to this track, which you follow alongside the Trent for 1.5km. **Note: in winter this low-level path can flood** – in which case, take the cliff-top route through the chalet park. On reaching a small fisherman's car park and turning circle, ascend the track right and in a few metres climb the bank left to walk high up on the Trent Hills. Follow this for a further 1.5km following the hedge away from the river and back again. Continue along the cliff top, down and up steps and back onto the cliff top until reaching a copse (Watson's Piece) then descend left to a stile. Over this, turn right and follow the path through the water meadows for 1.25km where you can see a modern housing develop-

ment on the opposite bank of the river. Here cross the stile, by the gate, and ascend the stony track up to Kneeton church.

Long Walk

3. Continue ahead to the main street and turn left. Follow the road to the right and at the next left-hand bend take the footpath ahead to the left-hand far corner of the field. Here pass through a gap, turn left and in 10m right. After 20m cross a bridge, turn right and follow a dyke on your right for 700m to a ditchboard. Over this, angle left to Slacks Lane. Turn right to the A46.

Short Walk

3a. Turn right just past the church onto a tarred road, and at its end turn left onto a headland path for 150m to a gap, left. Pass through this, turn right and continue straight ahead for almost 1km to Old Hill Farm. Cross over the farm track, then cross four arable fields to a wide track to bear left on to Kneeton Road. Turn left then, in 300m, bear right into Occupation Lane and, after 500m, take the footpath right. Now follow the route from point 8.

Long Walk

4. Cross over to the stile opposite then forward, keeping the fence on your left to join a farm track which leads to Spring Lane. Note the fine views of Flintham Hall and the lake. At the lane, turn left for 50m then right along a track. Where this turns right, go forward through a gate and cross the field to a second gate. Here turn half-right across a meadow to a footbridge. Keep ahead across a large arable field to a gap then angle right to a wide gap in the opposite hedge.

5. Take the track opposite for 400m to the corner of Barleyholme Wood and turn left as signed alongside a dyke, left. At the distant pylon, bear half-right to join a headland path with the hedge, right. At the field corner turn left and in 25m right go through a large gap in the hedge. Aim just to the left of two distant trees and cross two large fields to come onto Hawksworth Road at Car Dyke Bridge.

6. Turn right and in 1km just before the Screveton sign take the stile, left, to follow a hedge on your right. After passing through a small hand gate take the gate, right and turn left to follow the hedge now on your left, to a stile. Over this veer slightly right to a gate, seen ahead, to follow a path to a footbridge and then straight ahead to a track. In the next field, veer slightly left to a gap in the hedge ahead. Through this turn right and follow the hedge through two gates to a small green. Turn left and before reaching the white house ahead take the stile left. Turn right keeping straight ahead through three further gates to the road.

7. Turn right, go round the bend to a large house called 'Tree Tops'. Take the alleyway, right, passing the old whipping post and church to emerge onto

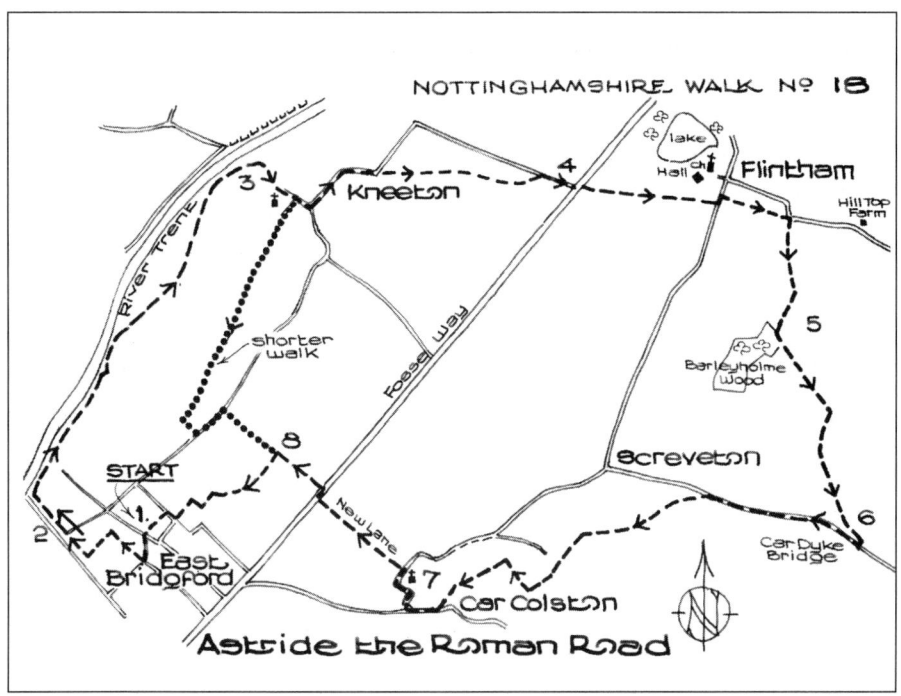

the Screveton road. Turn right and in 100m left down New Lane, which leads to the A46. Cross over diagonally right and proceed down Occupation Lane for 750m to a footpath sign, left.

Short Walk rejoins

8. Take the headland path for 500m to a small footbridge, then turn half-right across the field to a stile. Cross two fields to a path and cross the first stile on the left to a second stile to emerge onto a lane. Turn left, then right at the end of the lane to take the alleyway on the right, to another road. Turn left for 200m then right into Brown Lane. After a few steps take the path signed Main Street to enter the recreation ground. Follow the hedge left and enter another alleyway to meet the Main Street. Turn left for 50m back to the car park.

Points of Interest

Stokes Windmill, East Bridgford – Built by Henry Stokes in 1828 the mill was in use until 1912. The sails were struck by lightning in 1928 and the cap and machinery were removed around 1940. The mill was converted to a dwelling after the War and today stands proudly on the edge of the village. A tiled picture of a windmill can be seen on the wall beside the house door.

Flintham Hall – The conservatory at the eastern end of the Hall resembles the original Crystal Palace. The present building was built in the 19th century although there is evidence that a gabled house stood there in the 17th century.

Flintham Pinfold – 300m off route on the Sibthorpe Road stands the restored brick pinfold, opposite Hilltop Farm. A 'pinder' was responsible for rounding up stray animals in the village and one was elected in Flintham up to the Second World War.

Car Colston – Boasts the largest village green in Nottinghamshire with houses scattered around on all sides. It is not unusual to see cattle and horses grazing on the wide grassy expanses. The hall at the south-western end of the village dates from 1838 and can be seen from the roadside. The village was also the home of Robert Thoroton, the famous antiquary and historian of Nottinghamshire.

19: The Wolds Wander

A pleasant walk south of the Trent in the undulations of the Wolds countryside. Fairly easy walking mainly on bridle paths and some quiet country lanes.

Distance: Long Walk 20km (12½ miles); Short Walk 10.75km (6¾ miles)

Duration: Long Walk 6 hours; Short Walk 3 hours

Maps required: OS Explorer 260 Nottingham & 247 Grantham, OS Landranger 129 Nottingham & Loughborough

Terrain: Fairly easy and undulating

Starting point: Keyworth public car park (SK613308)

Refreshments: The Fairway, Keyworth. Griffin Inn, Plumtree. The Plough, Normanton-on-the-Wolds. Neville Arms, Kinoulton.

Bus Link: Nottingham

The Route

1. From Keyworth public car park, return to Bunny Lane, turn right towards church, then left into Nottingham Road. Continue downhill to where the road bends right, but go straight ahead to an alleyway on the left-hand side of The Fairway public house; this leads to Crossdale Drive then turn left.

2. Proceed to the top of Crossdale Drive to the school, and take another alleyway on the left. This soon turns right and right again around the school playing field. Turn left at the end of a garden to the remains of a stile into a field.

3. Keep to the right of the field with a hedge on the right-hand side. At a small plantation, the path bears right, through a wide opening in the hedge, into an adjoining field. Skirt this field with a hedge now on the left-hand side for 30m, cross over a wooden bridge and continue round the field with the hedge on the right-hand side. At the power lines and angle of the hedgerow, the official path is directly forward to the archway under the railway.

4. Pass under the archway to a stile at the side of an iron farm gate. Continue straight ahead to another stile with Chestnut Farm in front of you. Turn left to a stile on the right, just before The Poplars. (If required, the Griffin Inn is about 166m further along Station Road, at the crossroads.) Over the stile, go to the opposite corner to another stile leading into a paddock. Keep ahead to a stile leading into another paddock. Here go slightly left to a stile beside a metal gate in the far corner of the field.

5. Turn right along the cul-de-sac, this leads to the main A606 Melton Road. Cross over the A606, with great care, into lane signposted Normanton.

Continue along pavement through the village, which has many attractive properties. The lane bears right to a footpath sign on the left, just past Normanton Manor. (The Plough Inn is some 220m further along the lane.) Go over the stile onto a wide path and through a gate into a field. Carry straight on down a bank to a stile, still in the same direction, to cross a foot-bridge over a brook. Bear left to another stile then continue uphill and head for the end of a hedge, cross a stile to a farm road. Opposite, cross another stile, continuing uphill over a stile into a cultivated field. Cross the field following the footpath to cross another stile, here the path bears slightly left. (Take time here to savour the views of the Wolds and Nottingham.) The next stile is beside double metal gates at the side of a lane. Turn right on the lane to Clipstone. At the T-junction and Gulliver Cottage, turn right onto a bridleway, signposted to Laming Gap Lane.

6. Past the farm on the left-hand side the bridleway goes downhill, then turns sharply right, then left to pass through Cotgrave Forest. Continue on the bridleway to a T-junction. Turn right then immediately left to find an opening onto Laming Gap Lane.

Short Walk

6a. Turn right onto Laming Gap Lane. Walk 1km to reach A606 (Nottingham to Melton road). Cross road with great care and take footpath across field to railway bridge. Follow clear headland path for 1km to reach Keyworth at Stanton Lane. Go straight across on to Willowbrook Road and, at end, turn right on Selby Lane and return to car.

Long Walk

7. Go straight ahead, slightly downhill to Wynnstay Wood and Clipstone Wolds. Continuing on this lane, uphill, you meet the A46 Fosse Way. Turn right on the A46 for some 100m. Cross the A46 with care and, just before Owthorpe Lodge, turn left into a bridleway. This bears left after 30m and you continue for some distance in the same direction until you reach a copse. Bearing to the right, you join the driveway to Newfield Farm. Continue on the farm road, turning sharp right; when the road turns sharp left again, carry straight on at that point along a narrow footpath to the Grantham Canal at Devil's Elbow. Turn right and continue along the footpath with the canal on your left until you reach the poplar-lined driveway of Vimy Ridge. Turn left over the canal and turn sharp right, with the canal now on your right.

8. On reaching Main Street, Kinoulton, join this road and turn right. (The Neville Arms is some 950m to your left.) Pass the Primary school on the left and when the road bends left you find a stile on your right at the side of the gate just past Blacks Farm. Cross over the stile and bear right to the side of the farm. Continue on the bridleway going uphill until you reach Kinoulton Gorse woods. Bear to the right of the woods until you reach another

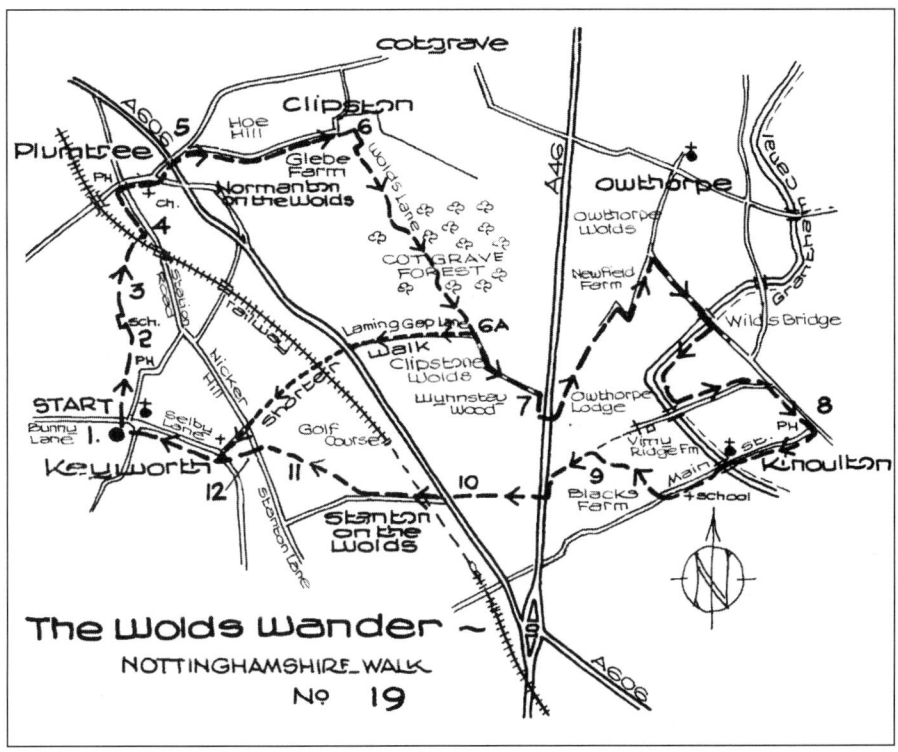

The Wolds Wander ~
NOTTINGHAMSHIRE WALK
No 19

bridleway crossing your path. Here turn left through the woods (this can be rather muddy).

9. When you leave the woods bear right for 22m and then left with a hedge on the right. At top of field, go diagonally left to a gap in the hedge, across two fields to join the A46 Fosse Way again. Here turn left and after 130m, find two farm gates on the right, go through the right-hand gate, onto a grass bridleway. Continue through a metal gate, with hedge on left. At the corner of the second field go through a gate on the left and immediately right to a wooden gate. Go straight ahead to join the A606 road opposite a petrol station.

10. Cross the A606 and continue into Browns Lane. Some 200m after the last house in this lane, find a stile on the right. Cross over, with hedge on left to the end of the field, to find a double stile near a small tree.

11. Go over the double stile and bear slightly right, aiming for a small copse, to find a wooden footbridge onto Stanton Golf Course. Keep to the left and note Stanton church on the left. Continue at the side of the course, avoiding the scrubland. At the rear of houses at the end of the golf course, ignore a stile on

the left (private) and take a path between the houses leads onto Stanton Lane.

12. Turn right on this lane and after 110m, opposite the entrance to the Golf Club, find a stile between houses on your left. This path continues to two wooden footbridges onto a school playing field. Across the field head for a small gap in the tall hedgerow, then cross scrubland to another stile at the back of the church. Cross this and continue through a small meadow to a metal gate and onto Selby Lane and Willow Brook. Go along Selby Lane, (sign posted Keyworth and Bunny), this takes us back to Keyworth and the car park.

Points of Interest

Vimy Ridge Farm – Originally called Pasture Hill Farm. The name was changed and the French-style avenue of Lombardy poplars was planted by the farmer as a memorial to a son killed in the fighting for Vimy Ridge in World War I.

Grantham Canal – Built by William Jessop and opened in 1797. Runs for 53km (33 miles) from the River Trent in Nottingham to Grantham. It was initially profitable but. like most canals. it lost business to the railways. It was closed in 1929 and abandoned in 1936 and has now lost both ends to road schemes. The original Trent connection was by Nottingham Forest football stadium. Some restoration is now in progress.

Keyworth – Although no longer a small village, Keyworth retains one unique feature – the church tower. Built in the 15th century, this is a tall buttressed tower above which rises an octagonal stone lantern which, in turn, is crowned by a short spire. In 1988, the Parish Council exchanged a parcel of land for the 'Keyworth Meadow', now a conservation area where many birds and various species of butterfly can be seen.

20: Flirting with Leicestershire

A walk in the extreme south of Nottinghamshire going through farmland of the University of Nottingham School of Agriculture to the banks of the River Soar and the preserved Great Central Railway. It also goes along the side of King's Brook, on the county boundary with Leicestershire.

Distance: Long Walk 22.5 km (14 miles); Short Walk 14.5km (9 miles)

Duration: Long Walk 7 hours; Short Walk 4½ hours

Maps required: OS Explorer 246 Loughborough and Melton Mowbray, OS Landranger 129 Nottingham and Loughborough

Terrain: Mainly field walking and gentle hills

Starting point: East Leake public car park (free) in Gotham Road (SK555264)

Refreshments: A number of public houses en-route in East Leake, West Leake, Sutton Bonington, Zouch and Normanton-on-Soar

Bus/Train link: Nottingham/Loughborough

The Route

1. From East Leake public car park return to Gotham Road and turn right, and right again into Main Street, signposted 'West Leake'. Pass the Nags Head public house on the left-hand side and the church on the right. Continue into Brookside and then bear right into Woodgate Road, signposted 'Hathern Station'.

2. At the top of the hill walk around the S-bend over a railway line (Great Central Railway) and, a few metres beyond, an iron farm gate on the right-hand side. Go through an opening in the hedge to walk on a bridleway. This bears left and, on the right-hand side, Ratcliffe Power Station can be seen. Continue passing Calke Hall Farm and go through a wooden gate, keeping the hedge on the right-hand side skirt the field and go through a metal gate onto a track to the gate of Manor Farm. Go into the farmyard and turn immediately left where you will see, at the rear of a farm building, a wooden gate beside a metal gate. Go through the wooden gate and proceed ahead and downhill with the hedge on the right-hand side to another wooden gate leading onto Brickyard Lane.

Long Walk

3. Turn right and follow the lane to the T-junction, turn right again along road and then left to pass in front of the Star public house. Immediately on the left-hand side, take a stile into a paddock then a further stile into a pasture.

Go slightly left to another stile and slightly left again over the next pasture to a further stile, then go across the corner of the field to another stile with a footbridge. Walk 5m to another footbridge, go through the hedge and turn left up the side of the field with the hedge on the left-hand side. At the corner of the field **do not go through the opening** but turn right with the hedge on your left. Turn left on a diverted route around the boundary of Glebe Farm to join existing path and turn left again.

Short Walk

3a. Go straight ahead across road into field opposite. Follow field-edge path and well-marked route for 800m with Hills Farm on your left and Cold Harbour Plantation on your right to reach Rempstone Road (A6006). Cross road onto bridleway into Limekiln Plantation and follow well-marked track (muddy in winter). At the end of plantation, follow field-edge path to Normanton Grange Farm seen ahead. Take diverted route (clearly way-marked) around farm building, pass barn and turn left through farmyard to follow track to a copse seen ahead. At this point turn left in field away from track and follow field path around field to a railway bridge. Cross the railway bridge and walk to Barn Farm, walking down driveway onto Leake Lane. Turn right and walk into Stanford on Soar. Turn left at junction into village to rejoin Long Walk (Go to point 8.)

Long Walk

4. Go straight ahead with the hedge on the left, over another stile and continue in the same direction. After four fields, you come to a cottage with a drive to a farm. Go straight across the drive into a narrow path (the Nottingham University School of Agriculture is on the right-hand side), cross over a railway bridge (Midland Mainline) and down a few steps to a driveway to several cottages. Here turn left along the drive with the stone wall on your left. This is Bucks Lane and the church is on the right. Bear right to the road and turn left on to Main Street, Sutton Bonington. Shortly on the right will be the Kings Head public house and 20m further on, also on the right, is Pasture Lane. Walk along Pasture Lane, which becomes a bridleway. Where it appears to turn right, walk slightly left along a field path with the hedge on the right. This leads to the canalised River Soar. **Do not go over the bridge** but turn left into Zouch.

5. Walk along the side of the river, it being on the right-hand side, and you soon pass the Rose and Crown public house on the opposite bank, continue to the road. (To go to the pub, turn right at the road.) Our route is to the left and, just past a farm on the right-hand side, go over a stile into a pasture. Going slightly left away from the river, make for a metal gate and go across another field to a stile with a footbridge and a further stile. Go across the field bearing slightly left towards houses, over the stile turn right along Moor Lane, Normanton-on-Soar. Keep to this road through the quiet village passing the

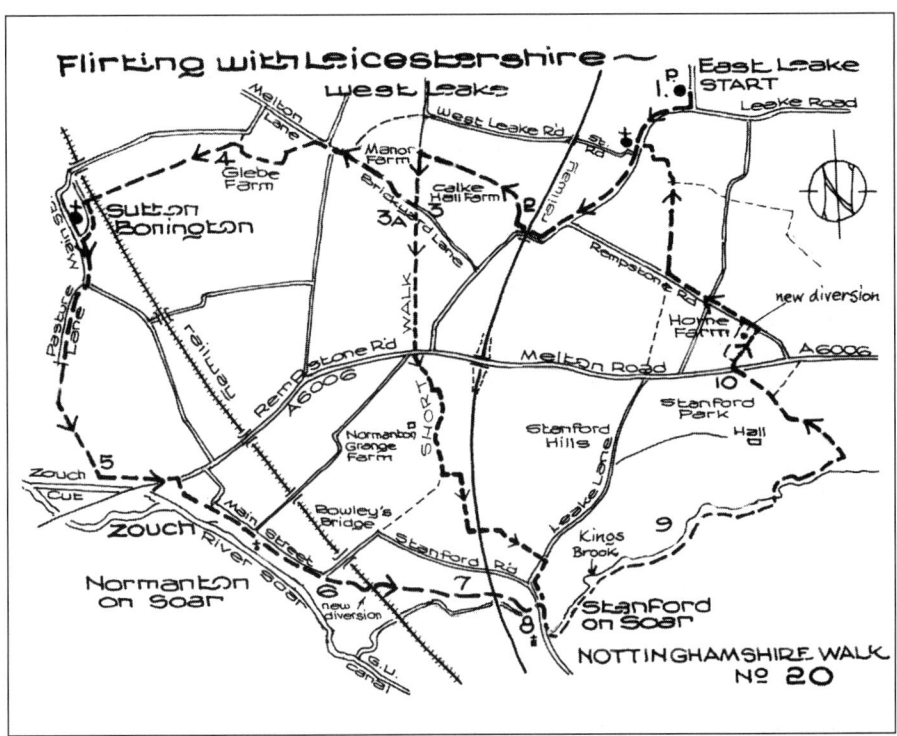

Plough public house on the right-hand side. Keep ahead on Main Street, passing the church, and, when the footpath ends, continue along the lane. Loughborough can be seen to the right in the distance.

6. When the lane turns sharp left at Bowley's Bridge, take the stile ahead at the side of a metal gate. Cross another stile at the side of another metal gate, and keep to the left-hand side of the field to reach the signal gantry above the railway (Midland Mainline). There is a tunnel under the railway, although you have to climb a wooden gate to go through it. This is a new diversion. On the other side of the railway turn right to the bank of the River Soar and then left along the edge of a field with the river on the right-hand side. In the corner of the field, go over a stile and footbridge. Continue to the right-hand corner of the next field to another stile and bear slightly left uphill to the left of a copse and away from the river. Go through an opening, still going uphill and follow a line of posts on the ridge.

7. You will soon see a small section of wooden fencing in a barbed wire fence. Go over the wooden fence and straight across a narrow field of some 30m to an opening in a wooden fence. Cross a single-track railway (Gt. Central Railway) and over the stile opposite, then bear right but keep just left of a copse

to a stile and then a double stile. Continue, keeping to the right of the field, to cross two stiles. Then turn sharp left with the fence on the left-hand side and the church on the other side of the same field. Walk towards the estate buildings beside a farm. Turn right at end of fence and exit field via kissing gate onto the road, turn right towards the church in Stanford-on-Soar.

Short Walk rejoins

8. Continue ahead to the sharp right-hand bend and on the left is a lane sign-posted 'Cotes and Barrow'. This is Stanford Lane where, after about 100m, you will see on the left a footpath sign on far side of a small bridge going over King's Brook. Go over the bridge to take the path and turn left. You now have King's Brook on your left-hand side.

9. Follow this path beside King's Brook for seven fields, then look for a way-marker indicating left to take you over a footbridge into woods. Bear right and follow the way-markers carefully with King's Brook now on your right-hand side. You will come out of the woods over a stile into a pasture. Proceed ahead over a ford/stepping stones into another pasture where you will see, on the left, a brick boundary wall of the Stanford Estate. At the side of the brick wall go through a wooden farm gate with the brick wall now close on the left-hand side, go up the hill through a pedestrian wooden gate. Continue in the same direction through another wooden gate and onto a driveway.

10. When you meet the Melton road turn left to pass the main entrance to Stanford Hall, immediately turn right down the drive towards Home Farm. Take new diversion off main drive, turning left and dropping downhill towards gate in next field. Walk to far side then turn right and walk though copse to Rempstone Road. Turn left to reach Loughborough Road and cross over to continue on Rempstone Road. Shortly on the right-hand side will be seen a finger marker next to a metal farm gate.

11. Turn right over the stile walking downhill heading to the right of the church spire. Go through kissing gate and follow the path over a footbridge and a fence uphill with the hedge on your left. At the top of the field the path turns right through a kissing gate into an alleyway between houses, turning left and right and down some steps into a cul-de-sac. This is Burton Walk – go straight ahead to another alleyway at the side of a school, turn left into The Nook, which bears right, then left. The church will be directly in front of you with the Three Horseshoes public house on your left. Here you turn right to go along Brookside and Main Street, back to Gotham Road and the car park.

Points of Interest

East Leake – The Post Office was originally the old manor house, built between 1715 and 1728. The church of St Mary was mentioned in the Domesday Book and stands on the site of much older buildings, being extensively restored in the

19th century. In the church is the 8ft Vamp Horn, known in the village as "The Shawm". Only five other churches have such an instrument, which was invented in 1670 by Samuel Morland, one of Samuel Pepys' tutors at Cambridge. It was used by the bass singer to lead the choir from the gallery to the church. Two Roundheads and three Cavaliers were killed in a skirmish locally in 1644, and they lie in unmarked graves near the church porch.

Brookside – The small village green has a brook running past the war memorial, and there are remains of the village pound, now furnished with seats. For a number of years there has been an annual tug-of-war across the brook which has developed into a carnival parade.

Stanford-on-Soar – The church of St John the Baptist dates from the 13th century. There are several interesting monuments in the church, such as the incised slab to an Illyngworth and his wife dated 1408, unique because it is the only alabaster slab in the county with indents for brass inlays. There is also a recumbent effigy holding his heart in his hand. Stanford Hall, standing in a land-scaped park, was the brick mansion of Charles Vere Dashwood.

Normanton-on-Soar – The 13th-century church stands on the bank of the River Soar. Extensive views over Loughborough can be seen from the churchyard. A rare royal arms of Charles II, in plaster, can be seen above the chancel arch.

Sutton Bonington – Has two ancient churches, a long main street and is the home of Nottingham University Agricultural College. The principle building, however, is the Hall built in the 18th century on the right-hand side.

The Great Central Railway – The London extension from Annesley to Marylebone was opened in 1899 and closed by Dr Beeching in 1967, although this section survives as a branch freight line to the British Gypsum works. The GCR (Nottm) runs steam trains from the Nottingham Transport Heritage Centre at Ruddington at the weekend. They have long-term plans to reconnect to the Main Line Steam Trust at Loughborough to the south and north to connect with Nottingham's new tram system.

The County of Lincolnshire

If you are fortunate to complete the ten walks in this county, you will have had a rewarding and enjoyable experience. People who have not yet discovered the delights of Lincolnshire for rambling imagine that the county is totally flat. This, however, is far from the truth since large areas in the Wolds are as high as hills in most other English counties. Indeed the highest point is at Normanby-le-Wold (168m) and compares favourably with neighbouring counties in East Anglia. Since recent local government reorganisation, the county can be split loosely into four parts. North Lincolnshire, West and East Lindsey, North and South Kesteven and the fens of Holland.

North Lincolnshire, formerly known as South Humberside, has the magnificent Humber estuary together with coastline which includes the holiday resort of Cleethorpes and the port of Grimsby. Epworth, situated in the north-west corner, was the birthplace of John and Charles Wesley, the famous Methodist brothers who were born in the early 18th century at the Old Rectory. The area also has two splendid windmills at Waltham and Wrawby, both still in working order, which are open to the public during the year.

West and East Lindsey are, perhaps, the jewels in the crown since they contain the Area of Outstanding Natural Beauty known as the Wolds. The main town is Louth and its church has the tallest spire in any English parish. Pretty villages includeTealby with its thatched cottages, Somersby, birthplace of Alfred, Lord Tennyson, Stainton-le-Vale and Oxcombe, on the Roman Bluestone Heath Road. Magnificent buildings can also be found such as Gunby Hall and Tattershall Castle, both in the care of the National Trust, whilst lesser-known ones like Revesby Abbey and Harrington Hall are worth seeking out.

North and South Kesteven are best known for agriculture rather than rambling. However, the River Witham flows through this region and forms a natural boundary on the north and west sides. The major settlements are at Sleaford, home of Money's Mill, Boston famous for its 'stump' and Grantham with its statue of Sir Isaac Newton who lived nearby at Woolsthorpe Manor. From a ramblers point of view some of the best walking lies on the Lincoln Cliff, also known as the Lincoln Edge, which stretches from the south of the city almost to Stamford in the far south of the county. Indeed, part of the Viking Way long distance footpath follows this escarpment passing the lovely limestone villages of Coleby, Leadenham, Fulbeck and Hough-on-the-Hill. Belton House and Grimesthorpe Castle are certainly the two most significant buildings in the area and should not be missed.

Holland is the most fertile part of the county due to large portions being reclaimed from the sea during past centuries. Spalding is the main centre and is world-famous for its bulb production and annual tulip parade, every May. Less well-known are villages such as Uffington with houses built from cream stone and Crowland with its triangular Trinity Bridge, dating from the 14th century.

As a conclusion, we must not forget the city of Lincoln, famous for its

12th-century cathedral, the Castle complete with prison cells and Ellis's Mill, a four-sail tower mill, which has been fully restored. Also Stamford, surely one of the best examples of a 'stone' town in the country. Nearby Burghley House and park just adds to the overall grandeur.

One thing of which not many people are aware is that the Greenwich Meridian Line of 0 degrees longitude passes virtually through the whole of the county. Towns such as Cleethorpes, Louth, Boston and Holbeach all stand on this famous time zone and most have plaques commemorating the fact.

Easton Church, Walk 30 *(Photograph: R. White)*

Highway Authorities

Lincolnshire County Council,
Highways & Planning,
4th Floor, City Hall,
Beaumont Fee,
Lincoln LN1 1BR   01522 552222

North Lincolnshire Council,
Public Rights of Way, Environment,
PO Box 42,
Church Square House,
Scunthorpe,
North Lincolnshire DN15 9XQ   01724 297391

North East Lincolnshire Council,
Environmental Services (Rights of Way),
Civic Offices,
Knoll Street,
Cleethorpes,
North East Lincolnshire DN35 8LN   01472 324468

Tourist Information

Lincoln: 01522 873256

21: Julian's Bower and The Trent Falls

An exhilarating walk looking down to the confluence of the Rivers Trent and Ouse. The stretch along the Humber estuary gives magnificent views of the world-famous suspension bridge. In the village of Alkborough, you can discover Julian's Bower, a mediaeval turf maze and the site of the Devil's Causeway, close to the remote hamlet of Whitton. This is surely one of Lincolnshire's classic walks.

Distance: Long walk 21/25 km (13/15½ miles); Short Walk 11km (7 miles)

Duration: Long Walk 6½/7½ hours; Short Walk 3½ hours

Maps required: OS Explorer 281 Ancholme Valley, OS Landranger 112 Scunthorpe

Terrain: Generally level, short climb onto the cliff.

Starting point: Burton upon Stather picnic area (SE 870188)

Refreshments: The Bay Horse and Ferry Boat Inns in Winteringham; The Butcher's Arms in West Halton.

Bus Link: Scunthorpe/Burton upon Stather

The Route

1. From the car park walk downhill to an information plaque and sign, which indicates this is the Nev Cole Way. Turn right and follow the cliff top path for 3kms, enjoying the splendid views across the River Trent, to pass Julian's Bower, an ancient turf maze, before entering the village of Alkborough via a gate. Turn left onto Bank Road, and walk into Churchside on the left side of the church.

Short Walk

1a. Turn right with the church on your left to a road junction. Turn right into Front Street (unmarked) to the road junction signed to West Halton. Turn left onto West Halton Lane and, 400 metres past the last house, turn right onto a clear track to Southdale Farm. Ignore the turn off to the farm and continue ahead underneath the power lines to bear left in 250 metres again on a clear track. Turn right at the road towards the village of Coleby. (Go to point 7 to continue.)

Long Walk

2. Forward down Churchside to a farm road. Just to the left are the restored Low Wells. To visit the Trent Falls, turn left downhill to a farm building 1 km away at a right-hand bend in the road. In 250 metres take the footpath left for

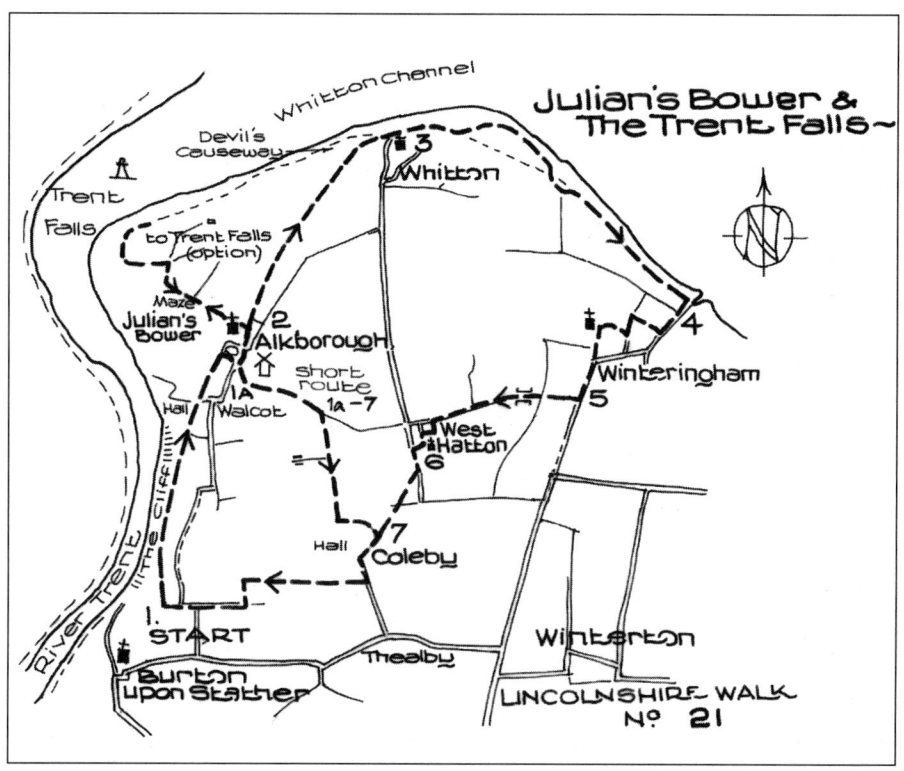

Julian's Bower & The Trent Falls ~

LINCOLNSHIRE WALK Nº 21

400 metres to meet the floodbank and 300 metres to the right will give you a marvellous view of the mouth of the Trent. To rejoin the main route, retrace your steps to Low Wells. Cross the farm road going up the slope with a stile right and continue on the ridge path turning right to a stile and another access road. Cross over to the footpath sign opposite, ignoring the direction arm since the Right of Way is left on the obvious headland path. In 1km, negotiate a small gully to meet a wood, left. Just past the end of the wood cross a stile, left, and continue in the same direction as previously to meet an obvious track coming up from the left. Looking back one sees the floodbank stretching back to the Trent, shown on the OS maps as the 'Devil's Causeway'. Now continue ahead to Whitton, in front of the church.

3. Turn left down Church Hill, noticing the anchor in front of a house called 'The Anchorage'. Where the road ends bear left, then right over a stile, to join the raised floodbank. Follow this for 4km to Winteringham Haven, enjoying the views of the bridge, estuary and distant wolds. Just past the Humber Yawl Clubhouse, turn right, walking on the raised path left to Haven Bridge. Over the bridge, follow the road, right, into Winteringham.

4. Enter along Low Burgage and take the footpath right signed 'Footpath 316 Kissing Gate' (next to a house called Havelock Place). At a path junction bear right to follow 'Footpath 316 Marsh Lane', over a footbridge, along the edge of a grass field to meet a track which leads onto Marsh Lane. Turn left and in 250 metres bear right down Western Green. At the T-junction, turn right down Meggitt Lane to All Saints' Church. Turn left with the road and, in 25 metres, take the alleyway, right, climbing the steps to a handgate and turning left onto a headland path. Keep ahead at a cattle grid to follow sign 'Footpath 312 The Cliff'. At the top of the slope, a panoramic view gives some relief from this always-windy spot. Continue ahead to a road and seat sheltered by conifers. Forward on the road for 300 metres to a sign, right: 'Footpath 313 West Halton'.

5. Descend the hill to a hedge, turning left then right to a small bridge. Over this, turn left and, in 10 metres, turn right keeping a drain on your right. Cross Halton Drain and join a track, subsequently tarred, leading to West Halton. At the telephone box, turn left down Cross Street and at the cross-roads right into West Street. At the next junction turn into Churchside bearing right to St Etheldreda's Church. Pass through the handgate to the left of the church, noting the sundial and plaque commemorating those lost in the Second World War, to emerge onto the road.

6. Turn left and in 200 metres take the stile right, just past Glebe Farm, then cross a paddock to a second stile, heading across an arable field to a large pylon near the roadside.

Short Walk rejoins

7. Continue ahead into Coleby until you pass the end of a stone wall on the right, to take a hedged track with a bridleway sign. Follow the obvious track with a water tower in the distance, for almost 2kms to a sharp left-hand bend to pass through a tree belt and then turn right onto another clear track. The water tower ahead is soon passed as you emerge onto a minor road. Continue straight ahead and where the road turns right, walk forward into the car park and picnic area.

Points of Interest

Julian's Bower – A mediaeval turf maze thought to have been cut by monks from nearby Walcot Priory. This is one of the few remaining mazes in Britain and was first recorded in 1697, although its true age has never been established. A plaque situated adjacent to the site gives a full description.

St John the Baptist's Church, Alkborough – The church tower was constructed in Saxon times whilst the remainder originates from the 16th century. A replica of Julian's Bower can be seen on the floor of the church porch and also in a stained-glass window above the altar. A large vertical stone cross stands adjacent to the porch. At the top, grooves can be seen which are thought to have been made by the sharpening of swords and scythes.

Low Wells, Alkborough – Circa 1850, these were restored on behalf of the local Parish Council in 1986.

Trent Falls – A bank of sand and silt built up by the tides at the mouth of the River Trent. Only exposed at times of exceptionally low tides.

Whitton – Was once an important port on the Humber estuary being served by the North Lindsey Light Railway in order to enable limestone, mined north of Scunthorpe, to be shipped across the Humber. A pier was built into the river and a packet called here en-route from Hull to Gainsborough. The railway line north of West Halton was closed in 1951 although it continued to be used for wagon storage up to 1954, when the rails were removed.

Winteringham – Was an important Roman settlement being on Ermine Street, which stretched from Lincoln to York. The Roman way crossed the Humber from Winteringham Haven, where a timber jetty has been seen when the river was very low.

West Halton – The Church of St Etheldreda has undergone many changes after a fire in 1692, although a window in the nave remains from the 13th century. The manor house, to the east of the church, dates from the 17th century, but has been much altered.

Coleby – Coleby Hall dates from three main architectural periods, the oldest being the early 17th century.

The Nev Cole Way – A 57-mile route from Burton Stather to Nettleton, created by the Wanderlust Rambling Club of Grimsby to mark the life's work of James Neville Cole MBE (1915-89). Nev was responsible for the formation of many of the RA groups in Lincolnshire and played a major part in the creation of the Viking Way.

The Humber Bridge – One of the longest single-span suspension bridges in the world with a main span of 1410m. The total length between anchorages is 2.2km(1.38 miles) and the clearance over high water is 30 metres. The Viking Way starts from the southern end and stretches 224km (140 miles) to Oakham in Rutland.

22: Step Through Time – Across The Line

A varied walk, which gives the discerning rambler a rare opportunity to cross the famous Greenwich Meridian Line at Humberston on the East Lincolnshire coast. Starting inland at Tetney, the route follows field paths right into Humberston with its ample supply of typical seaside attractions, then down the coast to Tetney Haven and Lock. We then join the Louth Navigation and finally discover the Tetney Blow Wells, situated in a lovely nature reserve.

Distance: Long Walk 22km (13½ miles); Short Walk 15km (9½ miles)

Duration: Long Walk 7 hours; Short Walk 5 hours

Maps required: OS Explorer 284 Grimsby, Cleethorpes and Immingham, OS Explorer 283 Louth and Mablethorpe, OS Landranger 113 Grimsby

Terrain: Flat, easy walking throughout

Starting point: St Peter's and St Paul's Church, Tetney (TA 316009)

Refreshments: The Plough, Tetney; The Crown and Anchor, Tetney Lock and numerous in Humberston.

Bus Link: Cleethorpes/Humberston

The Route

1. From the church walk westwards to the junction and turn right into Market Place. At the green, turn left and in 100 metres turn right onto a tarred footpath, adjacent to the Methodist church. At its end turn left up Stoney Way and, at the junction, forward (signed even numbers) for 75 metres to turn left into a cul-de-sac. Take the fenced path, right, next to no. 14, then at the next road cross diagonally left to the footpath opposite. On reaching Craftsman's Cottage, join a narrow metalled path which leads onto an access drive up to another estate road. Turn left and in 25 metres right onto yet another enclosed path. Follow this keeping a wire mesh fence on your right to cross a farm access track, then onto a headland path as waymarked to find a stile in the facing hedgeline. Cross a field to a stile into a paddock then ahead to another stile and footbridge. Cross the house drive to a stile then forward to a stile opposite. Over this turn right on to a track to the farm buildings to follow the waymarks going right then left to a gate.

2. Cross the field to the stile ahead to enter a grassy track which leads onto the A1031. Over the road go to the right of some large gates to enter another green lane for 150 metres. At the end join a headland path with a hedge right and at the third telegraph pole go through a gap in the hedge and continue

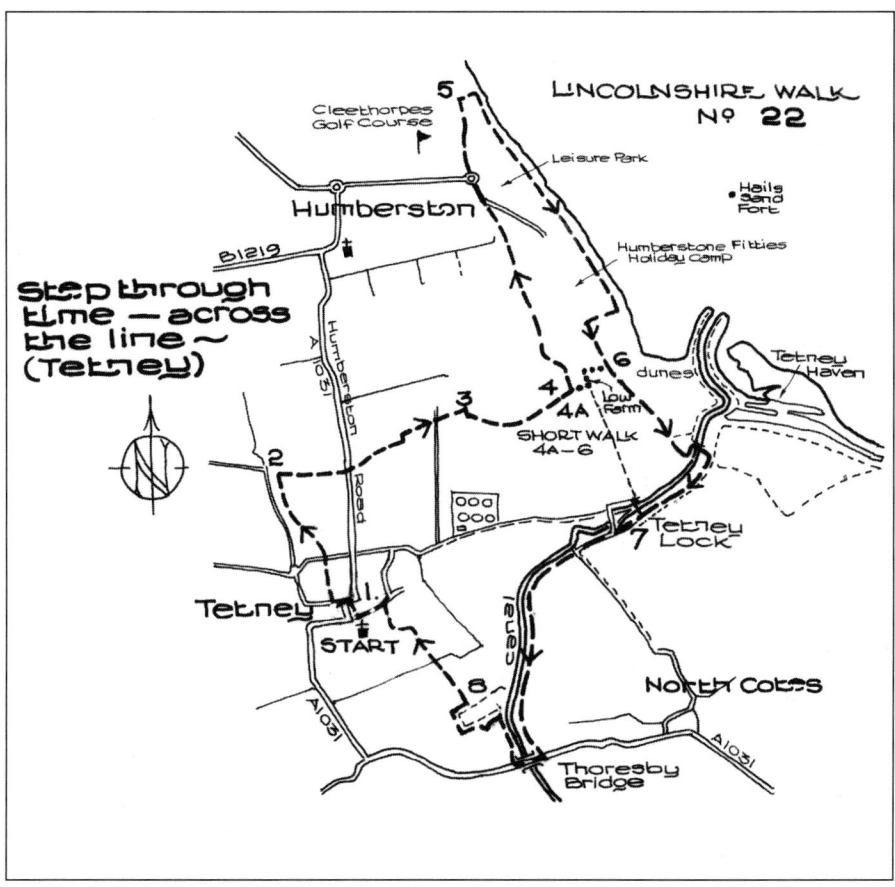

ahead in the same direction. Keeping the hedge on your left, follow it round to the left then turn right through a gap to a footbridge. Turn left, then right with the hedge line for 1 km.

3. At the fifth telegraph pole after the end of the hedge, bear half-right across the field aiming just to the left of Anglian Water's sewage plant to find a footbridge by a track. Forward onto the track for 750 metres to a three-way footpath sign.

Long Walk

4. Turn left over a shallow ditch, cross a small field to emerge onto a track. Continue ahead to walk alongside a caravan park passing through a turnstile by the side of some green iron gates. Keep ahead to join the access road to Thorpe Park then straight ahead to a large roundabout. Continue up Kings

Road towards Cleethorpes, passing the amusement park, for 800 metres to the new sewage plant.

Short Walk

4a. At this point continue ahead for 200m to a junction near Low Farm, turn left and in 100m right onto a headland path which leads onto the floodbank at point 6.

Long Walk

5. Turn right, pass the showground right, and over an embankment turn right onto a tarred path. In 250 metres you pass the Meridian Line marker and information cairn, whilst out to sea can be seen the two World War One forts – Bull Sand and Haile Sand. Continue to the end of the tarred path then onto the grassy dune, alongside the Humberston Fitties Holiday Park. After passing the Humber Mouth Yacht Club, follow the fence to the right into a car park by a lagoon. Turn left at the end of the water to join the floodbank path. In 600 metres, a footpath sign points right over a footbridge.

Short Walk rejoins

6. Ignore the footbridge and instead continue on the bank to pass underneath a redundant oil pipe to the Louth Navigation Canal. Turn left then right over the sluice gate bridge and right again to walk westwards alongside the canal's southern bank. In 1.5km, you join a road by the Crown and Anchor Inn at Tetney Lock.

7. Keep on the road for 150 metres to a stile right and rejoin the canal path for 2.5km to Thoresby Bridge. Turn right over the bridge and immediately right again, over a stile to walk back up the opposite side of the canal for 400 metres to a raised bank. Turn left alongside the bank for 400 metres, then right for 200 metres and right again for a further 200 metres to a large footbridge left.

8. Forward over the bridge onto a headland path and in 300 metres cross a farm track. Keep ahead to walk alongside a wood and, at its end, take the stile left. Here you can see Tetney Blow Well no. 4 in the corner of the wood. Continue across the field to another stile then halfway across this field cross a footbridge on your left. Then bear half-right to another footbridge. Over this and immediately over a third footbridge and forward with a hedge left, to walk by the side of a bungalow to come out onto Church Lane. Turn left up this road to the church.

Points of Interest

The Greenwich Meridian – The zero longitude line also passes through Louth and Boston, as well as Humberston in Lincolnshire. Up until 1884 there were numerous meridians, however at an international conference in Washington, 25 countries reached an agreement that the prime meridian, as established by the Astronomer Royal, Sir George Airy, should pass through Greenwich Royal Observatory. In 1930, a steel plate was set in position on the pathway at Humberston to test a new non-corrosive steel. This was presented by a Sheffield foundry and, as you can see, is still present.

Haile Sand and Bull Sand Forts – Built during the first World War in the Humber estuary at a total cost of £2.5 million, the forts had an anti-submarine steel net connected between them to protect the ports of Hull and Grimsby.

Tetney Haven RSPB Reserve – Designated as a reserve in the early 1970s, it is now home for various types of wading birds.

The Louth Navigation Canal – Opened in 1770 this 11¾-mile-long canal runs from Louth to Tetney Haven. It carried corn and wool from Louth and took coal and timber in the opposite direction. When the railway reached Louth in 1848, the canal declined and it was finally abandoned in 1924, but is still used for drainage purposes.

Tetney Blow Wells – These artesian wells were formed by water under pressure and escaping through flaws in the boulder clay. From 1948 to 1961, the wells were used as a watercress farm, but nowadays they are in the care of the Lincolnshire and South Humberside Trust for Nature Conservation.

Tetney Oil Terminal – Built by Conoco in the early 1970s, the large tanks dominate the skyline for miles around.

23: Warriors, Worshippers and Walkers

A walk for those who imagine Lincolnshire is flat and boring. It encompasses the churches at Tealby, Walesby, Normanby-le-Wold, Stainton-le-Vale and Kirmond-le-Mire and offers spectacular views of the countryside.

Distance: 23 km (14 miles). No Short Walk.

Duration: 7 hours

Maps required: OS Explorer 282 Lincolnshire Wolds North, OS Landranger 113 Grimsby & Cleethorpes

Terrain: Gentle slopes on road, track, field paths and grass

Starting point: Memorial Hall, Tealby (TF 157908). Park considerately in the village, or on the grass verges near the church

Refreshments: Kirmond-le-Mire Manor House, public houses and tea room in Tealby

Bus/Train link: Market Rasen

The Route

1. From the Memorial Hall go down the road on the Viking Way and then right at a footpath sign just before the ford. At the end of the path, 'The Smooting', turn left at the road and then right over a stile into a grass field. At the top right-hand of the field, a stile leads onto another road. Cross the road and turn left onto Footpath 123 to Walesby between houses, which leads into a grass field. Follow the hedge on your left until reaching a stile where this path joins the Viking Way. Continue forward on the Viking Way, ignoring the bridge on your left, passing through a wood near Castle Farm before turning left over a stile into a grass field.

    Follow the Viking Way signs to cross another stile in the middle of the field and continue straight on to cross a farm track leading to Risby Manor Farm. Continue across the next field and go down to a bridge and two stiles in the right-hand corner. In the next field, the path climbs steeply up to a stile, where the path leads to Walesby 'Ramblers' church which can be seen straight ahead. On leaving the churchyard carry on down the track into Walesby, where there is a more modern church, and follow the Viking Way signs out of the village to a point where the Viking Way turns right onto a stony track towards Mill House Farm.

2. Where the track divides take the left-hand fork and carry on through a gate to the end of the hedge on your left. Now bear slightly right towards a waymark

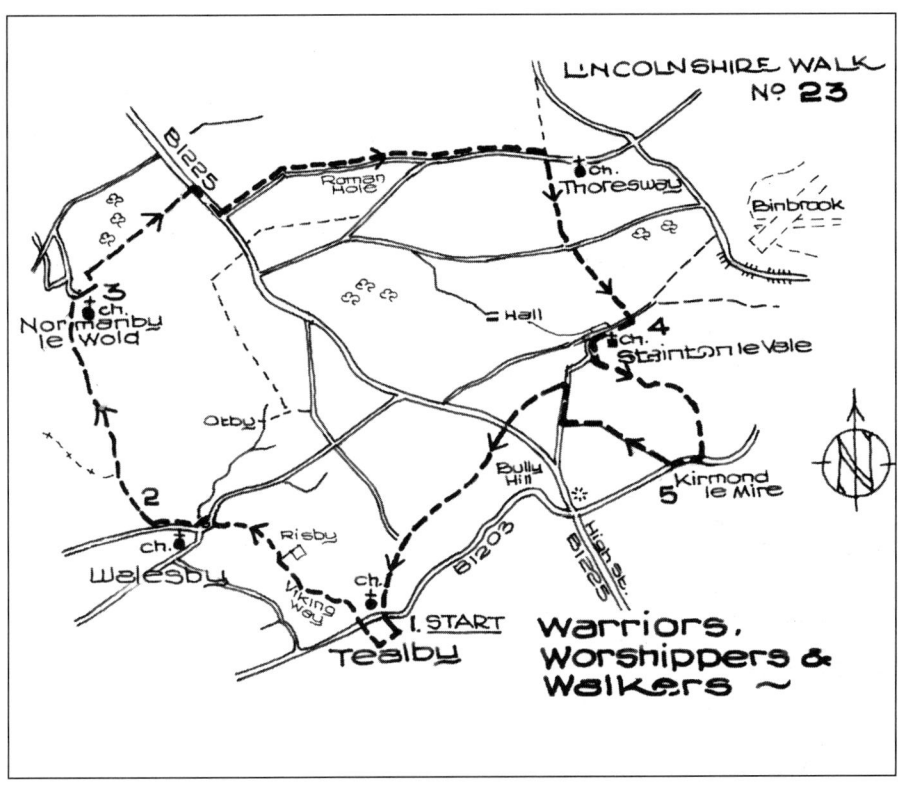

post halfway up the hill and carry on to a gate in the top right-hand corner of the field. A clearly defined headland path now takes you to the church at Normanby-le-Wold in 1km. The views from this path are spectacular and Lincoln Cathedral can again be seen on the left horizon.

3. On leaving the churchyard, turn right down a signposted farm road. After about 200 metres, where the track turns right, take the path on the left and then in another 200 metres pass through a gap in the hedge and turn right along the headland path. After passing through another gap and into the edge of a small wood, a derelict cottage will be seen on your left. Soon after passing the cottage, turn right through a gate into a large field and immediately turn left up the hedge side until you emerge onto a busy road. Turn right onto the road and then after 150 metres turn left at T-junction into a minor road.

Carry on down the road, bearing left at the road junction, for nearly 2.5km until you see a bridleway sign on each side of the road. Turn right up the hill skirting round a small spinney, then down the hill to turn right where the hedge ends, carrying on along a good left and right curving track to a minor road. Cross the road and turn left for about 30 metres, then right onto a good bridleway track, which goes through a gap in a belt of trees. From here, the 1250ft Belmont television mast can be seen. The track comes out onto a minor road opposite the church at Stainton-le-Vale.

4. Turn right on the road towards the village and after 200 metres turn left at the T-junction. Carry on past a seat and a telephone box for 500 metres to a point where the road turns right and a bridleway goes through a gap in the hedge on the left-hand side of the road. Follow the bridleway as it turns left along the hedge side and then bears right along the side of a wood, before it climbs steeply through another small wood. The path then bears slightly left and continues on a clear right-hand curve down to the manor house at Kirmond-le-Mire. On reaching the road turn right and walk uphill to the church.

5. On leaving the churchyard turn right onto the bridleway, which then turns left, then right, and rises steadily for about 800 metres before bearing left to emerge on a minor road. Turn right on the road and walk to a point where a bridleway is signposted on the left, just before an electricity power line crosses the road. Turn obliquely left onto the footpath and follow it until it reaches a busy road. Cross the road and carry on, heading for the gap between two woods on top of the hill in front. The path goes down to a stream with a footbridge and then uphill to a stile in the left-hand corner of the field and then carries on to a minor road. On the highest point of the track, Lincoln Cathedral can again be seen. At the road, turn left down a very narrow lane, until a crossroads is reached. Go straight across to reach the Memorial Hall on the left.

Points of Interest

Tealby – The Church of All Saints is built in ironstone and occupies a commanding position at the top of the village. It was rebuilt in 1871-2. The school, south of the church, is also of ironstone and was built in 1856.

Walesby – The Church of All Saints was also built of ironstone. It stands on a hill remote from the village and was little used after the late 1880s; it was restored in 1931. It was replaced by the Church of St Mary in the village in 1913-14. All Saints' Church is known as the 'Ramblers' church and local members of the Ramblers' Association hold services there twice a year. At the east end is a stained glass window dedicated to wayfarers.

Normanby-le-Wold – The Church of St Peter stands about 500ft up and was restored and partly rebuilt on old foundations in 1868. The interior is very interesting.

Stainton-le-Vale – The Church of St Andrew stands at the eastern end of this secluded village. Dating back to c1300, the interior was restored in 1886. Just inside the wrought iron gate of the church is a memorial to the men who died in the Great War 1914-18. Inside the church door on the left is a framed notice giving details of the church's history.

Kirmond-le-Mire – St Martin's Church is comparatively modern, being built in 1847. In 1975 part of a mosaic and traces of building debris were discovered, associated with a Roman villa. Inside the church is a memorial tablet to five children from the same family who died between the ages of two months and three years in the years 1760 to 1775.

24: A Roman Reminder

This is a superb winter walk, being on the flat but mostly over well-drained paths. Concentrations of wildlife can be seen during the winter months and, with no foliage on the trees, views are extensive. On a cold, clear winter's day you can truly, in the Lincolnshire way, 'see the sky'.

Distance: 18km (11½ miles). No Short Walk.

Duration: 5 hours

Maps required: OS Explorer 271 Newark on Trent, OS Landranger 121 Lincoln

Terrain: Flat, canal and riverside paths. Generally easy walking.

Starting point: Kettlethorpe church. There is plenty of parking in front of the church, but please take care not to block the entrance to Kettlethorpe Hall next door. (SK849758)

Refreshments: The White Swan and Wheelhouse Restaurant in Torksey.

Bus/Train link: Lincoln/Torksey

The Route

1. From the church walk through the gate into the grounds of Kettlethorpe Hall. Immediately to the right (west) is a stile. Climb this and head straight across the field still heading west. Another stile will take you through the hedge and over the metalled track. Take the footpath on the right-hand side of the ditch, maintaining your westerly heading. Go over the footbridge crossing the Sewer Drain – clean these days and supporting fish life – and the Sallie Bank.

2. The path then swings right, round to the north-west, up towards a small cottage. Turn left at the cottage and walk on down the vehicular track. The track bears round to the right and turns into a metalled road leaving you heading due north towards the power station. The road is called Sallie Bank Lane and passes through a small housing estate. You are now in the village of Laughterton. Turn left along the main road (A1133) and you can see the metalled road you are going to take leading off to the right. This road was originally known as Mill Lane, but these days is called Marsh Lane. The road name sign, to avoid confusion no doubt, has both names. Marsh Lane has a gravel surface as it nears the river with a Scout Association camping ground to the right and the East Midlands Sun Club for Naturists to the left.

3. Marsh Lane comes out onto the flood bank of the River Trent, turn right here

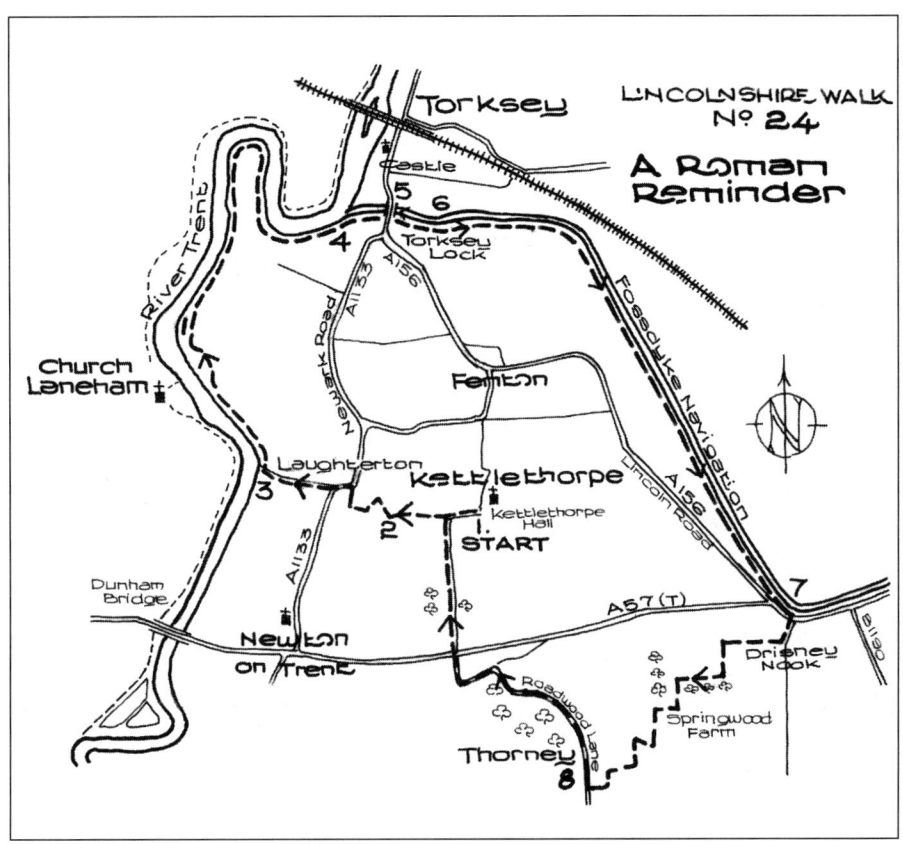

(north) and head for the power station. Follow the flood bank path north-wards, past the square tower of Church Laneham church on the westerly bank of the river. As you round the U-bend in the river, you will see Torksey Castle. Follow the flood bank path right round to Torksey. The gates along the path here are called 'clap gates', double gates hinged in such a way so that one side is always closed. Do not let them go when you are half-way through!

4. As you approach Torksey you will pass a modern, square building, which is a pumping station taking drainage water from the surrounding farmland up into the River Trent. The path turns to the right where the Fossdyke Naviga-tion runs into the Trent and you can see Torksey Lock ahead. Approach the lock and come out onto the A156. Should you be in need of refreshment here, turn right down the A156 and about 100 metres along on the right you will see the White Swan public house.

5. Walk across the road with Torksey Lock on your left and through the car

park, which has public toilets to the right, to follow the towpath on the southerly bank of the Fossdyke Navigation alongside Torksey Marina. Here you will find the Wheelhouse restaurant.

6. Continue along the elevated path and enjoy the peace and quiet, and of course the views. Just over halfway along this section, you will pass disused chicken farm sheds and, further on, some that are in use. Cross a stile by a five-bar gate to join the main road (A156). Walk along this in a south-easterly direction, passing the junction with the A57 and take the next turning on the right, Drinsey Nook Lane. The building on the corner, now an MG car spares business, was once called the Buffalo Inn.

7. Walk down Drinsey Nook Lane for about 200 metres past the chicken farm sheds. Immediately you have passed the chicken farm you will see a finger post indicating the footpath to the right (west) passing in front of a bunga-low. Go straight across the field, keeping the hedge and the ditch on your right. Still walking west, at the end of the field turn left (south) to the bottom of this field, turn right (west) again and then left (south), keeping Springwood Farm on your right. Walk down to the farm entrance. Turn right (west) here through the farmyard and cross the front of Springwood Farm keeping the farmhouse on your left. After 100m turn left over a footbridge to follow a waymarked path to emerge onto Roadwood Lane at Thorney.

8. Turn right (north-west) and follow the lane until you reach the A57. Cross the road heading north and take the track called Westmoor Lane. Pass Rough Wood on your left where paintball games are held and you may see people in camouflage clothes creeping about in the undergrowth. Continue along the wide and straight track until you reach open ground where you will see Kettlethorpe church and Hall away to your right. Climb the stile on the right and cross the field to reach the starting point of the walk.

Points of Interest

Torksey Castle – A mediaeval manor house attacked by Cromwell's army during the Civil War and now a ruined testament to the days when the River Trent formed the frontier between Royalist and Roundhead forces. Farmers in this area report ploughing up musket balls and cannon shot to this day.

Fossdyke Navigation – was originally engineered by the Romans nearly two thousand years ago to join the rivers Trent and Witham at Lincoln. Since the Witham runs into the sea at Boston and The Wash, it became possible to trans-port large loads over a huge area.

Buffalo Inn – was a haunt of the barge people using the waterways of this area and was closed by the church in the early 19th century for being a 'house of ill repute'. The building was used as a hospital for wounded soldiers during the Crimean War. Local legend has it that one of the owners of the inn, a man of eighty-one, married a girl of twenty. On their wedding night he strangled the girl and then hanged himself.

25: A Holy Trail through the Lincolnshire Wolds

One long and one short walk, through the beautiful unspoilt countryside of the Lincolnshire Wolds with marvellous views *en-route*. There are rolling chalk hills, secluded valleys sheltering old-world hamlets and their tiny churches. Also featured are Tetford at the heart of the Wolds, with its Tennyson connections, and a stretch along the Viking Way.

Distance: Long Walk 19.5km (12 miles); Short Walk 10km (6 miles)

Duration: Long Walk 6 hours; Short Walk 3 hours

Maps required: OS Explorer 273 Lincolnshire Wolds South, OS Landranger 122 Skegness

Terrain: Typical of the Wolds, undulating scenery with gentle hills, pasture and arable land, dotted with small copses and enclosed by varied hedgerows. The footpath network includes grass paths, farm tracks, country lanes and some arable crossfield paths. There are numerous stiles, some with high steps.

Starting point: Belchford church (TF 294754)

Refreshments: Public houses in Tetford and Belchford

Bus/Train link: Horncastle/Louth

The Route

1. From the church take Chapel Lane opposite. Where the road forks walk down Ings Lane on the right, at first a metalled road, then a track which becomes a grassy path turning left along the field edge before the track becomes evident again. The track climbs gently to reach Bluestone Heath Road with Ings Farm on your right.

2. Turn right and walk along the road for about 1km. Take the first turn on the left, signposted Oxcombe, and along the road to Oxcombe Manor. To visit the small church at Oxcombe: turn right just after the manor, cross the yard and walk through the gardens, the church is on the left hidden in the trees. The main routeOtherwise, after passing the manor house, turn left down a signed bridleway. Walk through the trees and take the track ahead towards Farforth House. At a junction of paths, carry straight on climbing steadily with Farforth House and farm on your right. A sharp right-hand turn takes you to the rear of the farm buildings and towards the road.

3. When you reach the metalled road, turn right and then almost immediately

left. Here the track passes in front of Farforth church. **To visit the church:** do not turn left yet, but continue straight ahead towards Farforth House Farm and the entrance is on your left. **The main route** continues on the track as it follows the edge of a copse, where the track veers away from the copse continue along the edge on the footpath. At the end of the copse, the footpath bears right downhill to skirt Jericho Plantation. The path is not obvious, but continue with the plantation on your right to a fingerpost just after the Olde Rectory. Here you emerge onto the road. Turn left to visit Ruckland church, otherwise turn right on the main route and follow the road downhill with care. Take the footpath on the left as the road climbs again and, after 90 metres, cross the Greenwich Meridian from the western to the eastern hemisphere! Continue past numerous lakes to reach Park Cottages. Follow the road round towards Worlaby House and skirt the estate buildings.

4. After the last house on your right, cross the metalled road to a waymarked stile in the hedgerow. Note the building at the bottom of the road; this was Worlaby church but it is now used for village functions. Follow a clearly defined field path before crossing two stiles leading to Bluestone Heath Road. Turn right for approximately 90 metres to a waymarked gap in the hedge on your left. Walk diagonally right to the corner of the field, turn left onto a track for 45 metres and then right through a gap in the hedge. Clip the corner of the field to another gap in the hedge and walk across two clearly defined field paths to the bottom of the hill. Go through the hedge to another field and walk towards a stile, which leads you through a cottage garden and onto Clay Lane.

5. Take the road opposite and walk through Little London into Tetford. Just before the church you find yourself back in the western hemisphere, having recrossed the Greenwich Meridian! At the junction near the church, turn right down North Road. **(For Short Walk go to 5a)** Take the first footpath on the left to cross one stile and then walk straight over a field to a footbridge. Bear left to the field boundary and then turn right along it to another footbridge. Pass through a wooden gate on your left and walk beside the stream to another gate here a passageway leads to the road. Turn right uphill to the road junction and then left along South Road. Walk approximately 50 metres and take the enclosed footpath on the right. On reaching open fields, continue ahead with the hedge on your right then at the junction of paths turn left and walk through two fields to the road.

Short Walk

5a. Continue along North Road until junction. Turn right onto West Road (by Wood Farm) and continue along road until road turns right, continue ahead onto Public Bridleway to Belchford. Follow well-defined bridleway path to Lowfield Lane (entrance to Low Yard Glebe Farm). Turn left to walk back to Belchford on metalled road (with care).

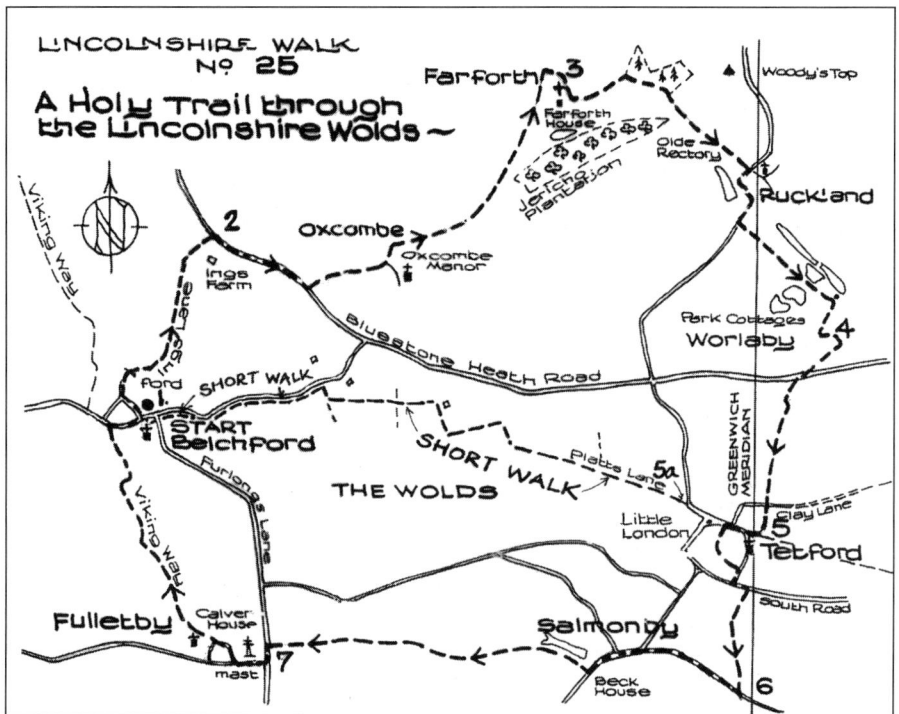

Long Walk

6. Turn right to Salmonby then turn left at a T-junction and after 180 metres take the left fork on to the Horncastle/Greetham road. Immediately after crossing Beckhouse Bridge, turn right onto Hill Farm track. After approximately 70 metres, climb the stile on your right and then a second stile, which takes you into a field with a lake on your right. Follow the path down to a bridge and then uphill to a stile near a tree. Turn left and walk along the field edge to a footbridge, continuing up and along the next field-edge to a stile. The path then begins to climb steeply across two fields and finally to a stile in the right-hand corner of the next field leading onto Furlongs Lane.

7. Turn left and then almost immediately right onto the Fulletby road. After approximately 45 metres turn right down Paradise Lane with the Fulletby radio mast clearly visible on your right. Follow the road round until you reach the School Lane sign. Carry on down this lane and just past Claver House on your right, you reach a double stile with a finger post pointing the route along the Viking Way. Follow this well waymarked path, turning left at the top of the hill and then right. Now its downhill all the way until you reach Dams Lane and back into Belchford.

Points of Interest

Belchford – The Church of St Peter and St Paul dates from 1783, being much restored at various times. There is evidence of a much larger church on the same site before 1153. During the Lincolnshire rising of 1536, the Rector of Belchford, Nicholas Leache, was one of the ringleaders who protested against the closure of the monasteries by Henry VIII. He was hung, drawn and quartered at Tyburn for treason.

Bluestone Heath Road – This is an ancient trackway later used by the Romans. It rises to the very summit of the Wolds and has a spectacular view site along its south side near Tetford.

Oxcombe – The Church of All Saints is a small, delightful building with an octagonal tower and polygonal apse erected in 1842. Some artefacts surviving from earlier times, include a bell dated 1637, a 15th-century octagonal font and several gothic-style family pews. Of particular interest is a memorial to John Grant, who died in 1799: "A good husband, tender father and sincere friend". Then comes a gap in the wording on the tablet, chipped out when considered distasteful: "He made £100,000 by farming, which had never been done before." There was almost certainly a church here in the 13th century.

Farforth – The present Church of St Peter dates from 1861, though the Domesday Book of 1086/7 mentions a church in Farforth. Of interest inside are two large Victorian embroidered panels, a memorial stone incorporated from an earlier building commemorating Geo. Dunham and his daughter Mary, who died in 1725, and the recently (1993) donated part-stained glass windows.

Ruckland – St Olave's Church is one of the smallest churches in Lincolnshire and was rebuilt in 1885. It is believed that the first church was built there between 1030 and 1086. Rev George Hall, who was the first incumbent from 1905-18 was known as the Gypsies' Parson. He was a true lover of the Romany and carried out a number of missions to them. He is buried in the churchyard beside his son.

Little London – This is an area of Tetford, thought to derive its name from the old Scandinavian *Lundr*, which means 'grove of trees'.

Tetford – St Mary's Church is built of green sandstone and is chiefly 14th-century with a 15th-century tower. Inside the church is a wall memorial to Captain Edward Dymoke who was 'Champion' to George II. His helmet and breastplate, which he wore at the coronation, are also there.

The White Hart Inn was host to the Tetford Literary Club, which was addressed by Dr Samuel Johnson in 1764 and claimed the poet Alfred, Lord Tennyson as a member. Nearby in the village of Somersby is Tennyson's birthplace at the Old Rectory, a private residence.

Fulletby – As the village stands at 130 metres, it is a good site for radio transmitters and the mast can be seen throughout the walk. Lincoln Cathedral over 20 miles away can be seen from Fulletby Top.

26: The Culverthorpe Circular

A pleasant and fairly easy walk, starting and finishing in a fine country estate and taking in five picturesque Lincolnshire villages and hamlets.

Distance: Long Walk 15.5km (9½ miles); Short Walk 12.5km (7.8 miles)

Duration: Long Walk 5 hours; Short Walk 4 hours

Maps required: OS Explorer 248 Bourne and Heckington, OS Landranger 130 Grantham and surrounding area

Terrain: Field paths, parkland, arable land, pastures, green lanes and some country roads. Gentle undulations but no real hills. Some of paths may be muddy in winter and overgrown or obstructed by crops in the summer, but are quite passable.

Starting point: Culverthorpe 'Stepping Out' car park (TF019399)

Refreshments: The Red Lion public house, Newton

Bus/Train link: Grantham/Sleaford. The bus service is very infrequent. Your own transport is practically essential.

The Route

1. Leave the car park by the tree-lined path near the notice board. After a few metres, this leads to a drive. Turn right along the drive, with a lake on each side, and walk for about 100 metres to a way-marked gate on the right.

2. Go through the gate into parkland with the lake on the right; follow the side of the lake to the far (eastern) end and turn left to join an estate road at a stile. Turn right at the estate road and follow it to leave the park at a handgate. Walk ahead through the hamlet of Culverthorpe and turn right at the road just past the farm buildings. Walk along the road for about 120 metres to a signposted footpath on the left.

3. Follow the way-marks as the path twists and turns along headlands for about 2.4km eventually to a metalled road near the village of Aunsby.

4. Turn left on the road and walk to the T-junction. A signpost on the road sign here points across an arable field towards Aunsby church (ignore the bridleway to the left). Walk along the path, heading slightly to the right of the church spire, and then through a grass field and alongside a house to reach the road in Aunsby, near a telephone box. This path can be muddy in winter.

5. Turn left through the village passing the church on your left and then a small works; soon to a bridleway on your right, just opposite Ash Cottage. Take the bridleway into a pasture for about 100m and turn left just on the other side of

the hedge for a further 100m; this will take you to a field gate. Pass through the gate and turn right.

6. Walk uphill along the bridleway, passing under some power lines, to a footbridge. Bear slightly left and walk across a large arable field to a metalled road at a right-angled bend. Turn right here along a track in a roughly westerly direction to the road at the small village of Dembleby. Walk on in the same direction through the village passing the church on your right.

Long Walk

7. For the main walk, follow the road round a left-hand bend and carry on to the busy trunk road (A52). Cross the road and walk up the hill on the signposted path, continuing virtually in a straight line for about 1km until you reach a grass field at a signposted footbridge. Cross the bridge and carry on in the same direction across the field, aiming at the left-hand house of the three you can see ahead. Climb the stile on to a metalled road and turn right into the village of Newton; take the right fork at the church and carry on ahead to the Red Lion where you can pause for refreshments.

Short Walk

7a. If you want to take a short cut, bear right down a lane just past the church. The lane degenerates into a track and after about 800m you will see a track going off to the right, which you ignore. Shortly afterwards your track bends to the left and it will take you, after about 1km to a junction with a green lane. Turn right here and you are back on the main walk at point 11.

Long Walk

8. Climb the signposted stile on your right as you face the pub and walk up through the grass field. Go through a stile in the top corner of the field into a rough grass area with a pond, sometimes dry, on your right. Follow the edge of the wood round to the left for a short distance until you reach a hedge. Turn right at the hedge and walk along it keeping it on your left until you reach a hedge at right angles. Carry on in the same direction with a hedge about 50 metres to the right to a footbridge. There are way-marks along this section but it is possible to miss them.

9. Turn half-left at the bridge and walk uphill across a stony field, aiming about halfway along the wood ahead. The entrance to the wood is not too easy to spot but the path through it is well waymarked. Go through the wood and bear left to cross a small, rough grass field and reach the A52 for the second time. Cross the busy main road and turn left for a few metres to a signpost at a gap in the hedge on the right; a sign proclaims the culinary delights of the Red Lion. Go through the gap into another very stony field and turn half-left.

10. The path leads slightly to the right of a group of trees, a short distance ahead. Here you will see a number of poles carrying power lines; pick out the nearer

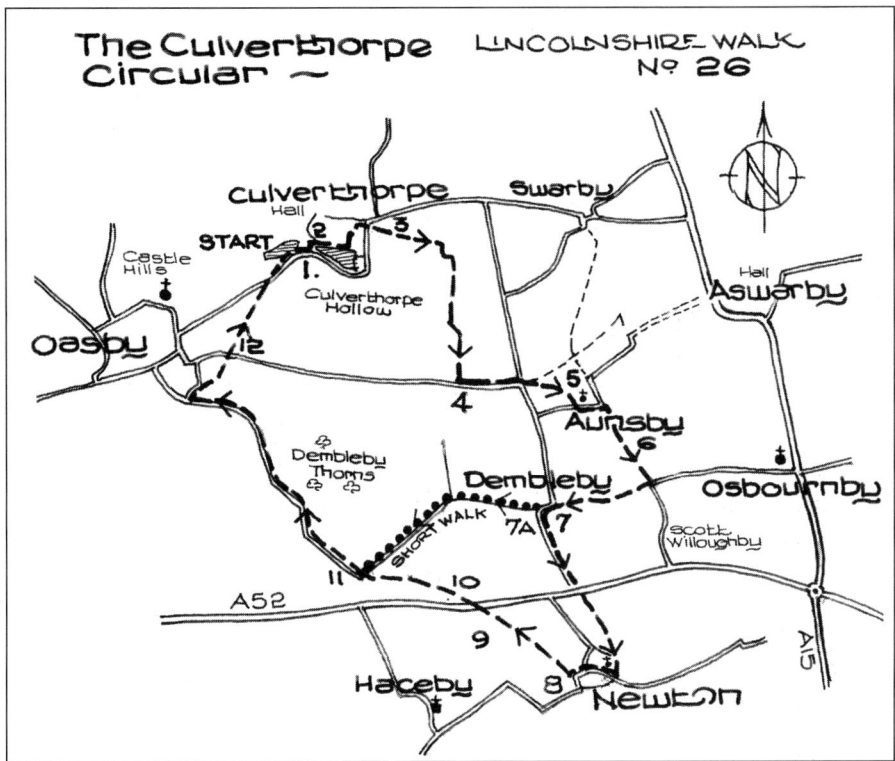

The Culverthorpe Circular ~

LINCOLNSHIRE WALK N⁹ 26

set which crosses your path and aim for the second pole from the left. It is in line with two other poles. Carry on past the pole (waymark) until you reach a farm track leading south from Dembleby Heath Farm. Cross the track and walk across a large arable field, heading towards the right-hand tree of a pair of trees, to a farm track at a waymark. Turn left here for about 300 metres and then turn right along a green lane. After about 50 metres, a track joins the green lane from the right.

Short Walk rejoins

11. Carry on ahead along the green lane, deeply rutted in places, until you reach the hamlet of Aisby in about 2.2km. Walk into the centre of the hamlet passing the green, with a telephone kiosk, on your right; turn right at the first road junction after the green, (opposite Goose Barn Lodge) towards Heydour. On the outskirts of Aisby, just past some farm buildings at a bend in the road, there is a gap in the hedge on the right with a signpost; at the time of writing this is well hidden in the hedge, so be alert! Go through the gap and turn slightly left; cross the rough grass field to another signposted stile leading to a quiet country road. Just before this hedge there is a sandy track for exercising horses but it does not pose any problem.

12. Cross the road and enter the arable field opposite; the path ahead has a slight dog-leg and leads to a small clump of trees concealing a pond. From the trees go through a gap in the hedge into the next field and turn half-right. Walk across this field to the corner to a metalled road at a signpost. Turn right and walk a few hundred metres back to the starting point.

Points of Interest

Culverthorpe Hall – This fine 17th-century hall was once the home of the Newton family whose most famous member was Sir Isaac Newton, the great scientist. The walk takes you through the fine park and past the lake. The hall is not open to the public but there are a number of walks, of various lengths, available on the estate. Leaflets may be obtained from North Kesteven District Council.

Aunsby – The church is of Norman origin but was greatly restored in the 19th century when the tower was dismantled and rebuilt stone by stone.

Newton – This village of grey stone has a fine church with a tall tower, the base of which dates from the 13th century. The picturesque Red Lion Inn is believed to be on the site of an eighth-century alehouse. The Inn has a high reputation for its carvery.

27: A Foxtrot from Ropsley

The walk starts from Ropsley village situated 9.5km east of Grantham and 4km east of Old Somerby taking in Ropsley, Little Humby and Boothby Pagnell via Ingoldsby and Kirton Woods.

Distance: Long Walk15km (9½ miles); Short Walk 7km (4½ miles)

Duration: Long Walk 5 hours; Short Walk 2 hours

Maps required: OS Explorer 247 Grantham, OS Explorer 248 Bourne and Heckington, OS Landranger 130 Grantham

Terrain: Field paths, tracks, green lanes and minor country roads

Starting point: Main Street, Ropsley (SK992343). Park opposite church and central green

Refreshments: Green Man and Ropsley Fox Inn, shop in Ropsley

Bus/Train link: Grantham-Ropsley Monday to Saturday only

The Route

1. With the church and green on your right-hand side, walk down Main Street passing the Green Man Inn to no.10 on the left (opposite the junction of Crown Hill Lane), birthplace of Richard Fox. Proceed now for approx 150 metres and, where the road bends left, take the footpath off right through gate and between stone cottages to enter a narrow tunnelled pathway between tall hedges. Exit over a stile and go forward along the end of the cottage gardens, cross the top end of a dirt access track and beyond some 30 paces to find the footbridge (path here is often indistinct among herbage). Over the stile, go forward with sprawling willow trees and Ring Dam on the right, then cross a narrow field to a footpath sign and stile in the hedge opposite and again over next field to the stile. Maintain direction half-right to midway of facing hedge. Cross bridge and stile and keep this line half-left across to far field corner. Proceed over the stile and forward approx 40 paces to the next stile on the right, and cross a broad sleeper bridge into a grassed field. Turn right and follow the hedge, passing a gate, to a stile in the far corner. Beyond this, in 75 metres, cross a further stile right into a lane. Go left along the lane into Little Humby village, a picturesque cluster of stone cottages about a central green.

2. Turn right along the road, over a ford and along the lane for approx 1.6km, passing lone 'New England' cottage on the right, to a sharp right-hand bend. Turn left here to follow a broad green hedge-bound track up a rise to a crossing green track.

Long Walk

3. Continue forward on the green lane shortly to pass beneath the canopy of a small wood, taking sharp right then left bends before coming to the road. Boothby Pagnell is right and Ingoldsby left. Across the road, offset to right is a stone track. Go forward on this initially to follow the west boundary of the Forestry Commission managed Ingoldsby Wood, ignoring turnings into the wood left. In 750 metres, now walking on a wide track with woodland on either side. Ignore the track departing right (signed permissive bridleway) and continue, again on the west edge of the wood with open fields right, to the south end of the wood and sleeper bridge over a dyke. Take this and in approx 75 metres turn right along a field-edge track descending to the road – Boothby Pagnell is again right and Bitchfield near left.

Short Walk

3a. Turn right here and follow the track to enter the south-east edge of Kirton Wood. (Go to point 6.)

Long Walk

4. Cross the road and turn right. Within 100 metres, before lone Bitchfield 'Old School House', take the bridleway left. Ahead is a wide vista of open farmland. The track initially dips to cross West Glen river, then rises to its previous level and turns right. Follow through left then right bends, maintaining height with the stream valley below right, to come to the road and Boothby Pagnell village (with the Norman manor house in seclusion right, just before). Turn right along the road to a T-junction with the church opposite.

5. Go left along the roadside path. As the road leaves the village and dips, take the footpath signed right. In 300 metres, over the river, the track bends left to follow a fence and then shortly right at the field end to continue east and upwards beside Boothby Little Wood. At the end of the first field, through a gap in the hedge, a waymark indicates the definitive path continuing half-left over a cultivated field, through the hedge to the right of the far corner and crosses to diagonally opposite corner. At the field corner, follow the footpath sign, right, over the dyke and through a tall hedge into an arable field. Strike a line half-left, aiming for the right-hand, east boundary of Kirton Wood. Go through a tall tree hedge to join a track and turn left into the wood.

Short Walk rejoins

6. Almost immediately turn right along a rutted track following the eastern perimeter northwards to wood end and multi-directional signpost. Go forward over a sleeper bridge and along the field-edge path with the dyke and hedge on the right, up to the field-end dyke (ignoring footpath waymark through gap right shortly before). Cross the sleeper bridge and continue with the hedge on the right to the field end. Go right through the gap and follow the track bending left around a tree-shrouded pond, through a gateway and then forward to the road.

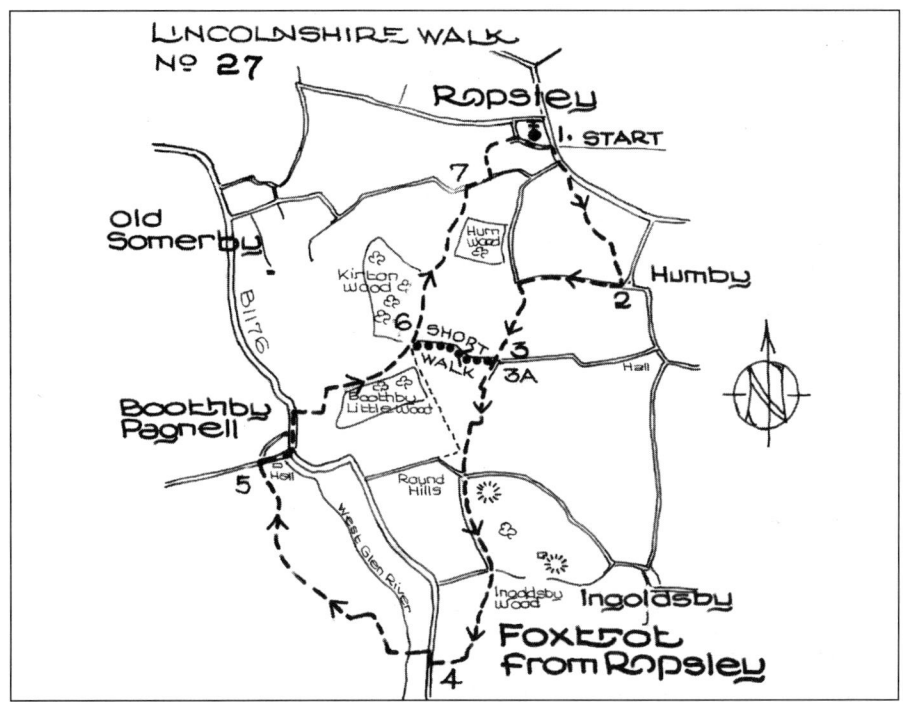

7. Turn right towards Ropsley. Just before the speed restriction sign, turn left across a footbridge to enter a mini-golf course. Maintain direction across to exit over footbridge in hedge line, turn right and continue down into the field end corner. Exit the field into the end of a cul-de-sac road, and forward to join Church Lane. At the churchyard boundary wall, find a small access gate some 20 paces left. Walk through the graveyard beside the church south entrance and on to exit gate at the east boundary. Follow the track down to Main Street and your starting point.

Points of Interest

Ropsley – the Church of St Peter dates from the 12th century and was constructed from local stone and timber. It has an eight-sided spire housing two bells and topped by a weathercock. The church register dates from 1558. Richard Fox, Bishop of Winchester, was born in Ropsley in 1448 and he founded Corpus Christi College, Oxford and The King's School, Grantham. This is marked by a tablet on the wall of no.10 Main Street.

Boothby Pagnell – the manor house is a grade 1 listed building, only part of the original building of Norman origin, dating from AD1200. It was owned by the de Boby or de Boothby family and later in the 14th century by the Pagnell family.

28: A House Of Correction and a Holy Well

This walk takes you from the wide street of Georgian houses at Folkingham to a lonely church and the site of an old priory at Sempringham and back through the picturesque village of Aslackby.

Distance: 15.3km (9½ miles). No Short Walk.

Duration: 5 hours

Maps required: OS Explorer 248 Bourne and Heckington, OS Landranger 130 Grantham and surrounding area

Terrain: Field paths and tracks with some country roads. No appreciable hills. The paths cross arable land and are sometimes obstructed by crops, they are likely to be muddy in the winter.

Starting point: Folkingham market square (TF072336) ample parking

Refreshments: Public houses in Folkingham. There is a public house in Aslackby, but it may be closed at lunchtime.

Bus/Train link: Grantham/Sleaford. The bus service is infrequent.

Some of the paths have been diverted and are not as shown on the OS maps. The diverted paths are clearly way-marked and are referred to in the text.

The Route

1. Walk down the broad main street, away from the Greyhound Inn (closed at time of survey) and turn left along a footpath immediately opposite Spring Lane. After about 50 metres, cross a track and climb over the stile ahead into a rather uneven grass field. Turn half-right and cross the field to its corner to meet a metalled road. The remains of the moat of Folkingham Castle and the impressive gatehouse of the House of Correction are on your left. Nothing remains of the castle itself.

2. Cross the road and turn left and walk for about 40 metres to a pumping station and bridge on your right. Cross the bridge and follow the signposted path to your left. The path has been diverted along the bank of a small stream on your left. Continue along the stream for about 900m and then turn right at the edge of a field to climb a gentle slope, with a ditch on your left, to a well-defined track. Turn left along this track and bear left in about 200 metres at a junction with another path; walk for about 1km until you reach a metalled road (Mareham Lane).

3. Cross Mareham Lane and take the footpath across a large arable field; aim slightly to the left of the electricity pole that is just to the left of the distant

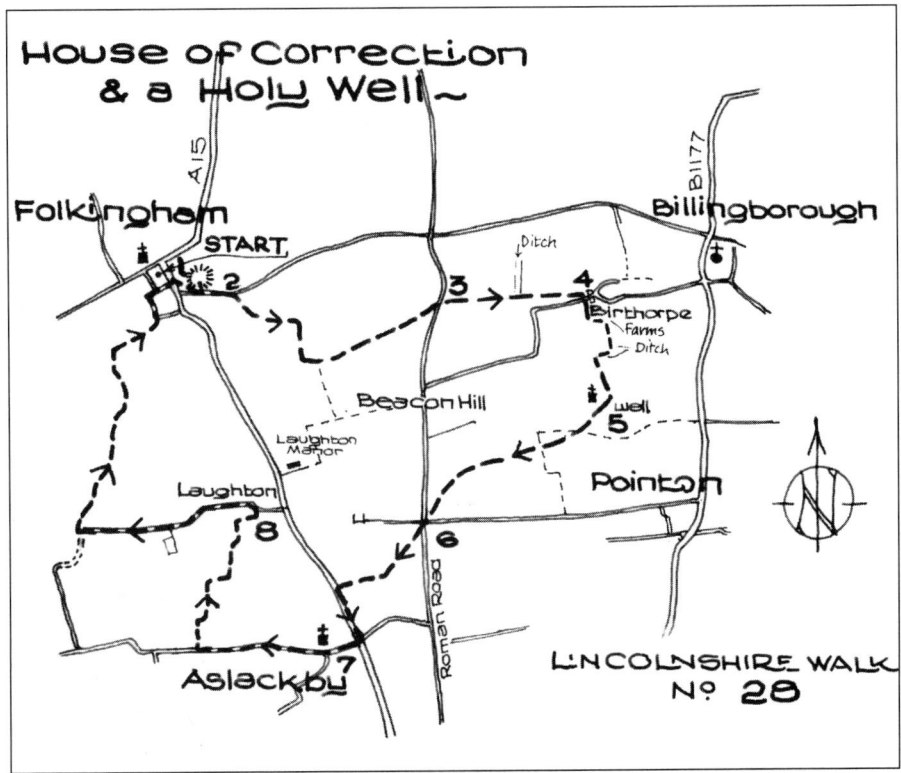

buildings at Birthorpe. After about 250 metres cross over the drain at a culvert, bear slightly right and continue until near the buildings at Birthorpe. (The map shows the path as a straight line from Mareham Lane to Birthorpe, but if you follow this you will have to scramble across the ditch.) On reaching the building turn right for about 50 metres to the metalled road. The path can be muddy in winter.

4. Cross the road and take the signposted footpath to the right of the farm build-ings. The path runs parallel to a ditch and roughly 80 metres to its right; after about 500 metres the ditch joins up with a bigger one which you cross at a culvert near some bushes. After crossing the culvert, head across the field aiming slightly to the left of the tower of Sempringham church. Cross a foot-bridge at the left end of a hedge and continue along a headland path, with a ditch on your right, to the church.

5. Enter the churchyard and walk for about 75 metres along the path, passing the church on your right, to a small group of trees. Take the path across an arable field to a clearly defined track; cross the track and go over the foot-

bridge. Turn half-right and follow the way-marked path. On the left, you will see some earthworks, which are all that remain of Sempringham Priory. Carry on over a track to a footbridge spanning a wide ditch; cross the bridge and bear very slightly left, aiming for a small group of trees about 400 metres ahead. Here you cross another wide ditch by a footbridge. Follow the headland path, with the hedge on your right to the far side of the field to where the ditch ends and walk diagonally across the field aiming for the buildings of Pointon Cottage Farm. You will come out onto the metalled road (Mareham Lane again) near the farm.

6. Cross the road and turn left and walk to the road junction; enter a field on the right at a footpath sign. Head diagonally across the field to the far corner. At the corner of the field go over a ditch board and turn right. Keeping the ditch on your right, walk to the busy main road (A15) where there is a milepost. Cross road and turn left and walk for about 500 metres, passing the Robin Hood & Little John public house on your left, to turn right into the village of Aslackby.

7. Walk through the village passing the church on your right. Just after the speed de-restriction signs, you reach a track on your right with a footpath sign. Walk up the track for about 600 metres and then turn off it to the right at a footpath sign, just past a plantation of mixed deciduous trees. Walk along the headland path for about 200 metres and then cross a footbridge into a field. Turn left and walk forward, keeping the hedge on your left. At the bottom of the field, turn right at a plantation of conifers. After about 100 metres, turn left to a footbridge over a stream. Cross the bridge and go straight on, following the diverted path, keeping the hedge on your left until you reach the hedge at the end of the field. Turn right here for 100 metres and then left onto the metalled road at Laughton.

8. Turn left onto the quiet country road and walk for about 1km to a green lane by a wood. Turn right along the lane and follow it through various twists and turns for about 2.5km to the outskirts of the village of Folkingham. Take the turning on your left at the road junction, where there is a triangular island in the road, and shortly afterwards cross a small stream by a footbridge at a ford. Soon after the ford you turn right and walk up Chapel Lane and right onto West Street to reach the main street and the market square.

Points of Interest

Folkingham – St Andrew's Church has a set of stocks and a whipping post. The imposing gatehouse is all that remains of the House of Correction, built after the Napoleonic Wars, where minor malefactors were subjected to a harsh regime. The Old Reading Room (for sale at time of survey) was a coffee shop of character and The Greyhound was a fine old coaching inn.

Sempringham – Some earthworks are all that remains of the priory founded in the late 12th century by Gilbert, son of a Norman knight. Due to a serious deformity, he was unable to carry out knightly duties and he took up a religious life. He founded the Gilbertine Order, which was open to both monks and nuns, and is the only religious order to be founded in this country. In spite of his severe physical handicap, he lived to a very great age and was canonised after his death. Close by is St Andrew's Church, even older than the priory and still lovingly cared for. It stands in splendid isolation among the large arable fields. There is a holy well in the churchyard. Some 350 metres along a track running roughly south from the church is a memorial to Gwenllion, the only daughter of Llwelyn, the last Welsh Prince of Wales. According to the plaque she was taken as a baby by the English soldiers and held prisoner at the priory until her death at the age of 54 in 1337.

Mareham Lane – This is an old Roman road.

29: The Blue and The Gold

A circular walk close to the town of Bourne taking in the picturesque goldstone village of Edenham and Bourne Woods, famous for the blue-bells in Spring.

Distance: Long Walk 23 km (14 miles); Short Walk 13 km (8 miles)

Duration: Long Walk 7 hours; Short Walk 4 hours

Maps required: OS Explorer 248 Bourne and Heckington, OS Landranger 130 Grantham and surrounding area

Terrain: Easy woodland paths, tracks and farmland, gentle hills

Starting point: Picnic area car park, Bourne Wood west of Bourne off the A151 (TF 077204)

Refreshments: Bar meals at village pubs in Edenham, Morton and Dyke

Bus/Train link: Bourne

The Route

1. Leave Bourne Wood (shown as Pillow or Pillar Wood on some maps) car park by the path in the south-east corner adjacent to the toilet facilities onto the track (riding) and turn right. Continue along the riding heading south and leave the woods in approx 200m through a gate onto a track passing between two fields. Turn right at the main road and immediately after the junction, cross the road with care and enter the corner of a field by way of a stile. Go up the field and follow the path alongside Auster Wood. Cross the lane and pass through Auster Lodge Farm (riding school) following the footpath down the field to cross a stream between two stiles. Turn left, then bear right through gate and continue with a small wood on the right. At the end of the wood cross a footbridge over the East Glen river and bear diagonally right across the field to go through a gate at the far end. Continue in the same direction up the hill and through another gate in the hedge into a third field. Cross this field to a gate in the top corner with a conifer hedge on the right. Scottlethorpe Grange is on the right. Go straight on along the track to a metalled road, turn right and walk through the hamlet of Scottlethorpe, which has some charming cottages. Continue ahead to the main road (A151).

2. Turn left and walk through Edenham village crossing the river Eden and passing the church with its splendid cedar trees in the churchyard. If you are not stopping at the Five Bells, turn right into School Lane and at the fork bear right to continue uphill towards Cawthorpe.

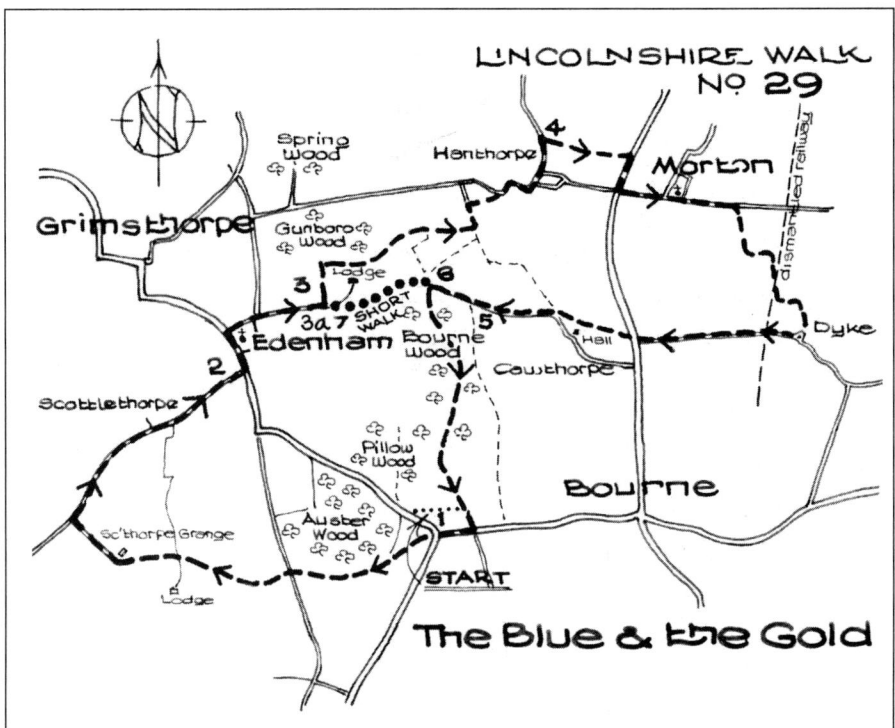

Long Walk

3. Just before the top of the hill turn left over the stile onto a path which has been agreed in conjunction with the Countryside Stewardship Scheme. As you walk this path over the fields (evidence of the old ridge and furrow system on the ground) to your left you can see over the East Glen River valley and Grimsthorpe Estate and pick out the castle in the distance. Turn right at the edge of Gunboro Wood and follow the path, striding out over fields to edge of Nab Wood (shown as Gunboro Wood on some maps). Bear left diagonally over the fields at the corner of the wood to a farm track, continue ahead and go left at the junction to head for the village of Hanthorpe.

Short Walk

3a. At the top of the hill pass Scoth Farm Cottages and continue on the bridlepath over fields to enter Bourne Woods through a gate. Proceed to the first main hard track (riding) where you turn right. (Go to point 6.)

Long Walk

4. Follow the road through the village and turn left towards Stainfield at the

T-junction. As you leave the village cross the stile in the hedge on your right to follow the path over several fields, a playground and the back of a row of houses, to arrive at the main A15 road. Turn right and walk for a few metres to Morton cross roads where you turn left and walk through the village towards the church, a handsome Gothic building and well worth a visit. Keep to the right of the church and head down Station Road where new houses mingle with old. Cross the stile and take the footpath on the right just beyond 'Bakers' Way' and adjacent to no.50a. Follow direction signs over fields/old railway track to the village of Dyke. Look out for the old crab apple tree where you turn right over the field. Turn right at the road and walk through the village passing the Wishing Well public house, follow the road out of the village, cross the main road again and take the footpath alongside the hedge opposite Dyke road end. Follow this path to cross a stile and bear right across a field to emerge onto a farm track to the north of the hamlet of Cawthorpe. This has very few dwellings but there are two fine houses: Cawthorpe Hall and Cawthorpe House. Cross the farm track and follow the bridlepath (Wood Lane) until you reach Bourne Woods.

5. Ignore the first track to the left and go through a gate and shortly turn left onto a wide forest track (riding).

Short Walk rejoins

6. Go ahead along the track and after 1km look out for the various wood carvings and sculptures and the splendid views east over the fen towards Spalding between the trees on the left. At the top of the incline are ponds dug out some years ago by the Forestry Commission. To explore the ponds and admire the sculpture turn left. Leave by the narrow path which rises steeply to the west above the ponds to return to the main riding, where you turn left. Continue for a further 1.5km to the car park on the right.

Points of Interest

Edenham – a pretty village with a good selection of stone houses and an attractive pub 'The Five Bells'. The village takes its name from the Eden stream, a tributary of the River Glen. The church, dating from Saxon times, contains monuments to the Bertie family who once occupied Grimsthorpe Castle.

Dyke – situated to the west of the Car Dyke, a Roman canal, this hamlet depends on agriculture for its prosperity. It does not have a church, but Redmile Farm is an attractive thatched.

Bourne Wood – There are many fallow deer and Chinese water deer (Muntjac) in the woods, together with blue tits, long tailed tits, jays and many other birds. During July/August you may spot a White Admiral butterfly, not often found this far north.

30: Stamford and Four Counties

A short stroll through part of the town before following the River Welland to Tinwell in Rutland. Then up to Easton on the Hill in Northamptonshire and across to Burghley Park in Cambridgeshire, before returning into Lincolnshire through more of the town.

Distance: Long Walk 16km (10 miles); Short Walk 10km (6 miles)

Duration: Long Walk 5 hours; Short Walk 3 hours

Maps required: OS Explorer 234 Rutland Water, OS Landranger 141 Kettering & Corby

Terrain: Mostly flat with 60 metres climb to Easton. Mainly on tracks with some field paths.

Starting point: Cattle market car park at the end of Station Road, Stamford (TF028068). Parking charge except Sundays

Refreshments: Several cafés, hotels and restaurants in Stamford. Public houses in Tinwell and Easton. Snacks at the Orangery at Burghley House in summer.

Bus/Train link: Bus service from Peterborough, rail link between Leicester and Peterborough

The Route

1. Turn left out of the car park taking the path over the river and across the meadows to Bath Row. Turn right towards the Town Bridge with Millstream to the right. At the end of a parking area turn left into a passageway (signed 'Tourist Information'), which leads onto St Mary's Hill. Turn left up the hill and left on to St Mary's Street. At the London Inn turn right up to Red Lion Square and proceed in the same direction up Barn Hill. Turn left at the top and on reaching Scotgate turn left and cross the road. Turn right into All Saints Place onto All Saints Street, continuing as St Peter's Street as far as Petergate. (The bastion of the Town Wall is at the end of this short street.) Turn left, opposite Petergate, down Austin Friars Lane which leads to Melancholy Walk alongside the Millstream.

2. Go through a gap into open meadow and follow path across the meadow to a riverside path. Follow this past a ford to a bridge, cross over the river and proceed in a westerly direction with the river on the right. Keep right at a path junction, still following the river, and after the pumping station, which feeds Rutland Water, walk under the A1 road. You are now in Rutland. (To detour to Tinwell cross over the bridge at the end of track (3) and follow stiles left through paddocks.)

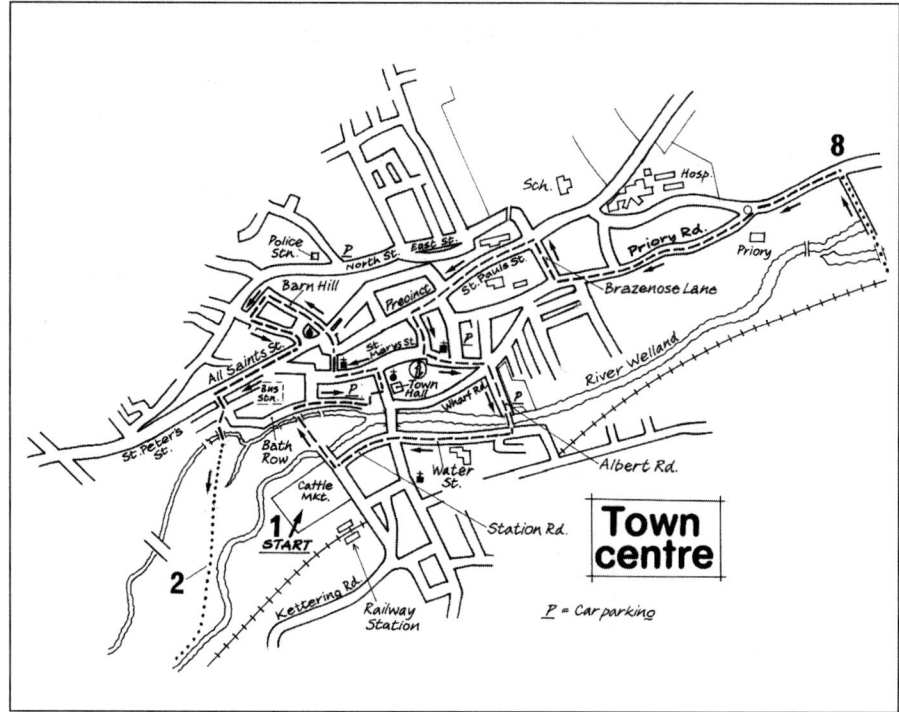

3. At the end of the track turn left with the fence on your right. Ignore the green track to the right and enter the next field. Take the path across this field to the white gate at the railway line and cross with great care. You are now in Northamptonshire. Cross over the railway and climb up the side of the field with a copse on the right initially. Proceed in the same direction across the open field, where there is a good view of Stamford with all six church towers visible. On reaching the corner of hedges, veer left with the hedge on the right. Turn right onto a gravel path and walk up to All Saints Church passing Eastons House.

4. Proceed through Easton on the Hill along Church Street and turn left at the memorial along High Street. This street leads out of the village up to the main A43 road (here turn right for the public house) followed left for about 100 metres before crossing to take the bridleway off to the right. Proceed along this track for 1km when a junction is reached.

5. At the junction turn left with the ruined Wothorpe Hall to the right. Follow the track right and at the next bend leave the track by the stile on your right. Take the direction of a sign to lead to the right of trees surrounding a pond. Continue past the ruined building and veer left and down to a gate and a

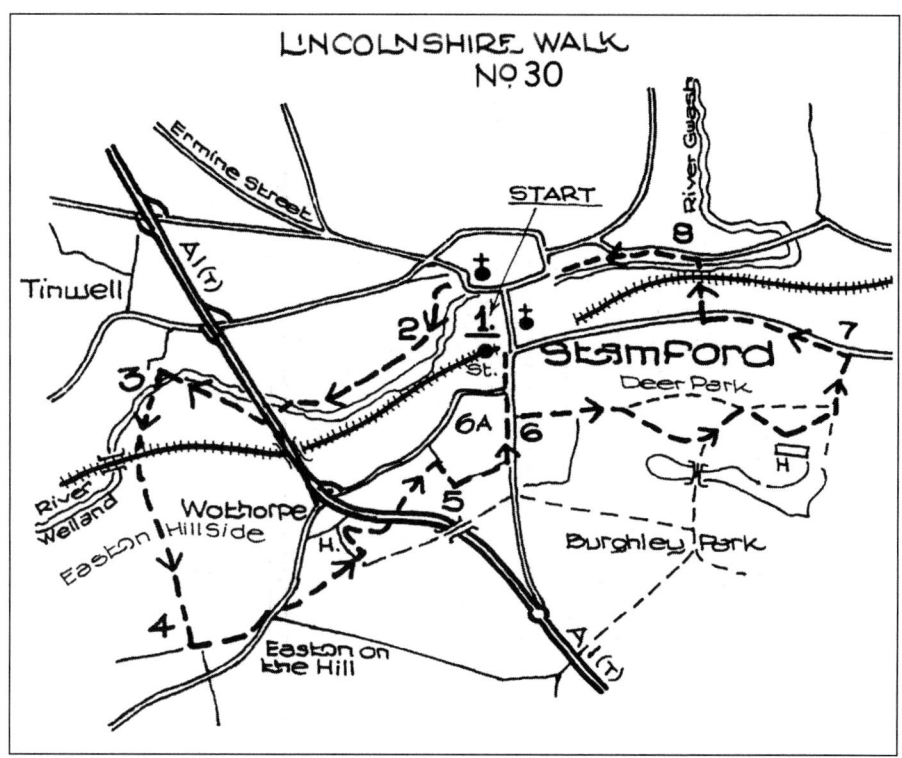

tunnel, which goes under the A1 road. You are now in Cambridgeshire. Go through the gate at the end of the tunnel and climb the steps right to walk along the field with hedge and A1 to the right. Turn left after 200 metres, crossing over a wall after 10 metres, and proceed with the wall now on the left to a stile. Cross the grass field to a stile and bridge onto a pebbled track between gardens. Continue in the same direction on the roadway through Wothorpe to a T-junction.

Long Walk

6. Turn left and after 200 metres enter Burghley Park through the Bottle Lodge Gateway to the right. Proceed through the park for 2km taking the roadway to the white gates into the deer enclosure. Go through the side gate and from this point either keep on the road or wander over the grass to the right to approach the house from the lake. From the house entrance, take the road that bears left down to the Pilsgate Lodge Gate.

Short Walk

6a. Turn left and continue along the road into Stamford, passing St Martins.

Turn left at the George Hotel and return to the car park at the end of Station Road. (You could enter Burley Park as in long walk and take a short walk along driveway and return.

Long Walk

7. Turn left and walk by the outside of the park wall for 1km as far as the second gateway. Take the bridleway right to the railway line and cross through the hand gates. Continue through the next gate into a meadow to cross over the river on a footbridge, then cross over the millstream on a new wooden footbridge. You are now back in Lincolnshire. Turn left on a track past Hudds Mill and then right to the Uffington road (A16).

8. Turn left and continue to south of the roundabout into Priory Road. Pass St Leonard's Priory on the left before crossing the road. Continue as far as Brazenose Lane and turn right up to the traffic lights. Turn left into St Paul's Street and proceed into the pedestrianised High Street as far as the library. Turn left down Maiden Lane opposite and left into St George's Square. Walk right of the church to the end of Blackfriar's Street and cross over a busy road to go down Albert Road. Cross over the river by the footbridge and turn right to walk along the riverbank. At the traffic lights, cross over into Station Road and back to the car park.

Points of Interest

Easton on the Hill – a village of lovely stone houses.

Stamford – The walk introduces the town and its ancient buildings. There are several plaques on the route noting points of interest and more information can be obtained at the Tourist Information Office in St George's Square.

Burghley House – was built by Queen Elizabeth I's Chancellor in the 16th century and the Park is the venue for the Horse Trials in September each year.

St Leonard's Priory – A fine example of Norman architecture with an ornate west front and fine arcade along the north side. The priory was founded by Benedictine monks in the early 12th century.

The Counties of Leicestershire and Rutland

Look at a map of England you can see that Leicestershire and Rutland are very nearly at the geographical centre of the land. They are counties of variety with the land rising on either side of the River Soar. To the west is the craggy and largely untamed Charnwood Forest, with Bardon Hill the highest point in the two counties at over 900 feet (278m). To the east, there are the rolling grasslands of the Shires and the ancient fortress of Burrough Hill. There is also Rutland Water, claimed to be the largest manmade lake in the country.

To the west, King Coal held sway for many years and the land is dotted with what the mining industry has left us. Many of these sites, such as Snibston Discovery Park, are now national attractions or are rapidly developing into wildlife habitats. Traces of railways and canals meander with the contours across the landscape, as evidence that this land was at the forefront of the industrial revolution. Stephenson's groundbreaking Leicester to Swannington Railway can still be seen. The Swannington Inclined Plane stationary engine is now in the York Railway Museum. The once-blighted landscape is now being brought back to life as part of the National Forest, with its headquarters at Moira. The industrial dereliction is being replaced by a landscape that will be the equal of the foxhunting areas elsewhere, with increasing areas of woodland and over 800km of linear access.

To the east, farming holds sway, and many of the

Bradgate Park, Walk 35 *(Photograph: Gordon Gadsby)*

fields show evidence of strip-farming in mediaeval times. The outlines of old villages, which were deserted and destroyed when the inhabitants were displaced by sheep, can still be seen. Quarrying of blue slate at Swithland and limestone at Barrow-on-Soar were the industries of old. The castles at Ashby-de-la-Zouch, Oakham and Belvoir and many similar monuments, serve the industry of the 21st century – Tourism. A host of other villages still survive amid a tranquil landscape. They offer the visitor such delicacies as Stilton Cheese, Melton Mowbray Pies and local beer.

Near the City of Leicester lies Bradgate Park with its acres of bracken, little woods and craggy rock features, also the ruined house of Lady Jane Grey, one of our many historical characters. King Richard III spent the night in Leicester before his ill-fated attempt to retain his crown at Bosworth Field. This is now preserved as the Bosworth Battlefield Centre. Cardinal Wolsey fell ill and died at Leicester and now lies buried at Leicester Abbey. Dr Johnson's first job was as an usher at Market Bosworth School. William Wordsworth spent time at Coleorton and immortalised in verse the ruins of Grace Dieu Priory. Daniel Lambert, one time Keeper of Leicester Gaol, who, when he died at the age 39, weighed 59 stone and measured 102 inches round the waist.

There is much for the visitor to see and enjoy in the two counties and with more than 3000 footpaths and other Rights of Way, much of it can be enjoyed on foot. At the last count, nearly 90% of the paths were in good or reasonable order and they pass through some very pleasant countryside.

Highway Authorities

Leicester City Council,
New Walk Centre,
Welford Place,
Leicester LE1 6ZG   0116 254 9922

Leicestershire County Council,
County Hall,
Planning & Transportation,
Glenfield,
Leicester LE 3 8RJ   0116 265 8160

Rutland County Council,
Rights of Way,
Highway Department,
Catmose,
Oakham,
Rutland LE15 6HP   01572 771117

Tourist Information

Leicester: 0906 294 1113
Oakham: 01572 724329

31: The Belvoir Horseshoe

The ridges of Green Hill, Longcliffe Hill and Hickling Standard form a natural horseshoe in the landscape around the picturesque villages of Upper and Nether Broughton on the Leicestershire/Nottinghamshire border. This, together with the beautiful woodlands and parklands between Grimston and Old Dalby, make this ramble across the Wolds, on the edge of Belvoir, one not to miss.

Distance: Long Walk 21km (13 miles); Short Walk 15km (9½ miles)

Duration: Long Walk 7 hours; Short Walk 5 hours

Maps required: OS Explorer 246 Loughborough and Melton Mowbray, OS Landranger 129 Nottingham

Terrain: Undulating countryside. Field paths and tracks. Can be muddy after rain.

Starting point: Nether Broughton church (SK696262)

Refreshments: The Red Lion and Anchor Inn public houses, Nether Broughton, The Black Horse at Grimston. The Crown at Old Dalby and The Plough at Hickling (off route)

Bus/Train link: Nottingham and Melton Mowbray

The Route

1. From Hickling road turn right into Church End, noting the commemorative plaque to Sir Winston Churchill on the churchyard gates and after 75m take the footpath left, adjacent to Church Cottage. Follow hedge on right to enter an enclosed track. At the end cross a double stile into a paddock, then forward to another stile and out onto King Street. Cross over bearing slightly right to enter a fenced track and forward to a stile, then in 75m to a gate. Turn right alongside the hedge to a stile by a gate. Keep ahead, passing the house on the left, to join Middle Lane. Turn left to the road junction with the Red Lion Hotel opposite.

2. Cross the A606 to the footpath signed through the public house car park to enter a field. At the far end, cross a stile and the field corner to follow the headland path alongside a hedge, right. Follow the hedge for 300 m to a stile on right, over this turn left to walk alongside a high deer fence. Go through two high steel gates then take the stile on the left, ignoring the main track. Go forward through two gates to a wide lane near Broughton Lodge

3. Cross the stile opposite then forward, bearing slightly left, to a gateway in the far left-hand field corner. Keep to the hedge on left for three fields to a gate-

way near some large trees. Now climb straight ahead to find a way-mark post and a stile directly below the power lines. Over this turn left to a farm track, then right alongside the hedge to the B676. Turn left and in 50m take the footpath on right, crossing a field diagonally left to a gate, by a sub-station.

4. Turn right into Wartnaby and just past the church follow the road to the right to a telephone box. Go through the gate signed 'Wartnaby Estates' to follow an obvious track for 1.5km to a minor road. Turn left and in 25m go right, through a gate. Keep ahead to a way-mark post at the bottom of the field, then ascend, veering right to a bridlegate by Saxilby Wood. Join the track to Barn Farm and, just past the buildings, go forward through a gate into a field. Keep ahead, crossing the route of the old railway line to another gate, veer left to enter a long field, aiming for the houses ahead. Pass through a gate, near a barn, to join the road in Grimston.

5. Turn right and follow the road passing the church on right, to take footpath, right, into an alley just past Red House Farm. Follow this alley and on entering a field turn left to pass alongside the rear of some bungalows. Walk up the narrow field to locate a double stile at the far end. Over these, take the stile in the left hedge (ignoring the one straight ahead) then right through a gate to walk up the grass field to a stile onto the B676 again.

6. Cross over to a stile by the gate into Old Dalby Wood. In 150m bear right as signed onto a clear path then in 300m descend to rejoin the main forest track. After 200m take the faint path on right, which leads to a stile at the wood edge. Keep ahead over the small hill to locate another stile into Fishpool Plantation. At the far side of this wood, emerge into a parkland landscape with Old Dalby Hall seen ahead. Continue forward passing to the right of the Hall to enter a small parking area, then out onto Church Lane. Turn left then follow the road on the right to Dalby Green. Cross the Green to an enclosed tarmac path between houses. This alleyway eventually leads to the Crown Inn at the foot of Debdale Hill.

Long Walk

7. At the Crown Inn turn left, up the gated road, admiring the view from a well situated wooden bench, to bear right to a gate leading onto a minor road. Cross the road to a bridleway opposite to enter a hedged track, which you follow for 1km to a gateway. Turn right, as signed, then left to follow a hedge on right, for 500m. Continue through a wide hedge, downhill to a minor road. Cross over, bearing diagonally left, to another bridleway, which you follow for 500m to a steel gate. After 100m, turn right in front of Wolds Farm, across a grass field to a gate, which leads onto a lane, which you follow to meet the A606.

Short Walk

7a. Turn right in front of the Crown Inn and follow the road round to the left to a

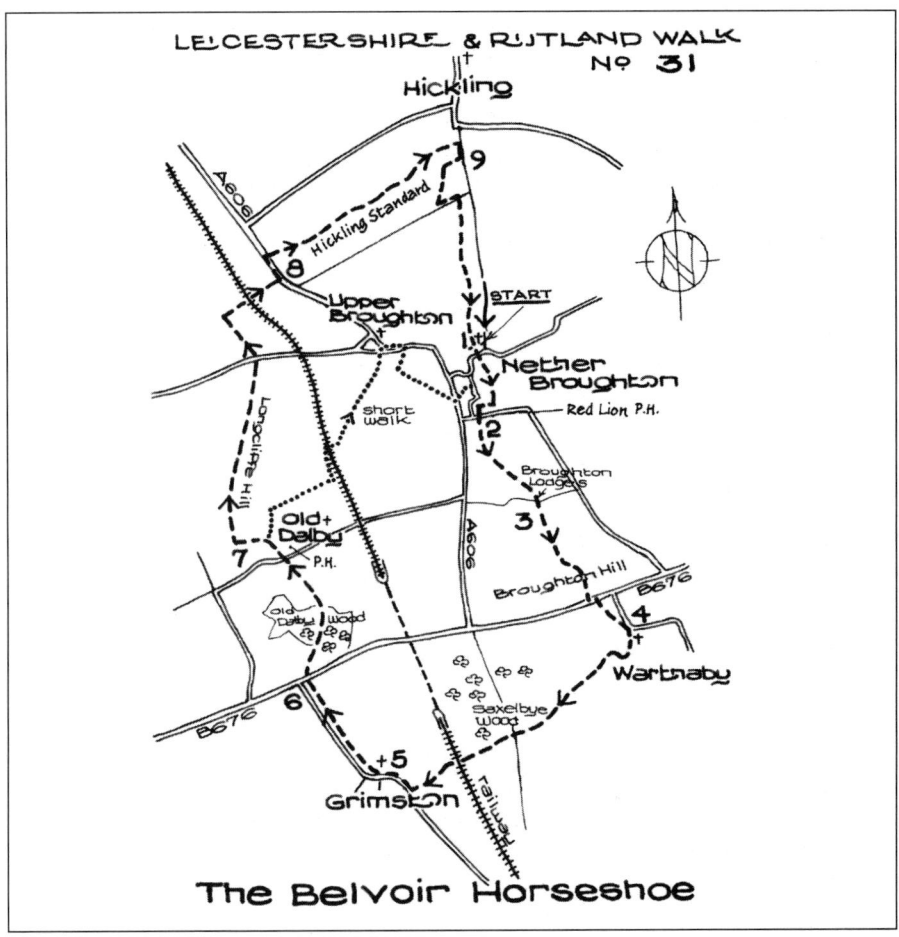

At the top: LEICESTERSHIRE & RUTLAND WALK Nº 31

The Belvoir Horseshoe

T-junction on Longcliffe Hill. Cross over diagonally left to a stile and follow the headland path along the field bottom. In the field corner, turn right over a track to the stile opposite, then forward over a second stile behind North Lodge Farm. Continue for 250m to a path junction turning left through the hedge then right on a clear headland path. Follow this, turning left in the field corner to a stile, right, which leads to a tunnel under the railway line. Through the tunnel, cross a stile, then turn left again on a headland path for 200m to a gap in the hedge. Pass through the gap then turn right to follow the Dalby Brook for 450m to an immature spinney.

At the far side, cross the stile to a second stile by a tree in the opposite hedge. In the next field, aim for a stile in the far left-hand corner. Over this, walk up the next field with the hedge on right for 200m to a ditchboard and stile, right. Continue uphill with the fence on right, to another stile, which leads into a paddock. Turn half-left, uphill to find a stile in the far corner, over this turn left onto a gravel track which leads onto Bottom Green in Upper Broughton. Turn right to join Melton Road and just before the speed de-restriction sign, cross the stile on right. Forward across three fields and at the far hedge turn left downhill to a stile in the bottom corner. Continue again, across an arable field to another to follow a headland path to a foot-bridge and the county boundary.

Walk uphill to a stile in the hedge, then turn to a stile in the right-hand hedge, continue in the same direction to another two stiles and emerge onto the A606, opposite the Anchor Inn. Cross the main road to the footpath through the public house car park, which leads into a small play area and eventually emerges onto Chapel Lane. Turn left to the junction with Middle Lane, then left again back to the church. (Note the 17th- and 18th-century houses en-route.)

Long Walk

8. Turn left on the grass verge for 250m to a stile on right to enter a grass field. Walk up the right-hand hedge for 500m to a stile, right, opposite Hill Top Farm. Over the stile, turn left to another stile in the facing hedge line. Follow the hedge on right, for 900m to cross a stile near the trig point. With the hedge now on your left, go forward over two fields to another stile at the end of Hickling Standard. Over the stile turn right and take another stile, turn left with hedge on left, go down to stile in the corner onto a sometimes muddy track (Long Lane) which takes you into Hickling.

9. Turn right on the road for 100m, then right again at the footpath sign. Forward between fences then veer left across the field to a stile. Over this turn left to a double stile then forward following the hedge on right, across three fields to a road. Turn left and in 100m turn right over a stile. Continue ahead over four fields to a long footbridge over a stream at the county bound-ary. Ascend slightly right, to find another stile into an arable field with a hedge on left. Follow this for 200m to another stile, then descend veering slightly right to a stile in the bottom right-hand field corner. Now continue in the same direction aiming to the right of Nether Broughton church, to ascend to an enclosed path to the right of an impressive house. Follow this to emerge onto Church End, turning left to return to the church.

Points of Interest

Wartnaby – The village name means 'watch hill' and was obviously a look out point over the surrounding countryside. Adjacent to the main door of St Michael's and All Angels' Church is situated a plaque commemorating the plant-ing of oak trees to Sir Winston Churchill and John F Kennedy. The church also has an unusual twin bell-tower. King Charles II is alleged to have stayed at Wartnaby Hall.

Grimston – The picturesque village green has a set of stocks beneath an impressive oak tree, whilst opposite is the beautifully converted Old School House.

Old Dalby – The 300-year-old Crown Inn is a converted farmhouse, which has retained many of its original features. At the rear of the building there is a petanque pitch. The church was rebuilt in the 19th century and contains several interesting old tombs. Behind the altar is a 16th-century tomb of a lady between her two husbands with her five children below. Nearby is the former Ordnance Works, now an industrial estate.

Upper Broughton – There are several timber-framed cottages in the village, such as the 17th-century Willow Cottage. In the churchyard is a fine collection of early 17th-century slate headstones.

Nether Broughton – The 13th-century ironstone Church of St Mary is well worth a visit. It was restored in 1881 when the aisle windows were installed. In the churchyard is a First World War memorial monument whilst adjacent to the main gate is a plaque to Sir Winston Churchill.

32: In Search of The Source of The Witham

Despite being one of Lincolnshire's main waterways, the River Witham's origins are in the Leicestershire Wolds, just to the east of the village of Edmonthorpe. This lovely walk explores the surrounding countryside visiting the 'stone' villages of Market Overton with its picturesque village green, complete with stocks, Sewstern situated on an old Salt Way and Wymondham, allegedly the true home of Stilton cheese.

After completing the walk, why not treat yourself to a delicious cream tea in the beautifully restored Wymondham Windmill tea-room?

Distance: 18km (11½ miles). No Short Walk.

Duration: 5½ hours

Maps required: OS Explorer 247 Grantham, OS Landranger 130 Grantham

Starting point: Nurses Lane, Wymondham, by the churchyard gate (SK852186)

Terrain: Tracks and field paths over rolling countryside. Can be muddy after rain.

Refreshments: The Berkeley Arms & General Store, Wymondham. The Blue Dog, Sewstern. The Black Bull & Post Office/Store, Market Overton.

Bus/Train link: Grantham/Melton Mowbray

The Route

1. Enter the churchyard through the south-east gate and leave through the lych gate into Church Lane. (Note the old Reading Room on right and the National School Room on left as you approach the main road.) Turn right towards South Witham and in 250m take the footpath, left, Buckminster. Bear right across the meadow to an electricity pole, then forward towards a yellow-topped post on the old railway embankment. Cross this then turn right on the headland path, which you follow round to the left and in 200m to a footbridge, right. Over this turn left to a stile then in 200m cross the foot-bridge, right, to turn left again keeping the hedge on your left to emerge through a gate onto a minor road.

2. Turn left and in 15m take the footpath right following a way-marked head-land path alongside a dyke for 1.5km to a wide hedged track. Cross over, still alongside the dyke, then forward for 1km to pass to the right of Manor Farm and onto a minor road. Cross to the stile opposite and follow the hedge left to

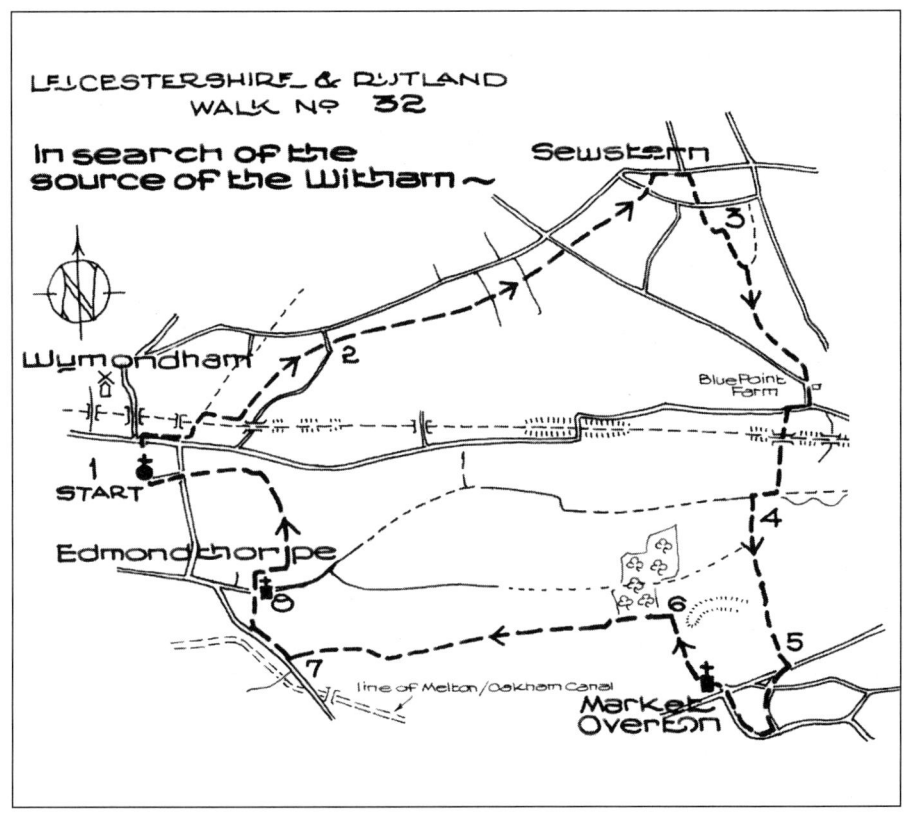

another stile and road. Turn right into Sewstern, then opposite the Blue Dog Inn, turn right down Church Lane.

3. At the end take the left of two signed paths through a gate, then forward veering slightly left across the meadow to a double stile in the hedgerow. Cross this and turn left along a headland path crossing into the next field, keeping the hedge on your left head for the signpost through the hedge facing you. On reaching the sign turn right and keeping the hedge on your right walk for 1.25km to meet a track. Turn right and in 30m left onto a wide hedged track (The Viking Way). Follow this passing Crown Point Farm, left, to a road.

4. Turn right for 250m then left down the access road to Pasture Farm. Keeping the buildings on your right, go through a gate and in 20m over a stile. In 100m cross a narrow stream – this is the infant River Witham. Its source is difficult to establish but it must only be a few metres to the right. Ascend slightly to a stile, but do not cross it, instead turn right for 100m to a gate. Through this, turn left, initially on a track, which improves, to a tarred surface. This passes through a small industrial estate and eventually leads onto Thistleton Road, Market Overton.

5. Turn right and in 100m left down Bowling Green Lane. At the end turn right onto Main Street to pass the picturesque village green and village store, to a T-junction. Turn left onto Teigh Road and in 50m right down Church Lane. Follow the track for 1km admiring the views from the ridge and where a hedge comes in from the left, turn left aiming for the yellow topped post at the corner of the wood.

6. Follow this clear track for 1.5km and when it turns sharp left, continue ahead into an arable field, veering slightly right to another way-marked post. At the post, turn left to a third way-marked post by a gate. Cross the next meadow aiming for a gate just to the left of The Lodge.

7. Turn right on the road and in 250m take the footpath right passing through two gates to ascend a meadow with a stone wall on right. At the house, go through a gate then forward through the yard, to another gate. Turn right onto the main road in Edmonthorpe.

8. Opposite the church take the footpath left ascending the field, veering slight left to a stile in a wire fence. Turn right for 250m and at a T-junction, left into a sometimes enclosed track. Follow this for 600m to enter a meadow via a gate. Forward keeping the hedge on your left to another gate, then bear left to a footbridge. Continue ahead along Wrights Lane to meet Edmonthorpe Road. Cross this into Nurses Lane, which you follow to the right and your starting point.

Points of Interest

Wymondham – On entering the churchyard note the base of the Market Cross just to the right of the main entrance. This was originally positioned next to the Berkeley Arms until it was moved. Also, read the inscription on Samuel Pears' grave, opposite the west wall of the 13th-century tower. The church has a 15th-century belfry and a grand array of medieval carvings. Outside the lych gate is the old Reading Room built around 1675 at the instigation of Sir John Sedley who died in 1638 and left £400 for the education of local children.

For many years, Stilton cheese was produced here and it is claimed a Mrs Paulet first made it in 1730. Its fame spread and she started supplying the landlord of the Bell Inn on the Great North Road at Stilton.

Just to the north of the village on Butt Lane stands the 19th-century windmill. Inside the machinery is still intact whilst the six sails removed in 1922 are now being restored. Nowadays, the mill is a tea-room and the adjacent buildings house craft shops.

Sewstern Lane – Probably Lincolnshire's oldest highway and was certainly used by the Romans and could date from the Bronze Age. At one time, it was the main route between Stamford and the River Trent. Use of it declined during the 17th century but it continued to be used mainly by drovers taking their animals to market.

Edmonthorpe – St Michael's Church stands close to Edmonthorpe Hall. The church dates from the 13th century with 15th-century additions. It contains various monuments to the Smith family. Edmonthorpe Hall was destroyed in 1943 when a cook threw a rolling pin at a white cat and in the process knocked over a pan of fat.

The Melton to Oakham Canal, which ran to the south of the village was closed in 1847.

33: The Blue Stone on The Wreake

Two circular walks in the Wreake Valley starting from Frisby and linking the villages of Rotherby, Rearsby and Gaddesby.

Distance: Long Walk 16km (10 miles); Short Walk 13km (7½ miles)

Duration: Long Walk 5 hours; Short Walk 3½ hours

Maps required: OS Explorer 246 Loughborough and Melton Mowbray, OS Landranger 129 Nottingham & Loughborough

Terrain: Mostly meadowland, some crop fields

Starting point: Old Village Cross, Frisby on the Wreake (SK693176)

Refreshments: Bell Inn, Frisby on the Wreake, Wheel, Coach & Horses, Rearsby, Cheney Arms, Gaddesby.

Bus/Train link: Leicester/Melton Mowbray

The Route

1. Leave Frisby on the Wreake by the Old Cross at top of Water Lane and take the footpath way-marked 'Leicestershire Round', down a gravel drive and across fields to a minor road. Still following 'Leicestershire Round' signs, take left-hand path. Near the end of the fourth field, at the edge of Rotherby village, turn right towards the railway line. **(Cross this with care.)** Go over two fields to a bridge, the site of the Old Mill. Cross the bridge, turn left and walk along the bank of the River Wreake. Hoby village is on your right.

2. Still on the river bank, the path passes between the river and a house, then crosses the bridge and turns right. Shortly leave the river, **(again taking care crossing the railway line)** and go straight ahead to Rotherby, entering the village through the gate by the church. Turn right along metalled road.

Long Walk

3. At Hoby Road turn right, then left into Brooksby Agricultural College. Continue along drive following yellow markers through the grounds, bearing left at cottages near the church into a field. Bear right across fields to the road by a fishing lake. Turn left, way-marked 'Equine Centre' and follow the road round Hall Farm.

Short Walk

3a. At Hoby Road turn left at Brooksby, cross the A607, follow bridleway marked 'Mid-Shires Way' south-east for 2.7km. Turn right at the road by Carlton Lodge Farm to join the main route at Gaddesby at the junction of Park Hill, Rotherby Lane and Pasture Lane. (Go to point 6)

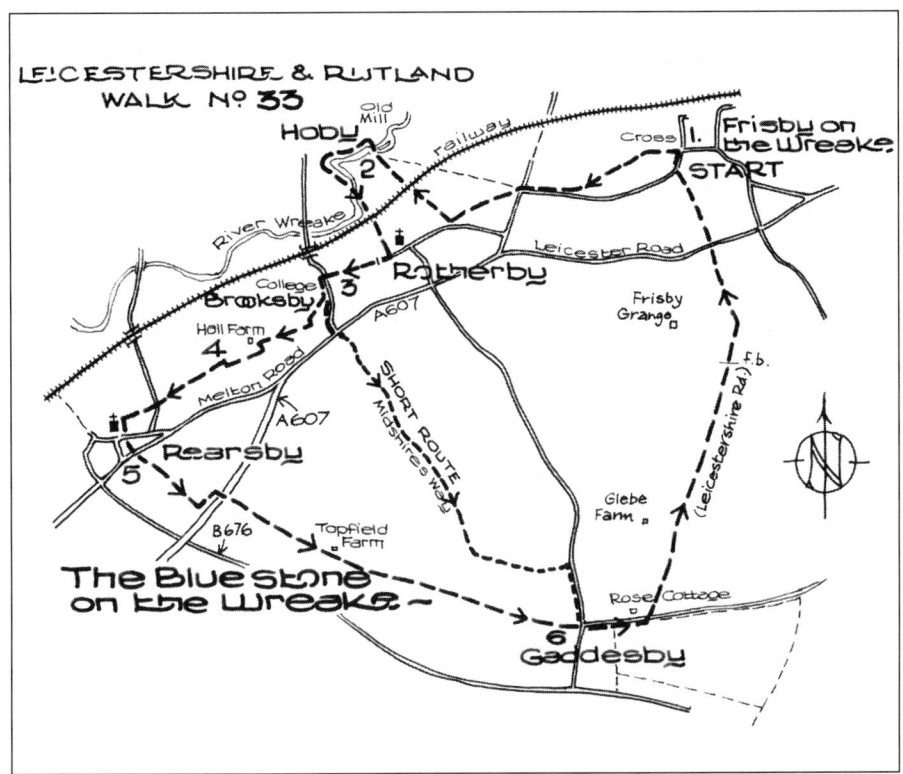

4. Do not enter the Equine Centre but follow the track swinging right then left becoming a footpath in field, continue to follow footpath over the hill, the village of Rearsby is now in view. Keep alongside the hedge into walkway leading to a metalled road in front of houses. At the end of this, cross road into Church Leys Avenue and follow walkway left round the church. Turn left and cross the old packhorse bridge over the ford in Rearsby village.

5. Turn left, then right by the post-box. Cross the A607 to a footpath, continue over playing field and one further field, turning left in front of an oak tree. Turn right to cross the bypass just before the end of the field. Follow the way-mark signs over the fields with the hedge on right. After four fields, cross a stile and continue over one further field and stiles through Topfield Farm. Continue straight ahead on tracks and fields, following way-marks to reach the village of Gaddesby at top of Park Hill.

Short Walk rejoins

6. Continue over the road and down Pasture Lane. Just past Rose Cottage, take the footpath on the left. You are now back on the 'Leicestershire Round'.

Follow the well way-marked path over fields for 3.5km, crossing the busy A607 near the near remains of an old Stump Cross. Continue ahead to Frisby on the Wreake, on reaching Rotherby Lane turn right into the village.

Points of Interest

Frisby – The church has a Norman base tower. A 10ft high Market Cross stands opposite the Bell Inn and there is an ancient Stump Cross on the main road.

Rotherby – A pretty village with an interesting church and Leicester City Greenhouses which are sometimes open to the public.

Rearsby – The seven-arched packhorse bridge was built in 1714. In Mill Road there is a house dated 1661 with an E-shaped gabled front and another house nearby dated 1613 with a timber frame.

Gaddesby – At the corner of Chapel Lane and Cross Street stands a large glacial Ice Age erratic, known locally as the Blue Stone, from which John Wesley preached when visiting friends in the village. The church, 13th to14th-century, is said to be the most beautiful church in the county. Inside are mediaeval benches and box pews and a mounted statue to Col. Cheney who had five horses shot from underneath him at Waterloo.

Brooksby Hall – The home of the Villiers family for 500 years, where the Duke of Buckingham was born in 1592. Later residents include Lord Cardigan of Balaclava fame and Admiral Beatty of Jutland.

34: An Iron Age Vista and Capital of Coritani

A circular walk starting from the Iron Age Fort at Burrough Hill, with fine vistas and linking several villages including the site of St Mary and St Lazars Hospital at Burton Lazars and Little Dalby Hall.

Distance: Long Walk 17km (11 miles); Short Walk 12km (7½ miles)

Duration: Long Walk 5½ hours; Short Walk 3½ hours

Maps required: OS Explorer 246 Loughborough & Melton Mowbray, OS Landranger 129 Nottingham

Terrain: Undulating countryside and field paths. Can be muddy.

Starting point: Burrough Hill Fort Car Park (SK765115)

Refreshments: Public houses in Thorpe Satchville, Great Dalby and Burton Lazars

Bus/Train link: Oakham/Melton Mowbray

The Route

1. From Burrough Hill Fort car park, follow the signs marked Burrough Hill Fort and Dalby Hills Path, along the farm track. At the end of the farm buildings, take the footpath to the left indicated by a marker post, through a farm gate. Go directly across the field to a stile and continue over it along the field boundary with the hedge on the right, to a double stile in the corner of the field, which leads onto a stone track. Turn left along the track, passing Burrough reservoir to reach Somerby Road, turn right into Burrough on the Hill village. **As there is no footpath on this road, take care.** Note the views on the left over the Wreake Valley.

2. On entering the village and reaching the Church of St Mary the Virgin, go right through the main gate, past the church porch, to a stile in the left-hand corner of the churchyard. Go across the field with a wall on the left to another stile, then diagonally right heading for the corner of a bungalow garden, to a stile which leads on to Melton Lane.

3. At the lane turn right and walk downhill for about 200m to where it bends right. At this point, take the path on the left into a field (the fingerpost at this point is hidden in a bush and is virtually invisible when walking downhill). Continue along the field boundary with the hedge on your right and at the bottom cross into the next field, then a footbridge and stile. With a hedge and brook on the left, continue to a footbridge, then head diagonally left over an open field to a marker post and a stile on the crest of the ridge. In the

distance, the red roofs of houses in Thorpe Satchville can be seen, the next destination. Descend the other side of the ridge, over a footbridge in the hedge line, with Adams Gorse Spinney on the left. Climb up the next ridge to the end of the spinney, then head diagonally right over the crest of the ridge, to the right-hand corner of the field. Cross over a footbridge through a gap in the hedge, then bear diagonally right to the corner of the next field to cross a double stile and footbridge. From here, turn left and with the hedge on the left, cross two fields, aiming for Thorpe Satchville village hall. Cross some playing fields to emerge on the B6047, Great Dalby Road.

4. Turn right along the main road, passing Bakers Lane junction to a fingerpost on the left, at the side of the entrance to Satchville Hall Lodge. Heading diagonally right, follow the marker post over the estate grounds, through a copse of horse chestnut trees to a double stile. Turn right after crossing the stile keeping to the field boundary, with the hedge on the right, then continue over the fields to a fishing pond at Hall Farm. Take the stile at the right-hand corner of the pond and with the hedge on the right, climb gradually uphill to a tarmac lane.

5. Turn left along the lane and before the entrance to the farm buildings on the right, take the footpath right, by a fingerpost. Cross directly over an open field aiming for a field gate, after passing through this walk gradually downhill, along a field boundary with the hedge on the left, to a double stile. Go straight ahead to cross a footbridge and stile. Then, with the hedge on your right, walk along the field boundary aiming for a double headed fingerpost and field gate to gain the main B6047 road.

6. Turn left and climb uphill along the road, using the grass verge as there is no footpath. After 200m at the top of the hill, take a footpath left at the fingerpost. After crossing a small field to a stile, turn right and follow the field boundary to the bottom of the field. Find a gap in the hedge with a wooden fence and a marker post half hidden in the hedge. Climb over the fence and head directly uphill to the crest of the ridge to a stile. Cross this and walk downhill through a horse paddock to a field gate and pass between the house and outbuildings onto the drive to a gravel path between the houses. You then enter Great Dalby on Main Street, opposite the war memorial.

Short Walk

7a. Continue along Main Street, past The Royal Oak public house. After the public house car park and opposite Hawthorn House, take the path to the right marked by a fingerpost. This leads to a stile to cross an open field, aiming for the hedge corner directly opposite, to find a stile with a four-fingered signpost. Turn left and with the hedge on your left follow the field boundary, to a path across an open field, emerging onto a tarmac road.

7b. Cross the stile opposite and with the hedge on the left, continue for 800m over three fields to a field gate with a footpath marker arrow. Pass through

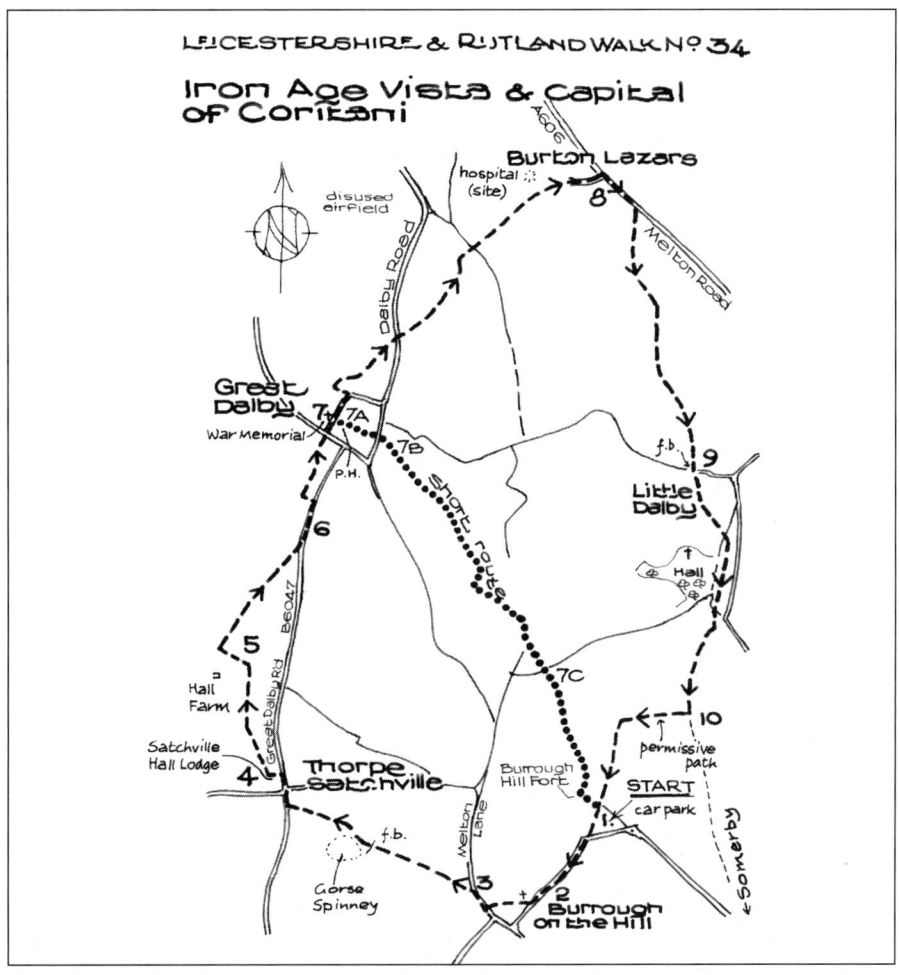

LEICESTERSHIRE & RUTLAND WALK Nº 34

Iron Age Vista & capital of Coritani

Burton Lazars

hospital (site)

disused airfield

Dalby Road

Agge

Melton Road

Great Dalby

War Memorial

P.H.

short route

Little Dalby

Hall

f.b. 9

6

B6047

5

Hall Farm

Great Dalby Rd

Satchville Hall Lodge

4

Thorpe Satchville

7C

Burrough Hill Fort

permissive path

10

START car park

Somerby

f.b.

Melton Lane

Gorse Spinney

3

2 Burrough on the Hill

the gate and walk uphill with the hedge on the left. When it ends, aim diagonally left to a large gap in the hedge and wooden fence. On entering the next field turn right, with the hedge on the right follow the field boundary to a stile and fingerpost, leading onto a green lane. Ahead, on the skyline, note the ramparts of the Iron Age Fort on Burrough Hill, our ultimate objective. Continue left, down the green lane to where it meets a stone track at some farm buildings. Follow the track to the right around the buildings, where they end, take the path marked to the left across an open field to find a bridge over a stream. Go straight ahead across the next field, passing an old oak tree in the centre, to aim for a gate and fingerpost in the far hedge.

7c. Cross the tarmac lane to a fingerpost indicating a path to the right. Follow the field boundary with the hedge on the right to climb uphill to a wood, Burrough Hill Covert. Continue ahead, along the edge of the wood to the corner of the field with a line of willow trees, where there is a gap onto a wide path. The path climbs uphill, through a double set of gates, to join Dalby Hill permissive path. Follow the marker posts for this path to the summit of the hill and the entrance to the Fort. Here an information board gives the history of the Fort. Follow the track back to the car park and the end of the walk.

Long Walk

7. Walk straight ahead down Main Street past The Royal Oak public house. When the road bends right, you find a stream and a footbridge immediately in front of you. **Do not cross the bridge**, but take the concrete road on your left. This passes Brook House and leads to Great Dalby waterworks. Just before the waterworks, take the footpath indicated by a fingerpost to the right, aiming diagonally right to climb uphill to a stile and open fields. Follow the marker posts over the fields to a stone track. This is part of the disused Second World War airfield of RAF Melton Mowbray. Cross over the track and fields until a concrete taxi-way is reached, running parallel to the main road. Walk left along this, passing an entrance gate, to reach the B6047 road. Cross the road to a fingerpost, going diagonally left across a large field to a marker post adjacent to a solitary hawthorn bush. On reaching this, cross a tarmac lane and continue in the same direction across the next field to a small gate, to join a bridleway. Pass through the gate, then with the hedge on the right, continue across the field to a field gate and a stone track. Follow the track until it turns right to enter the hall grounds. This is the site of the St Mary and St Lazarus Hospital. Keep straight ahead, through a field gate and a small gate to reach the driveway to Hall Farm. Continue along the driveway to the main entrance gate to join a tarmac lane, this leads through Burton Lazars village to gain the main A606 Melton road.

8. At the road junction, turn right and walk past Gartree Stud to a fingerpost on the right, in an entrance to farm buildings. As you stand with your back to the road, in the distance on the left you can see the farm buildings of Manor Farm and the church steeple of Little Dalby on the ridge behind them. These are the next objectives. Bearing diagonally left, follow the marker posts across a number of fields. After passing a mediaeval moat on the left, turn left across a concrete bridge, then right to cross further well-marked fields. The path leads to the left of the farm buildings to a stile and a tarmac lane. Turn right along the lane and pass Manor Farm to a road junction.

9. Cross the road and walk up the lane opposite marked 'No Through Road', passing Hollies Farm on the left. Where the lane bends right at a large stone trough, go through the small gate in front and climb straight uphill with Little Dalby church on your right, to a marker post on the crest of the ridge.

From here, follow the edge of the wood, crossing a footbridge to a lane leading to Little Dalby Hall, with the walled gardens of the hall on your right. From the lane, take the footpath indicated by the fingerpost marked Somerby and cross the field, aiming to the left of the farm buildings, to a stile, which leads onto a stone track. Turning left, walk uphill along the track to reach Buttermilk Hill Spinney, where there is a sign indicating the permissive path of the Dalby Hills Walk.

10. This path is maintained by the Ernest Cook Trust and is closed on occasional Thursdays during the shooting season. The notice board indicates whether the path is open or closed (see note below). If open, follow the path marked by the marker posts along the lower slopes of Burrough Hill and through a wood. On emerging from the wood, the permissive path continues straight ahead, but the path we require curves to the left and ascends to the crest of the hill. From here, bear diagonally right and follow the marker posts across the field to a metal pedestrian gate opposite the farm buildings. Go through this and then right along the lane to Burrough Hill Fort car park and the end of the walk.

Note – If the Dalby Hills Walk permissive path is closed, continue straight ahead at Buttermilk Hill Spinney, climbing uphill and across the fields to reach Somerby village. On entering the village, turn right and walk along Burrough Road to the car park.

Points of Interest

Burrough Hill – An impressive Iron Age hill fort. It is possible that this fort was the capital of the Coritani before Leicester took over this function as Ratae Coritanorum in the early Roman period. The hilltop nearly 600 ft commands a fine view in all directions.

Burrough on the Hill – A hilltop village with some ironstone 17th- and 18th-century farmhouses. Cheseldyne Farm (north of the church) was the birthplace of William Cheselden, surgeon to Queen Anne. The Church of St Mary is 13th century. The Duke of Windsor, when Prince of Wales used to stay at Burrough Court (burned down during World War II) when he rode with the Quorn Hunt. He met Mrs Wallis Simpson, the future Duchess here on one occasion.

Thorpe Satchville – A well-known centre for hunting for several generations. St Michael's Church, mainly 17th century but with Victorian alterations, stands on the village green.

Great Dalby – The village lies in a valley close to Burrough Hill. The nave of St Swithin's Church was rebuilt in a gothic style after being destroyed when the mediaeval spire collapsed in 1658.

Burton Lazars – The village gets its name from a former lazar house (leper hospital) founded by Roger de Mowbray. The hospital disappeared at the Dissolution, but for 400 years it was the most important lazar house in England. Earthworks to this long vanished building can be seen to the west of the church.

Little Dalby – A small village with a Victorian church and a hall, home of the Hartupp family from the late 16th century until the 1950s. The hall's main claim to fame is a housekeeper to the Hartupps, a Mrs Elizabeth Orton. In the reign of Queen Anne, she perfected the recipe for Stilton cheese. This Leicestershire cheese's name comes from the inn in the village of Stilton on the Great North Road, but it had been made for many years before that.

35: A Kingdom to Delight

A walk around Bradgate Park, then going north through farmland across the Great Central Railway line to the outskirts of Quorn, returning via Woodhouse and Swithland Wood.

Distance: Cropston Leys to Swithland Wood via Quorn 12.8km (8 miles), Bradgate Park circuit 6.5km (4 miles) Combined Walk 19.3km (12 miles)

Duration: Long Walk Cropston Leys 4 hours; Short Walk Bradgate Park 2 hours, combined Walk 6 hours

Maps required: OS Explorer 246 Loughborough and Melton Mowbray, OS Landranger 129 Nottingham and Loughborough, OS Landranger 140 Leicester and Coventry

Terrain: Easy paths and tracks

Starting point: Hallgates car park by Cropston Reservoir (SK542114).

Refreshments: Tea rooms at Newtown Linford; Bradgate Park at weekends; Public houses in all villages en-route.

Bus/Train link: Loughborough/Leicester

The Routes

N.B. Short Walk is paragraphs 1-5 inclusive, Long Walk is paragraphs 6-12 inclusive and the Combined Walk is paragraphs 1-12 inclusive.

Short Walk

1. Turn right through gate into Bradgate Park to the next gateway and here veer right to follow path along perimeter wall on the right. Keep ahead for about 1.6km passing covered reservoir and small pond on your left.

2. Just before the corner, divert left along path to the top of the hill to Old John Tower for magnificent views all round. To the left of the tower descend slightly to an archway in the wall and go though the copse to the war memorial. Keep ahead and just before rocky outcrop turn right, descending to cross a wide track to join perimeter path at the yellow post.

3. Turn left and keep ahead for about 1.2km with wall on your right. Follow the wall round to the left until you reach park exit to Newtown Linford car park. A short diversion out of the park to the road ahead brings you to a garden centre and tea-rooms to the right.

4. Return to the park and either follow tarmac path, or more interestingly follow the streamside towards the ruins of Bradgate House. Ignore paths to

the right by the bridge and left to the ruins. Keep on main track to the visitor centre.

5. About 200m after the visitor centre take a grassy path on your left and just before the gateway go right to the top of a stony outcrop for fine views across the reservoir. From here a clear track leads back to the Hallgates car park (Cropston Reservoir).

End of Short Walk

Long Walk

6. Exit the car park, cross the road, turn right and take the footpath over stile in the left-hand hedge after a short way. Cross the field to a stile in the top right corner, across the next field and follow yellow markers taking narrow path between wire and hedge. Go over the stile to join a track, turn left and go ahead through gate into a spinney. Keep ahead and turn right at T-junction in track (yellow post) and go to road.

7. Turn right and almost immediately left onto a bridle path. Go through gate and head for the top left direction across the field. Keep ahead, go through three gates and turn left on the road into Swithland.

8. A short way beyond the public house on your left, take the path on the right signposted Quorn. Go over the stile and keep ahead up right-hand side of the field. Turn right over the stile near the top right-hand corner, into a short alley soon to climb over the left-hand side fence and go up the left-hand side of the next two fields. Go along the top of the field and follow a narrow path by a ditch over a stile and continue to a road. Turn right to the railway bridge. You may get good views of steam trains on the Great Central Railway.

9. Beyond the bridge, take path on left over the stile, firstly following the railway but shortly veering to the right across the meadow to a yellow-topped post. Turn left to follow path next to the iron railings, over the bridge and then left to go up the side of the field. By a gate go over the stile on your right and follow the path to the left, soon meeting the stream. Follow this path for about 800m to go over a stile and emerge by houses onto the road at Quorn.

10. Turn left along road and shortly as the road goes to the right, turn left onto the bridleway towards Woodhouse. The lane soon becomes a path. Keep ahead, under the railway and follow the earthy hollow round to the right emerging along a field side. Turn left at the track. Follow this, turning right after a short way and then – almost immediately after a sharp left turn – go sharp right (signposted Woodhouse). Ignore bridleway signposted Rushey Fields Manor ahead.

11. Emerge after a short distance at the end of Vicary Lane onto the main road at Woodhouse and turn left. Fork left down School Lane by the church. Note Pestilence Cottage on your right just before the road bends to the left. As the

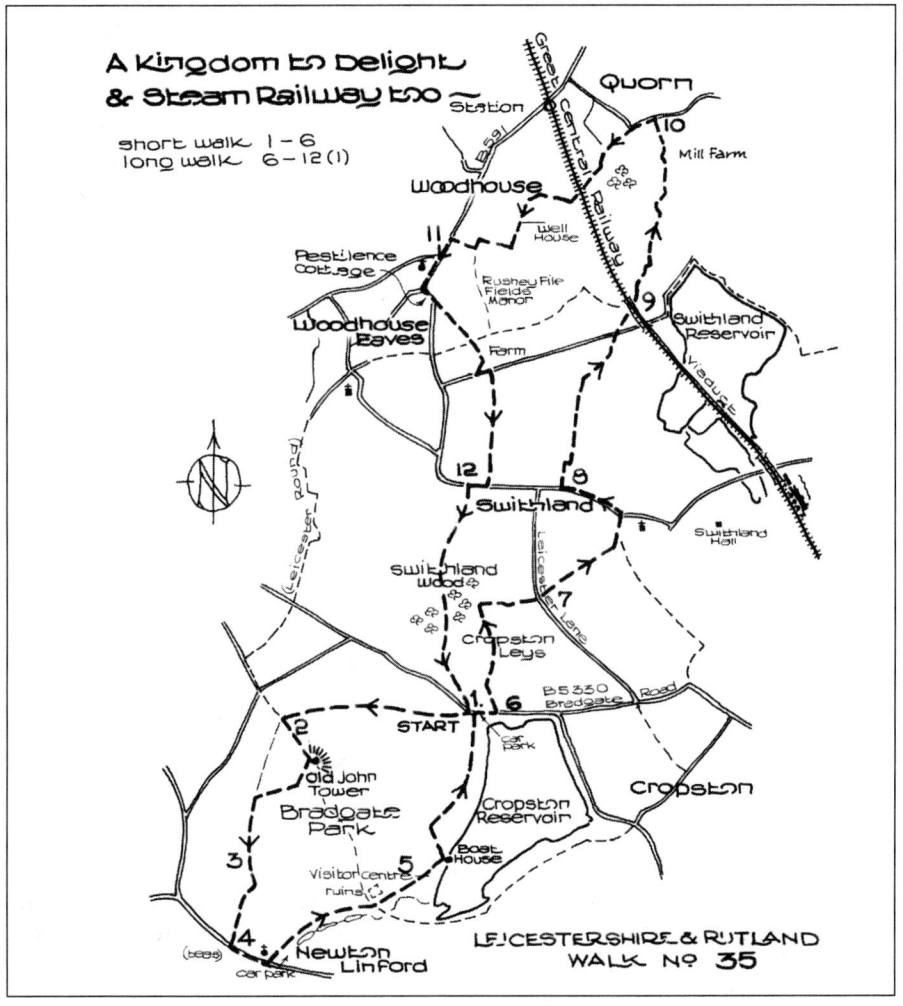

A Kingdom to Delight
& Steam Railway too ~

short walk 1 - 6
long walk 6 - 12 (1)

LEICESTERSHIRE & RUTLAND
WALK No 35

road turns to your right take a path over a stile on the left to Rushey Fields Farm. Go along the left-hand side of the field and over two stiles, across a brook, over a stile and almost immediately right to a stile in the field edge. Go left up the farm track, but just before the farm, take stile in the right fence and diagonally skirt buildings to stile in left-hand of field (approx. one third along) and on to a lane. Here, turn left and shortly take stile in right hedge by a gate for a path to Swithland. Go down left-hand side of field, over stile and diagonally across next field to far right-hand corner. Take stile, go over brook and keep ahead down two fields to emerge onto the road at Swithland.

12. Turn right along the road and as you leave the village, turn left onto a path by the side of a house just before the 30 mph de-restriction signs. Go over two stiles to enter Swithland Wood. Keep ahead, ignoring paths to the left and right, for about 1.2km. As you approach the road, take a path to the left, down slate steps by the left-hand side of the wood. Very shortly, take a foot-bridge and stile on your right into a meadow and head diagonally left towards the buildings. Take a stile just to the right of these onto the road. Turn left past Horseshoe Farm to the starting point car park almost immediately right.

Points of Interest

Bradgate Park – A former estate of nearly 1000 acres on the edge of the village of Newtown Linford. Given to the City and County of Leicester in 1928 by the industrialist, Charles Bennion, for the people of Leicester "to be preserved in its natural state for their quiet enjoyment". In the park Thomas Grey, 1st Marquis of Dorset, built a mansion at the end of the 15th century. In 1537 the 2nd Marquis, also Thomas, and his wife Lady Frances had a daughter, Jane. When Lady Jane was sixteen she was married to Lord Guildford Dudley, son of the regent, the Duke of Northumberland. The Duke had induced the weak young King Edward VI to bequeath the throne to Lady Jane. The king died and Lady Jane Grey became Queen of England. Her reign lasted nine days, when she was thrown into the Tower of London with her husband, charged with treason and they were beheaded. She was 17 years old. After Jane's execution, the oak trees in the park at Bradgate were topped and are still visible today. The Grey family continued to own Bradgate until the early 20th century. The tower known as Old John was built as a memorial to a family retainer 1786.

Newtown Linford – a former Forest village on the edge of Bradgate Park. There are some interesting old buildings including cruck cottages, and the Church of All Saints is well worth a visit.

Cropston and Swithland Reservoirs – the reservoirs were built in 1866 and 1894 respectively to supply water to Leicester. Cropston Reservoir to the east of Bradgate Park complements the natural beauty of the park.

Swithland and Swithland Wood – one of the best known Forest villages, famous for its slate quarries, which produced roofing material from Roman times onwards. The slate was also used for headstones in churchyards. In the woods, there are many examples of former quarry sites. Visit the Church of St Leonard, mostly 13th century and notice many fine headstones, including the slate wall monument to the slate workers.

Woodhouse – once a forest settlement in the 12th century lying on the northern fringe of Charnwood Forest. The Herrick family lived at Beaumanor for over three hundred years. St Mary's Church is a mix of dates but mainly 17th century.

Woodhouse Eaves – one mile south of Woodhouse, this is a pleasant Forest village now very much built up but with some cottages on Maplewell Road built entirely of rough stone and slates from the Swithland quarries. The Church of St Paul was built in 1837 and enlarged in 1880. Nearby Beacon Hill, iron-age earthwork, rises to over 800ft and gives commanding views of Charnwood Forest and beyond.

The Great Central Railway – The London extension from Annesley to Marylebone was opened in 1899 and closed by Dr Beeching in 1967. The 13km (8 ml) between Leicester and Loughborough were saved by the Main Line Steam Trust and is now the only preserved railway with a double track. Steam trains are run at the weekend and on some weekdays in the summer.

36: A Rutland Retreat

A circular walk in a beautiful part of Rutland, starting from Braunston in Rutland and going over undulating countryside to visit Launde Abbey Retreat. Some of the paths are often ploughed out so careful navigation is required.

Distance: Long Walk 13km (8 miles); Short Walk 10km (6 miles)

Duration: Long Walk 4 hours; Short Walk 3 hours

Maps required: OS Explorer Map 233 Leicester and Hinckley, OS Explorer Map 234 Rutland Water, OS Landranger Map 140 Leicester, Coventry and Rugby, OS Landranger Map 141 Kettering and Corby

Terrain: Field paths and tracks. Undulating countryside, some paths may be obstructed by crops and are mostly muddy in winter

Starting point: Braunston in Rutland church. (SK833067)

Refreshments: Braunston in Rutland public houses.

Bus/Train link: Leicester/Melton Mowbray

The Route

1. From the church take the minor road towards the village of Ridlington. Walk up the hill and at the top, where the road veers sharp left, turn right and walk along a tarmac road – Wood Lane.

2. The lane becomes a grass track which we follow for 1km. On leaving the track keep the hedge on the left through a gap and turn right. The path follows the right-hand hedge to the corner of a field, take the first gate of a pair onto a wide hedge lined farm track.

3. Continue forward along this track, through the next field gate, then turn right and continue along a rutted undulating track to a further field gate. This leads onto the Oakham-Leicester minor road.

4. Turn left and take a field gate on the right of the two footpaths (**not left footpath**). Go through gate and over fields past a pond on your right, keeping the hedge to your right, to a field gate at the Launde-Oakham minor road.

5. Turn right for a few metres and take footpath on left to follow hedges, firstly on your right, then left, then right again. Take farm gate on left of houses and farm buildings to Withcote Hall (very muddy).

6. Pass farm buildings, taking path on left along farm track, around the lake to reach some cattle sheds. Upon entering a large field, go due south over the field to a further field, out of view for some time. Descend to footbridge over

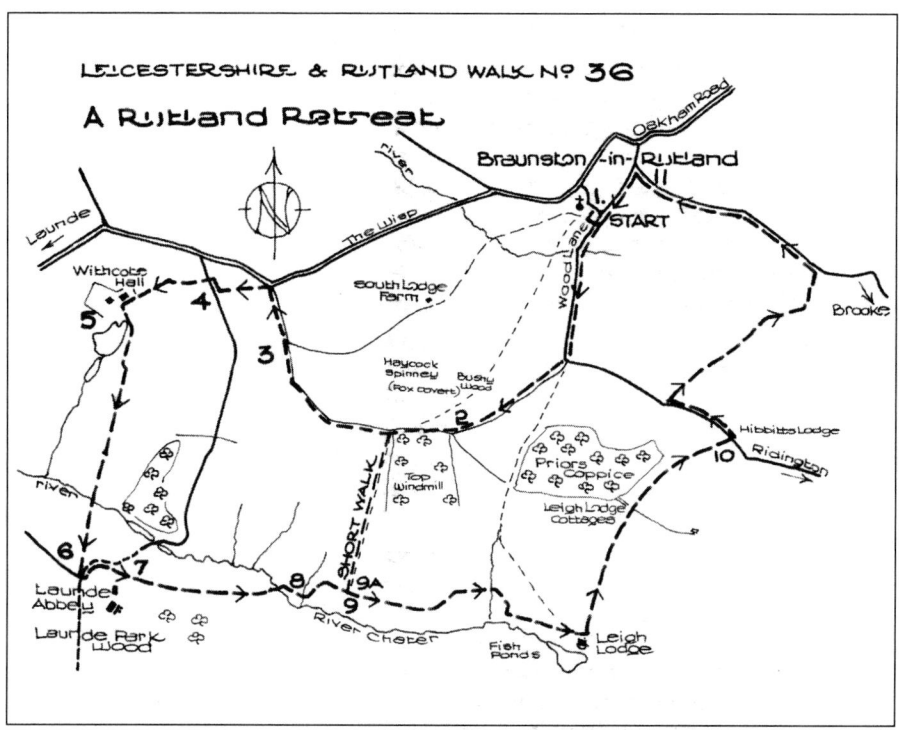

the River Chater. Cross the bridge and ascend to bear left over another large pasture field to a footpath sign near a cattle grid at the road and Launde Abbey. You may visit Launde Abbey at this point

7. Turn left for a few metres along the tarmac road. Turn right to go near the boundary of the Abbey and fishponds. Continue through field gates, then on entering another large field, veer slightly left, keeping the large Launde Park wood on your right. You eventually see the field narrow, to find a field gate and bridge in a small copse in the far left-hand corner.

8. Cross the bridge over the stream to turn right and follow paths to a paths junction.

Long Walk

9. Go straight ahead into a field; follow the path on the edge of the grass field, with a hedge to your left. Cross field to descend into a plantation, then cross a large field, to a wide track. Take the path straight ahead to reach Leigh Lodge. Follow the farm track to the left for 1km to reach the Braunston-Ridlington minor road.

Short Walk

9a. Turn left for two fields. On reaching the top of the second field, turn right and retrace route to Braunston.

Long Walk

10. Turn left along the road and after 250m take a bridleway on your right to cross fields to reach the Braunston-Brooke minor road. Turn left and continue along the road into Braunston in Rutland, turn left at the T-junction to return to the church.

Note – At the time of publication, the bridleway was closed due to the presence of badger setts, but a diversion should be in place shortly. Please follow this clearly marked route.

Points of Interest

Braunston-in-Rutland – This village lies on the hillside above the infant River Gwash. The church of All Saints is mainly 15th century but there is evidence of some Norman building in the chancel arch and the doorway.

Withcote Hall – This was one of the great houses visited by Leland during his survey for Henry VIII. The owner of the hall at the time of the Civil War was Smith of Withcote who supported the Parliamentarians and later forfeited the lordship to the Crown. The parish church stands within the grounds of the hall and has some fine 15th-century glass.

Launde Abbey – Built on the site of a former priory, this impressive Tudor house was owned by Thomas Cromwell who awarded it to himself at the time of the Dissolution of the Monasteries. His son, Gregory, died in 1551 and his wall tomb is in the chapel together with memorials to the Simpson family who bought Launde Abbey in 1763. The chapel is part of the house and is sometimes open to the public.

Brooke – A remote village well worth a visit. It lies in a shallow valley with sweeping views. St Peter's Church is a most charming place with a 13th-century tower and an Elizabethan north aisle. Half a mile to the north-west of the church is the site of Brooke Priory, a small Augustinian house founded around 1150. Nothing remains of the monastic buildings except extensive earthworks.

37: A Gardener's Delight

A pleasant circular walk in the footsteps of the late BBC Celebrity Gardener Geoffrey Hamilton, visiting Rutland Water, Empingham, Exton Estate and village including the grave of Geoffrey Hamilton and also the opportunity to visit his Nursery

Distance: Long Walk 20km (12½ miles). See note at end; Short Walk 11km (7 miles)

Duration: Long Walk 6 hours; Short Walk 3½ hours

Maps required: OS Explorer 234 Rutland Water, OS Landranger 130 Grantham, OS Landranger 141 Kettering & Corby

Terrain: Easy field walking, reservoir-side paths

Starting point: Sykes Lane car park, Rutland Water (car park charge) (SK936083)

Refreshments: Public houses at Empingham, Exton and Whitwell. Café at Sykes Lane car park

Bus/Train link: Oakham and Stamford

The Route

Long Walk

1. From the large car park, walk towards Rutland Water and turn left heading towards the dam of the reservoir seen ahead. Just before reaching the dam take a track that goes up its bank to the top.

Short Walk

1a. From the large car park, take the path towards Rutland Water. Turn right and follow the main path towards Whitwell car park.

1b. At Whitwell car park leave the main path and follow path to exit road. Turn right and walk along the road to reach its end. Walk along track, away from access road, to reach Whitwell village and the A606 road.

1c. Cross the road **with great care**, turn right and walk 150m to a footpath on the left, at Noel Arms public house. Go through car park into beer garden, to ascend flight of steps into a field. Follow field footpath across several fields, to reach the Exton to Empingham minor road.

1d. Turn left to walk to a road junction, here turn right and walk to next junction to join the **Long Walk**. (Go to point 14.) You may go into Exton village to visit the Parish church and Geoff Hamilton's grave, then return to this junction.

Long Walk

2.   Walk across the dam for 300m then turn to the left off the dam, aiming for a surveyor's concrete column seen ahead and a metal gate. Go through the gate and across a field aiming for its right-hand corner and stile. Follow a clear path through a wood and into two fields, clearly way-marked, to a field gate. Go through this to walk down a track into the village of Empingham and the A606 road.

3.   Turn right, cross road and walk to St Peter's Church. After visiting the church, continue along Church Street to Main Street. Cross this to take the Exton Road out of the village. Ignore the first path near Highfield Close, but take the next path on the right-hand side on reaching the plantation near a bench.

4.   Walk into the field along the headland path to the rear of the plantation, then go across the field parallel to the road, to a stile. Go over this and across a field, to the far hedge, to gain a further stile.

5.   Go over this stile aiming for a hedge on the right-hand side, then go straight across the next field aiming for the plantation seen ahead. Follow the track through the plantation, crossing two stiles then straight across a further field passing a telegraph pole. At this point, aim for Horn Mill Cottage, seen ahead, to a stile at the road.

6.   Turn left and walk uphill, passing Horn Mill Trout Farm to a stile on the right.

7.   Go over the stile, to walk along a farm track to gain a further stile and descend to a concrete bridge over a stream. Our path heads up to the plantation seen ahead.

8.   **Do not** enter the plantation, but turn left and follow the boundary fence along a clear path towards a larger plantation seen ahead. **Do not** cross the river, but go over another stile and walk straight on to a further track and lake. Go straight on, heading for a stile at the side of another field gate. Cross this field, when Fort Henry comes into view, aim for this eventually to see a stile in the left corner of a field.

9.   Go over the stile onto an access road. Turn right and walk for 50m to a footpath on the left. Follow this path along the field edge with excellent views of Fort Henry. Eventually the lake disappears, then follow the river, still on the field-edge path. Continue into the plantation, following a path in a straight direction, eventually to climb some steps, to a further path junction.

10.   Turn left on a footpath and walk straight on (ignoring a left turn) for 2km to a path junction. (This is the Viking Way.)

11.   Turn left and continue to a handgate/stile into a field over a ditch board, then veer left across the field to the far left-hand corner, to a stile next to double field gates. Turn left and walk to a track junction seen ahead.

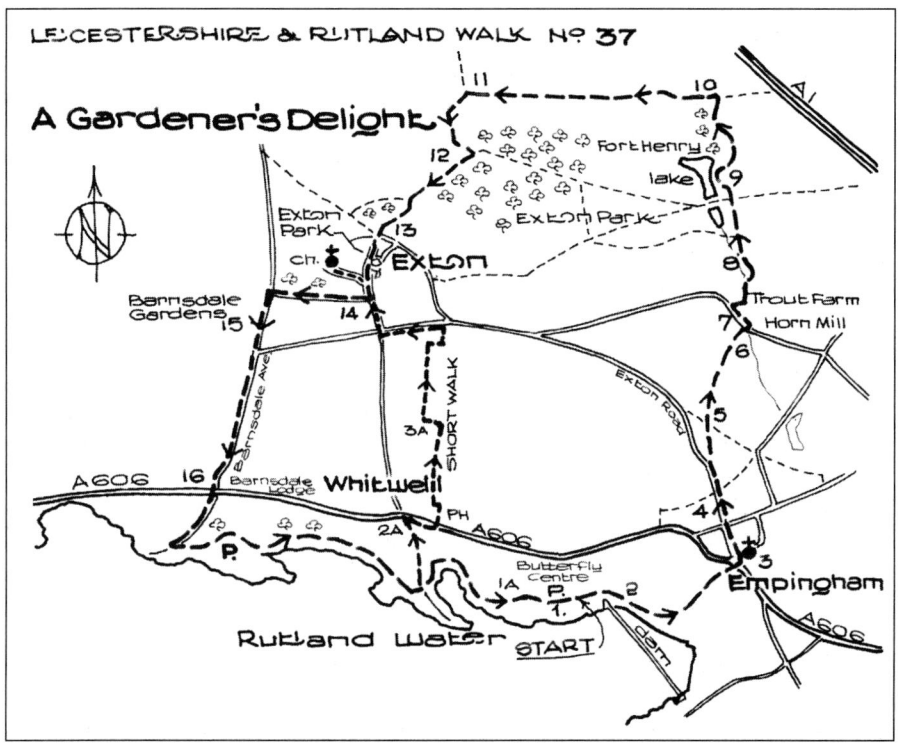

LEICESTERSHIRE & RUTLAND WALK No 37

A Gardener's Delight

Fort Henry

lake

Exton Park

Exton Park

ch.

EXTON

Barnsdale Gardens 15

14

Trout Farm

Horn Mill

SHORT WALK

Barnsdale Ave

Exton Road

3A

A606 16 Barnsdale Lodge Whitwell

PH A606

2A

Butterfly Centre

1A

P.

T.

dam

Empingham

A606

Rutland Water START

12. Turn right and follow a wide track, until you reach a further junction. Turn left and carry straight on, ignoring a gate, to a farm and Exton village.

13. Walk through the village. Turn left and then right, going past the Market Cross. Then walk past the School and the Fox and Hounds Inn. Continue out of the village to reach Church Farm. (A further detour can be made, by turning right up the track to Exton Parish church. On reaching the church, you can view Geoff Hamilton's grave in the top left-hand corner, near a seat.) After returning to Church Farm, continue out of the village to a road junction.

Short Walk rejoins.

14. Turn right and continue along the road to a further road junction. Turn left, to find Barnsdale Nursery on the right.

15. After visiting the nursery, continue straight along the road to reach the A606 at Barnsdale Lodge Hotel.

16. Walk across the road and descend to the path at the side of the reservoir. Turn left and walk past Whitwell car park, to return to Sykes Lane car park.

Points of Interest

Rutland Water – The largest reservoir in Britain was formed by damming the River Gwash and was originally known as Empingham Reservoir. Several villages, including Nether and Middle Hambledon, are submerged under the reservoir, which holds 136,500,000 litres (30 million gallons) of water. There are picnic sites and facilities for sailing and fishing.

Empingham – The River Gwash flows to the south of the village. St Peter's Church is one of the largest and prettiest in the county; it has a little crocketed spire and a beautiful interior.

Exton and Exton Park – The Old Hall, now a ruin, was built by the Haringtons at the time of Elizabeth I and destroyed by fire in 1810. It was the home of the Noels, the Viscounts Campden, and the Earls of Gainsborough. The New Hall was built in 1852. The Church of St Peter & St Paul was struck by lightning in 1843 and rebuilt in 1850. It contains fine monuments to the Harington and Noel families. The thatch and limestone village is worth a visit, especially Pudding Bag Lane. Geoff Hamilton, the TV gardener is buried in the churchyard. His nursery, on the edge of the village is open to the public. The beautiful 1000-acre estate park contains the lovely Fort Henry which dominates the lake, formed by damming the North Brook.

Note – Walkers not wishing to visit Barnsdale Gardens may walk 14 to 3a, 2a to rejoin the main route at Whitwell car park. This diversion also cuts out 2km of road working.

38: A Walk Through Time

A great sense of history is all around on this walk, from the glorious Ashby Canal with its many coloured narrow boats, to the steam rising in the distance from the Battlefield Line Railway. Walk through villages and across fields which witnessed one of the most famous battles in English history, the Battle of Bosworth Field.

Distance: Long Walk 21km (13 miles); Short Walk 15km (9 miles)

Duration: Long Walk 6 hours; Short Walk 4 hours

Maps required: OS Explorer 232 Nuneaton and Tamworth, OS Landranger 140 Leicester Coventry and Rugby

Terrain: Canal towpath and field paths

Starting point: Shackerstone village (SK 374067)

Refreshments: The Rising Sun, Shackerstone; Shackerstone Station tea-room, weekends and Bank Holidays; Moore Arms, Norton-Juxta Twycross; Twycross Zoo refreshments; Curzen Arms Hotel, Twycross

Bus/Train link: Tamworth/Coalville

The Route

1. From the Rising Sun in Shackerstone village turn right to walk over canal bridge (Turn Bridge No 52) to second fingerpost on left signed Snarestone. With canal on left, walk as far as Bridge No 58 at Gopsall Wharf, approximately 3.6km.

2. Turn left over bridge passing entrance to Gopsall Wharf picnic site to follow minor road for 365m to a T-junction with the main road, turning left along road for a short distance.

3. Turn right at junction signposted Norton-Juxta Twycross and Austry, to take footpath on right in corner of field. Walk straight across field to waymarked gate in hedge onto Culloden Farm drive. Turn right, then left around farm buildings, through two metal farm gates and heading for stile on left and then through second stile to enter field. Turn left at footpath crossroads. Maintaining same line of direction, aim for white building and Norton-Juxta Twycross church tower. As you enter the village, head to the left of the white building to pick up public footpath sign and enter village at the 30 mph signs.

4. Follow road around to the right, passing church on the right, to pass to left of no.6, and take the hedged footpath opposite a public house. Turn right, then left into Chapel Lane, cross into field and with hedge on right go through

double gates to the road. Turn left, then right over stile into Twycross Zoo grounds. (Path diverted through grounds.)

5. Walk half-right at waymark heading for an untidy field corner to find a concealed stile. Bear half-left down field towards Lea Grange Farm, go through hedge and turn left. Cross stile next to metal gate and go half-right, still heading for the farm buildings. Cross a concrete farm bridge and go through a gate, heading for left of farm buildings. Go through a blue metal gate and bear to left of buildings, to turn left after first barn.

6. The route goes towards Orton Wood, aiming for a stile in the top left-hand corner with a ditch board and barbed-wire fence. Head again for a stile in the top left-hand corner of field. Then walk around next field with hedge on right to cross another ditch board and stile. Continue straight ahead, at bend look for waymark and ditch board, which may be concealed, to enter the wood.

7. On entering the wood, turn left and walk along edge of wood with a ditch on your left. Pass into a field bearing right to cross through a gap in the hedge. Continue keeping hedge on your right to a stile that leads between some bungalows.

8. Turn left along Hallfield Close and sharp left past the village hall onto a road in Twycross village. Turn right down Main Street, passing the Curzon Arms Hotel. At the village green, fork left into Church Street.

Long Walk

9. Continue down the main road for some 1.3km to a large lay-by. Take the footpath at the rear of the lay-by, heading straight across the field to a stile. Continue in the same direction to waymark and further stile. Cross a third field, again in the same direction, with hedge initially on your left. Follow trees in old hedge line and head for bottom right-hand corner gap. Enter a very narrow field and walk down the left-hand side to emerge on a minor road, through a metal gate. Go along tarmac lane straight ahead, following it round past Temple Mill.

Short Walk

9a. Take the footpath left through the churchyard signposted Little Twycross following the path to a stile. Follow yellow waymarks across two fields aiming for a stile midway between Farm House and a grey barn, to emerge on a minor road in Little Twycross. Turn right, then left over a stile with a fingerpost. Cross a field half-right to a stile in a hedge. Turn half-left to another stile, and cross a large field half-left to a stile. Aim for the left-hand side of Gopsall House Farm. Continue in the same direction across a field heading for a stile in the top right-hand corner. This is hidden by abandoned farm machinery. Turn right to a gap in the hedge, then half-left aiming for a lone tree and the edge of the wood. (The Race Course.)

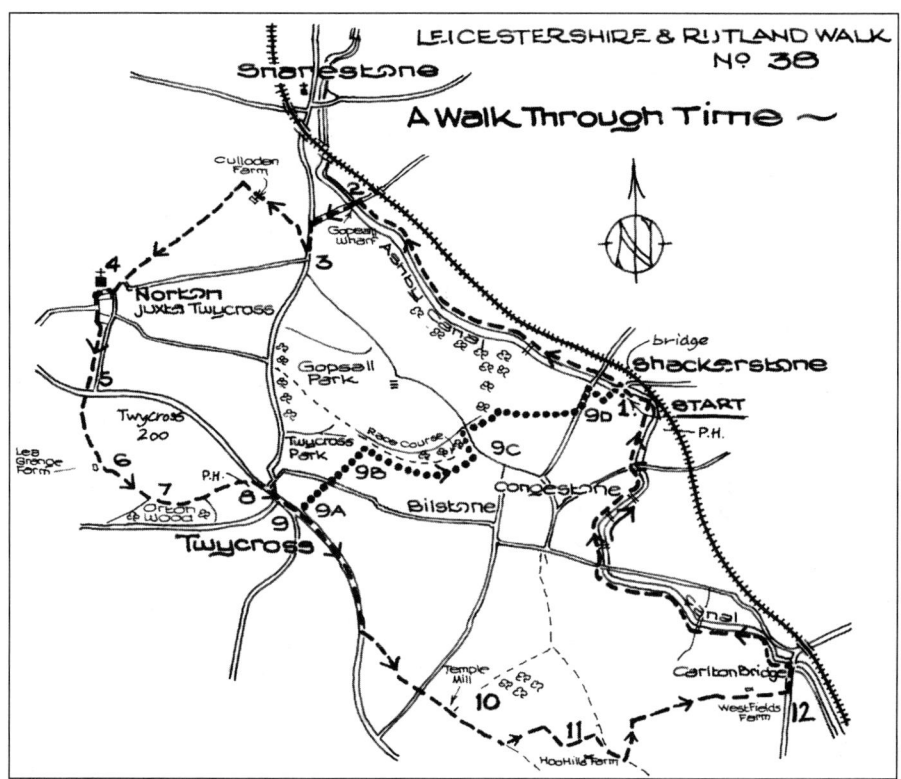

9b. With the wood on your left-hand side, walk along the field edge. Just before the end of the third field, look for a waymark on left of the wood. Follow yellow waymarks in same direction as before, but now inside the wood on a wide green path. Leave the wood by a stile and signboard, turning left initially. Once over the brow of the field, turn right and walk with a wire fence on the left. The buildings of Castle Farm are ahead and you cross the farm track.

9c. Continue in the same direction, with fence and hedge on your left, to a ditch board and stile. Still in the same direction, go round a field edge. As the hedge on your left gets higher, you reach a metal gate in the far right-hand bottom corner. Cross stile and turn left along a track. Almost immediately, turn right over a ditch board and through an iron gate. Continue in the same direction as before, with a high hedge on your left. Cross stile by a metal field gate, then turn right in front of the second metal gate, and walk along an avenue of trees on your left.

9d. At the end of the avenue, cross a ditch board and a small field to a stile to turn left onto a minor road. Shackerstone village can now be seen ahead, walk along the road back into the village and your starting point.

Long Walk

10. Where track turns left to Temple Farm continue ahead, with hedge on left, for one field. Turn left at waymark post and continue with a spinney on the right. At the end of this, cross into field on right through gap and aim for the small farm buildings on the rise. Reach the hedge and turn right to walk alongside it to a waymarked gap on the left. Pass through the gap and go diagonally right to a stile.

11. Head up the hill, with Market Bosworth church spire in the far distance, to cross stile and continue with hedge on right. After crest of Hoo Hill, turn left at cross hedge towards West Field Farm. Walk downhill with hedge initially on left and then on right, and continue left round corner of field to cross stile on right. Continue towards farm with hedge first on your left, then on right to emerge onto a farm track. Walk between West Field farm buildings onto a metalled drive, to emerge on a minor road. Turn left towards Carlton Bridge and the Ashby Canal.

12. At Carlton Bridge (No 44) turn left onto canal towpath, with canal on your right walk for 4km to bridge No 52 and your starting point.

Points of Interest

Ashby Canal – The Ashby-de-la-Zouch Canal, built in 1804, winds its way from Marston Junction to its current terminus north of Snarestone, passing through pleasant rural landscapes. This section of the Ashby Canal north of Carlton Bridge is rich in wildlife, being designated a site of special scientific interest (SSSI). This designation is mainly due to the diversity of aquatic plants, with several species of dragonfly during the summer months.

Shackerstone – The base for the Battlefield Line. Shackerstone is a pleasant village dating back to Saxon times. The motte of the 12th-century castle is visible as a mound besides the canal. Nearby is Gopsall Hall where Handel stayed with his friend Jennes, when his Messiah was performed at Church Langton in 1759.

Battlefield Steam Railway Line – A five mile standard gauge steam passenger line which runs from Shackerstone to Shenton. Trains run every Saturday, Sunday and Bank Holiday Monday. At Shackerstone there is a museum, souvenir shop, café and car park. At Shenton passengers may alight and walk up the trail to the Battlefield visitor centre or down the road to the canal towpath.

Bosworth Battlefield – Historic site of the Battle of Bosworth Field 1485, between Richard III and Henry VII. Comprehensive interpretation of the battle with extensive visitor centre, including exhibitions, gift shop and cafeteria.

Twycross Zoo – Open daily throughout the year except for Christmas Day.

39: Six Tons and a Ham
– The Langtons of Leicestershire

The walk has panoramic views of rolling hills and pretty villages. The highest point is a 147-metre trig point on Langton Caudle. The shorter walk will suit people who enjoy visiting the churches and villages along the way.

Distance: Long Walk 20km (12 miles); Short Walk 15km (9½ miles)

Duration: Long Walk 6 hours; Short Walk 4½ hours

Maps required: OS Explorer 223 Northampton and Market Harborough, OS Explorer 233 Leicester and Hinckley, OS Landranger 141 Kettering & Corby

Terrain: Undulating countryside

Starting point: Tur Langton church (SP714946)

Refreshments: Public houses in Tur Langton, Thorpe Langton and Welham

Bus/Train Links: Leicester/Market Harborough

The Route

1. The first path sign is 50m on the left of the Crown Inn, on the opposite side to the Church of St Andrew. Walk up a lane with buildings on the left, cross a stile, to another stile in front. Go right, beside a hedge stretching down a field, to a stile over a ditch where the next marker can then be seen ahead. Over the next stile, the path crosses a large field to the left of the corner of a wood. An alternative horse track runs up the left-hand side to the top of the field, where a marker into a lane can be seen. Turn right towards the village of Shangton in the valley, passing a Transco Gas Terminal. Turn left at the road junction, following a lane into Shangton. At the T-junction turn left, then right, through a garden with a finger post.

2. Go through the garden follow the path into afield, with a barn on your right and a wood in front of you. On meeting a hedge on your left, go over a stile in the hedge and keep right until the path turns left towards a gap between two woods. Here you can see a house on a hill in the distance. Follow the way markers until you reach a lane. (This was originally a Roman road, going all the way to Colchester.)

3. Turn right and walk to the road (B6047). Cross over and follow the Roman road. When a farm road bears left, turn right, to walk along a farm track, keeping a hedge on the left. (The Langton Caudle and trig point can be seen

in the distance and the Shangton Care Village is in the valley on the right.)
Cross over a stream bridge and continue up the hill to a road signpost to
Stonton Wyville.

4.   Turn right and take the farm track, into Stonton Wyville. (The
     'Leicestershire Round' joins the walk from the left in the village.) Turn left,
     go over a bridge and then cross a busy country road from Tur Langton onto a
     field track.

5.   Turn left at a signpost to Welham and go diagonally uphill. Follow the
     'round' yellow markers with an arrow, until you reach the trig. point, with
     excellent all round views.

Long Walk

6.   The bridleway goes slightly left to a waymark post across the field to a gate.
     Pass through the gate, to walk over the middle of this large field, following
     the direction of a line of hedges, which appear from your left. The path meets
     this hedge at the bottom left-hand corner. Follow the way-markers, stiles
     and gates, bearing left along the top of the ridge, until Welham village
     appears, then head in the direction of its Parish church. At the road, turn left
     towards Welham and at a high wall, just before the church, turn right down a
     narrow lane between the farm buildings.

Short Walk

6a. Leave the trig point downhill with hedge on the right and cross the stile,
     bearing right, to follow the marked path down the valley, through a spinney.
     Swing right to join a long field with a track and a ford, then a further track
     into Thorpe Langton. Turn right along the road, then left. Turn right again to
     pass the church on your left. Follow a walled path into an open field and
     continue to a red-bricked farm. Turn left here and follow a green lane into
     the open field ahead. At a way-marker, turn right along a hedge. (Go to point
     9.)

Long Walk

7.   This lane, with hardly any traffic, continues for some distance until a fishing
     pond is reached on the left. Almost opposite, a bridleway turns off through a
     hedge on the right.

8.   Follow the bridleway track until you meet the road into Thorpe Langton.
     Turn right and then through a gate on your left, following a footpath running
     diagonally to another stile, with a way-marker.

Short Walk rejoins

9.   Follow the hedge on your right, then a series of way-marked stiles to pass
     Park Farm on your right. In open fields move slightly left, then join a hedge
     on your left towards the village of East Langton. Going slightly right of the

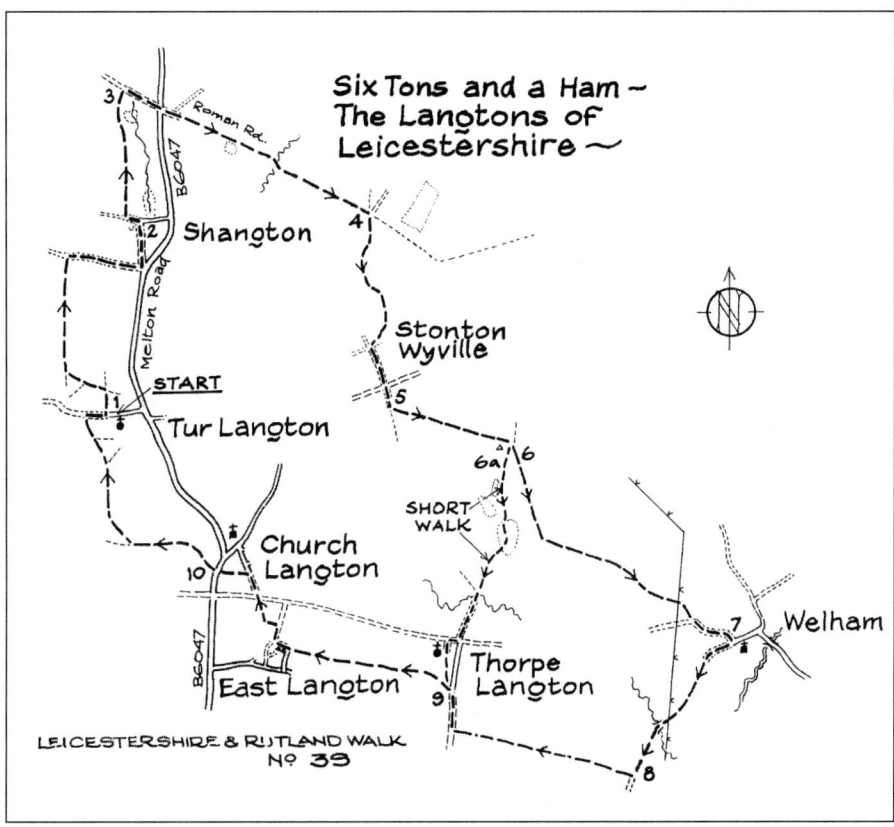

Six Tons and a Ham ~
The Langtons of
Leicestershire ~

Shangton

Stonton
Wyville

START

Tur Langton

SHORT
WALK

Church
Langton

Welham

East Langton

Thorpe
Langton

LEICESTERSHIRE & RUTLAND WALK
№ 39

field corner, swing left along the side of an old hedged way to a road. Turn
right and right again until you arrive at a road junction. Take the path opposite the Bell Inn, round the side of the cricket pitch, then turning right in a
field, which at the top, leads to a road junction. Taking the lane in front into
Church Langton, turn left on a path just before the 30mph sign. This leads to
the Melton road and the car park of the Langton Arms. (The parish church of
St Peter can be seen further up the road.)

10. Cross the road from the Langton Arms to a stile. Following the path sign to
the right, pass through a farmyard, to the path sign straight ahead into a field.
Follow the way-marker signs over further stiles until you arrive at a small
clump of trees. Here the path heads into the middle of a large field. Continue
until you have woods on either side and a small hedge in front, then turn
right onto a farm track. At the next way-marker, turn right and cross a double
stile. (Tur Langton church is now in sight.) Cross the next two fence stiles
and take the path to the left of the tennis court. Pass into another field, then

turn right, to arrive at a cottage drive. Follow this driveway onto Tur Langton's main street. The Crown Inn and church, where you started the walk, are on your right.

Points of Interest

Tur Langton – is one of several villages in the area which are always referred to as "The Langtons". The red-brick St Andrew's Church was rebuilt in 1866 on a new site. The remains of the old church can be seen at the west end of the village near the 17th-century manor house.

Shangton – a small and secluded village in attractive countryside. The Church of St Nicholas is largely unrestored 14th century and built of ironstone, although the chancel was rebuilt in 1873. The earliest period at which headstones appear in churchyards is the late 17th century and there are some fine examples in this churchyard.

Stonton Wyville – a small village with a 13th-century church which was not very sympathetically restored in the Victorian period. The Brudenell family, who own the manor house, came here in the reign of Henry VIII and the tomb of Edmund Brudenell, squire of Stonton, who died 12th May 1590, is in the church of St Denis. The Bishop of Salisbury was baptised here in 1337.

Thorpe Langton – another of the Langton villages. St Leonard's Church is late 13th century and was rebuilt in the 17th century. The old village, now gone, stood close to the church. The Baker's Arms was built around 1720.

Welham – a tiny village on the county border with Northamptonshire. The mediaeval village lay to the south of St Andrew's Church and the present village was much rebuilt by Francis Edwards in the early 18th century. The Old Red Lion is one of the best surviving examples of this rebuilding.

Church Langton – the Church of St Peter is the mother-church of this area and it dominates the countryside. In the churchyard there is a long series of Kendall headstones. The Rectory was built in 1784-86 by William Hanbury and, except for four years from 1778-82, the Hanburys were rectors successively from 1753 to 1899.

The County of Northamptonshire

For centuries the valley of the River Nene provided a rout for invaders and the Jurassic Way was a major pre-Roman route. Nowadays, Northamptonshire is a county unknown to many.

It has a rich history of noble families, estates, castles and country houses. It was a playground for kings, with extensive royal hunting forests. Remnants of these can be visited at Salcey Forest, Yardley Chase and Rockingham. There are less happy royal associations. The county has two Eleanor Crosses marking the places where the coffin of King Edward I's Queen Eleanor rested on its journey to London. One is in the centre of the village of Geddington, the other at Hardingstone, near Northampton. Mary Queen of Scots was beheaded at Fotheringhay. Richard III was born there and the imposing remains of the Perpendicular church house, the monuments of members of the House of York.

Eleanor Cross at Geddington, Walk 43
(Photograph: Bob Coles)

Other events of national significance were the unsuccessful Gunpowder Plot, hatched at Ashby St Ledgers, and the defeat of the forces of Charles I, by Oliver Cromwell at Naseby.

There are many ancient and majestic churches in this county of 'spires and squires'. Saxon churches are to be found at Brixworth, Earls Barton, Brigstock and Green's Norton. Northampton has the Norman church of St Peter and the round church of the Holy Sepulchre. The magnificent St Mary's church at Wellingborough was designed by J.N. Comper.

Northamptonshire is a county of attractive limestone and ironstone villages. Sheep, cattle, boot and shoe making and iron and steel manufacture have, at different times, given the county its economic prosperity.

H.E. Bates was born in Rushden, J.L. Carr lived in Kettering and the writer and illustrator 'B B', as Denys Watkins-Pitchford was known, lived at Sudborough near Brigstock. Each took inspiration for their writing from the people and landscapes of the county. Earlier literary figures associated with Northamptonshire were John Dryden, Thomas Fuller and Thomas Gray.

Two great missionaries have connections with the county, William Carey who helped to found the Baptist Missionary Society, and David Livingstone. Livingstone's journals were brought to the village of Twywell by one of his native companions.

There are four major named footpaths in the county, the Nene, Grafton, Knightley and Jurassic Ways and there are many other paths, by-ways and bridleways to explore.

Highway Authority

Northamptonshire County Council,
Public Services – Transport & Streets (Rights of Way),
2nd Floor,
Riverside House,
Bedford Road,
Northampton NN1 5NX   01604 238159

Tourist Information

Northampton: 01604 622677

40: Foxton Locks and The Grand Union Canal

An interesting walk in the beautiful Leicestershire countryside following part of the Grand Union Canal (Leicester Section) with the unique Foxton Locks and site of the famous inclined plane boat lift. In contrast there are some quite hilly sections through lovely pastureland with fine views and the pretty village of Gumley, Saddington and Laughton.

Distance: Long Walk 19.25km (11¾ miles); Short Walk 10.25km (6½ miles)

Duration: Long Walk 6 hours; Short Walk 3 hours

Maps required: OS Explorer 223 Northampton & Market Harborough, OS Landranger 140 Leicester and Coventry, OS Landranger 141 Kettering and Corby

Terrain: Undulating field paths/ tracks, long stretch of towpath and numerous stiles

Starting point: Foxton Locks car park. (SP692892) – Pay and Display

Refreshments: Public house, shop and tea room at Bridge No.61, Foxton Locks, public houses in Gumley, Saddington and Mowsley

Bus/Train link: Market Harborough/Leicester

The Route

Long Walk

1. Take the woodland footpath to the canal as signposted from the car park. Turn right, cross bridge No.60 and follow canal on your right, passing Top Lock Cottage and the flight of locks. Halfway down the flight notice on your right the canal museum and site of the inclined plane, both well worth a visit.

2. Carry on under bridge No.61 passing Foxton Bottom Lock and wharf basin. Keep to the left and then cross Rainbow Bridge No.62 to walk along the towpath, now to the right of the canal. Cross the canal again at bridge No.63, a high narrow footbridge. You are now on part of the Leicestershire Round. Continue straight ahead to a stile in the hedge and cross the next field keeping the sewage works on your right and aiming towards some gates. Halfway across the field, the stile and waymark become clear at the side of the gates. Bear diagonally left to another waymark and stile. Walk uphill, keeping the hedge on your left, to a kissing gate. Carry on along a narrow path beside a house to the main street in Gumley village.

Short Walk

2a. Follow the Long Walk route but cross the footbridge **before** bridge No.61 and then cross back over bridge No. 61 on to a bridleway. After passing through a pair of metal gates, walk close to the right-hand boundary to a wooden gate at the bottom of the field. Cross the road and continue through another field to a gate on the right in the hedge. Turn left along the lane and over a stream for approximately 195m before turning right on to the bridleway. Almost immediately turn left as waymarked. Walk with the hedge on your right to a gap leading to a track towards Gumley Lodge. After 90m on the track bear right to a waymark and a gate. Turn left and continue through two fields with a hedge on your left. Walk across the middle of the next field to a stile and straight ahead through two more fields to a road. Cross over to the stile and then aim half-right through paddocks to two gates leading into the village of Laughton. Turn left and walk along the road to the village green. (Go to point 6).

Long Walk

3. Turn right to continue the walk or left for refreshment at the Bell Inn. Where the road bends to the left walk straight ahead towards the church. (Note the interesting Tower House on your right.) Keep to the left of the church and take the footpath straight ahead to a kissing gate. Cross the field and pass between two magnificent beech trees to a metal gate. Cross the road to a stile just on your left. Walk through the next three fields keeping the hedge on your right. At a crossroads of paths, veer left towards the top of Smeeton Gorse and pause to admire the sweeping views. Cross the stile and bear right to the point where the hedge meets a fence and walk with the hedge on your right to a stile. Cross the field aiming for the third tree on the left on the horizon to a stile. From here there is a good view of Saddington Reservoir. Follow the path round the field edge to a stile in the opposite hedge and continue downhill as waymarked into a pretty valley. Cross the three footbridges and walk alongside a fence and over two stiles then bear slightly left uphill and down to a double stile. Walk ahead through a narrow field to a stile and a passageway into Saddington village.

4. Carry on up the lane straight ahead which passes to the right of the old Baptist Chapel and through a passageway to a gate. Walk on the track to your left to the road. Cross over to the footpath opposite and bear right until half-way along the hedge where there are three stiles. Turn left keeping the pond close on your right to a gateway. Take the left footpath signed Leicestershire Round and carry straight on through several fields to Arnesby Road. Turn left and walk along the road to a T-junction.

5. Turn left and after 270m take the footpath on the right towards Saddington Lodge Farm. (**Note:** At the time of publication there is a proposal for a diversion here. Please follow the clear waymarks.) At the junction of paths, go

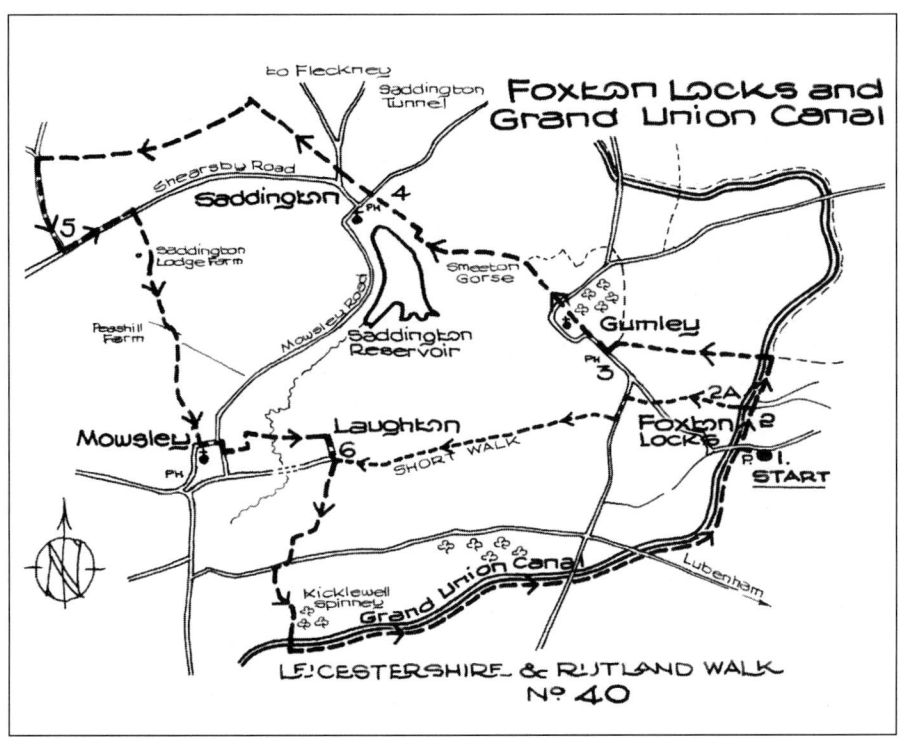

LEICESTERSHIRE & RUTLAND WALK
Nº 40

straight ahead through the farmyard to a gate on the left. Turn right and walk towards a gate. From the gate, walk diagonally half-right to another gate in the hedge and bear left to the corner of the next field. Pass through two gates and over a stile to climb gently bearing left to stile in the middle of a hedge-row. Continue ahead, with the old buildings of Peashill Farm on your right, to a stile. Carry on through the next field with the hedge on your left to a stile in the corner and keeping the hedge on your right, climb a double stile about halfway along the hedge. Cross over a track and walk straight ahead, noting the remains of a three-field system with very deep ridges and furrows in the next two fields.

Continue with the hedge on your right, cross a double stile and bear left downhill to a track. Follow the track uphill for about 90m and then take the footpath across the stile. (Note the site of mediaeval fishponds on your right.) Climb to the left towards an enclosed footpath between a house and a shed. This takes you into the village of Mowsley. Turn left and where the main street bends sharply to the left, continue straight ahead. Follow the road as it turns to the right and take the footpath on your left concealed beside a gate. Walk down the field, turning left at the bottom and continue along the field edge to the double stile. Follow the hedge to your right to a footbridge over the Laughton Brook and climb uphill bearing right to a metal gate, then head towards the right of the farm buildings to a short track leading into Laughton village. (Note the mud-and-wattle walled churchyard as you turn right towards the village green.)

Short Walk re-joins

6. Go through the gate near the telephone box and bear right to the corner of the field. As you walk down you can see traces of a mill mound on your left. Cross over the footbridge and walk diagonally right to a double stile in the corner. Continue left, keeping the tree in the distance well to your right to locate a waymarked stile leading to the road. Turn right and, after 90m, turn left and walk downhill. As you cross the stile at the edge of Kicklewell Spinney, there is a lovely view with the Grand Union Canal meandering below. Continue down two more fields to bridge No.51 over the canal. Cross the bridge and turn right down to the towpath and then right again to walk under the bridge. Now you follow the towpath all the way to bridge No.60 and retrace your steps to the car park.

Points of Interest

Foxton Locks – This is a unique staircase flight of ten locks; two groups of five with a passing pound between them. It is one of the longest staircase flights in the canal system and was opened in 1814 and constructed on the advice of the famous engineer Thomas Telford. At the side of each lock is a large pound into which water is passed when a lock is emptied. It takes an average of 45 minutes to negotiate the locks, using 25,000 gallons of water per passage. For this reason, the inclined plane boatlift was opened in 1900. A boat using the incline could be moved up or down the 75ft in as little as 8 minutes and with little loss of water. In simple terms, the lift worked with two tanks, one at the bottom level and one at the top level into which boats could be floated. The tanks were supported on wheels and ran on rails up and down the slope. One boat tank acted as a counterweight for the other and with the help of a steam engine, as one ascended the other descended. In 1909, the locks were reinstated for night traffic when the plane was not operating. However, in 1911 the plane was abandoned due to irregular traffic making it uneconomical to run. The locks have been in use ever since. All the machinery was sold for scrap in 1928

The site of the inclined plane is now under restoration. The lift's former boiler house has been restored and is now a museum with working exhibits.

Gumley – This pretty village once boasted a Hall next to its Church of St Helen, which dates from the 14th century. The Hall was demolished in 1964, having been built by Joseph Cradock in 1764. He lavished money on it, even to the extent of having his own private theatre. He may have been influenced by his friend, the actor David Garrick. Only the stable block of 1869 remains with its

Italianate clock tower intact. This is now being converted into private residences, having once been used allegedly for SAS training. In the grass verge on the bend opposite to the clock tower is the flat bed of what was formerly a Victorian weighbridge platform. It was made by H. Pooley & Son of Liverpool and London. It was last used in the 1920s and is thought to have weighed corn from the Gumley Hall Estate and coal from the nearby Debdale Wharf.

Saddington – The reservoir and dam were built in the 1790s to feed the canal. There is a particularly fine view of it from the car park of the Queen's Head public house. The Church of St Helen dates from the 13th century, though much of it was rebuilt in 1872.

Mowsley – The Church of St Nicholas was built around 1300 and underwent restoration in 1882.

Laughton – There are some lovely thatched cottages in this delightful village. St Luke's Church with its mud and wattle walled churchyard dates from the 12th century. In Victorian times, the side aisles were removed and the openings filled in, as can clearly be seen on the outer walls each side of the entrance porch. This resulted in a certain Colonel William Cole, Lord of the Manor and his wife being buried outside and not in the church as was originally intended. A wall plaque states that the Colonel served King Charles I and his three successors and was a commissioned officer for 58 years. He died in 1698 at the age of 85 years.

41: A Mediaeval Meander

A beautiful Northamptonshire/Rutland cross-border walk around the River Welland, Wakerley, Great Wood and Westhay Wood visiting the villages of Barrowden, Wakerley, King's Cliffe (option) and Duddington.

Distance: Long Walk 16km (10 miles). No Short Walk.

Duration: 5 hours

Maps required: OS Explorer 224 Kettering, Corby and Wellingborough, OS Explorer 234 Rutland Water, OS Landranger 141 Kettering and Corby

Terrain: Attractive paths, linking woodland and delightful stone villages

Starting point: Barrowden (Green) (SK947001)

Refreshments: Pubs in Barrowden, King's Cliffe and Duddington

Bus/Train link: Stamford/Corby

The Route

1. Walk east along the Main Street and bear right into Mill Lane, then right at the end following Jurassic Way signs – the path has been recently diverted. Follow the waymarked route to cross the river and go ahead under the disused railway into Wakerley.

2. Turn left along the village street and turn right after the Exeter guest house (formerly a public house), still following the Jurassic Way. Pass to the right of the church and continue across the field to a road. Turn right along the road, which soon swings left alongside woods. Turn right into the woods as waymarked and bear left to join a wide track. Keep on this main track as it passes to the left of a car park and picnic area, bearing left, then turn right as waymarked, through a barrier, on to another wide track. Turn left at the next T-junction, then right on to a grassy track. This descends to a valley, turning right and left, eventually leaving the wood via a stile. Bear slightly away from the wire fence to a stile among the trees. Bear left to a double gate and continue to the A43.

3. Cross with care and go downhill to turn left at a gate and follow the waymarks uphill with Fineshade Abbey stables on the left, partly on an enclosed path. Pass through some woodland and then across a field before turning right along the road to Top Lodge Visitor Centre. Here turn right, then right again on the track signposted to the sawmill and follow this wide track for about 2.5km to the sawmill.

4. Here turn left, still on the Jurassic Way, (or go ahead past the saw-mill and

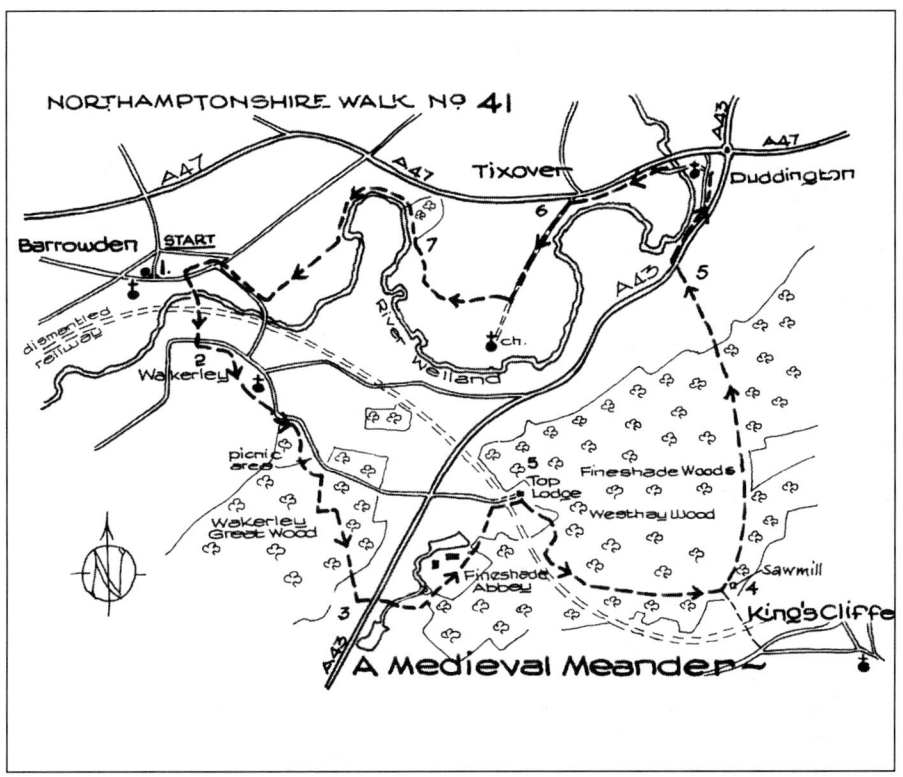

turn right for King's Cliffe – an extra 2.5km to the church and back). Follow the grassy track through the wood, which becomes stony for a short distance – watch out for the grassy track straight on where the main track begins to swing left to arrive at the A43.

5. Turn right along the A43, then left at the Royal Oak into Duddington village, and left again at a triangular green. Pass the old mill, cross the river and turn left alongside the A47 to Tixover.

6. Turn left off A47 to follow the village street as it bears left to end at a farm. Tixover church is ahead and well worth a visit (see points of interest). Return to farm and continue past this, and bear right along a stony track, with a hedge on the left. Where this track ends bear slightly right along the headland, still with a hedge on the left, shortly to enter an attractive wood which slopes down to the river on the left.

7. Continue with the river on the left through fields, until it turns away sharply – here go ahead with a hedge on the right to the road. Turn right along the road to Barrowden.

Points of Interest

Barrowden – A fine stone village of narrow streets and secret corners. The centre is a complex of small greens with a very traditional and well-populated duck-pond, all overlooked from the terrace of the inn. Nearby Durant House is the most notable in the village. The church, hidden away, is manly 14th century, remarkably wide, with a graceful west tower and spire, conspicuous in the view from the mediaeval bridge over the Welland. It was a royal manor at the time of Domesday, with a regular market and fair until the time of the Black Death – its open fields were not enclosed until 1880-82. Thomas Cook is associated with the Baptist Chapel in the village.

Wakerley – A scattered village, greatly decayed from the time when it was granted a Fair Charter in 1263. Hence the church is almost isolated and the manor house between it and the river has only earthworks visible. Wakerley Great Wood is one of the largest surviving parts of the ancient royal hunting ground of Rockingham Forest. It has been administered by the Forestry Commission since 1927, and many leisure facilities have been provided alongside the production of timber.

Fineshade – A Norman castle occupied the site until the time of King John – traces are visible by the stream. An Augustinian priory was founded c1200 and survived until the Dissolution. The Kirkham family bought the remains and converted them into a house, later replaced by a Georgian mansion. What survives today is chiefly the fine stable block of this mansion. The nearby woods are ancient and rich in wildlife. Top Lodge, formerly a farm of the abbey, houses the Forest District Office, and leaflets are available to guide the visitor around the points of interest.

Duddington – One of the most attractive villages in the county, seemingly roofed throughout in Collyweston slate. The bridge and mill feature in many photographs, having been featured on the cover of the OS Landranger Map 141. Many of the houses, including the manor, date from the 17th century. The church is a mixture of styles, with a low broach spire oddly positioned at the corner of the chancel. The interior contains many monuments to the Jackson family, resident at the manor for over 300 years.

Tixover – The church is isolated in the water-meadows and is mainly Norman. It is still lit by oil lamps, which creates an Edwardian ambience, in keeping with the furnishings and unfinished Roll of Honour. It originally served a village which disappeared, probably as a result of the Black Death. Later villagers rebuilt a village further north leaving the church standing alone. Tixover Hall in the village has an 18th-century east front.

42: The Nene Valley Wander

This walk takes you from Northamptonshire into Cambridgeshire and back along well-defined paths beside the River Nene and through woodland.

Distance: Long Walk 16km (10 miles); Short Walk 9.5km (6 miles)

Duration: Long Walk 5 hours; Short Walk 3 hours

Maps required: OS Explorer 234 Rutland Water, OS Explorer 227 Peterborough, March, Wittlesey, Chatteris, OS Landranger 142 Peterborough, Market Deeping and Chatteris

Terrain: Riverside , undulating woodland, can be muddy in places.

Starting point: St Mary the Virgin and All Saints Church, Nassington (TL062962)

Refreshments: Public houses in Nassington, Wansford and Yarwell. Teas at Yarwell Village Hall in the summer months.

Bus/Train link: Stamford and Peterborough

The Route

1. Starting from the church in Nassington, walk down the road towards the Black Horse public house on the corner of Fotheringhay Road. Turn right and after a few metres cross the road to join the Nene Way, over a stile. Follow the Nene Way and at the stepping stones (now closed) keep to the west bank of tributary to Yarwell Mill. Follow the Nene Way across two fields to Yarwell village. Turn right at road into the village; where the road turns sharply left, the Nene Way continues ahead for about 1.3km to Wansford. On reaching the A6118 turn left and then left again by church

Long Walk

2. Almost immediately turn right into Old Leicester Road. Follow for 500m. Turn right to take path to reach A47. **Cross with great care** and follow the path, keeping the hedge on right until reaching Meadow Lane in the village of Thornhaugh.

Short Walk

2a. Carry straight on for 900m to a bridleway on the right. Take this bridleway through Old Sulehay Forest. On emerging from trees continue ahead for 250m to join a minor road. Turn left and rejoin Long Walk. (Go to point 6)

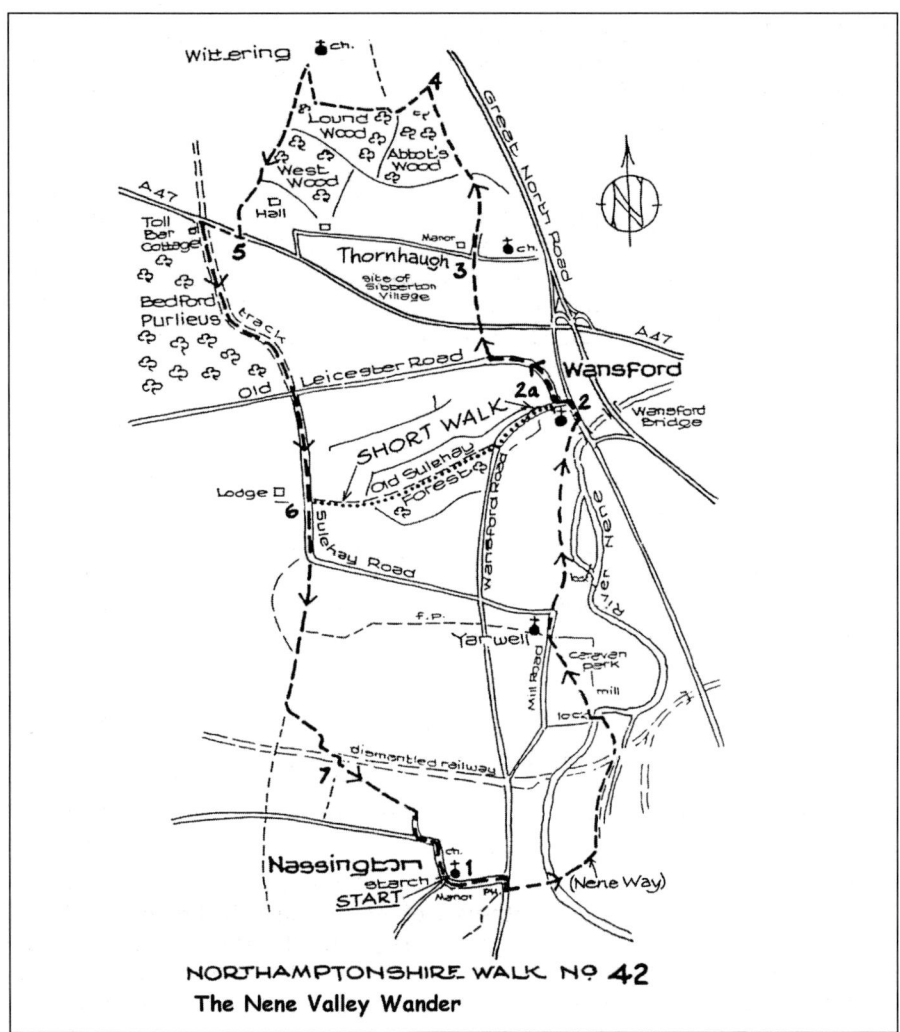

NORTHAMPTONSHIRE WALK Nº 42
The Nene Valley Wander

Long Walk

3. At the end of Meadow Lane, cross to the right of the manor, to pass through a metal gate. Follow the path down to a stream and turn left over a stile and a little bridge. Now follow the course of the stream until you reach Abbot's Wood. Turn right and follow the path until you reach an obvious corner, where you turn left. As you emerge from the trees, along the northern edge of Lound Wood, you will see the spire of All Saints Church, Wittering, to your right.

4. A wooden gate and stile, leads you into a grass field. Cross the field to a stile on the edge of a small wood. Turn left along the edge of the wood and climb two stiles into a field. A corridor of hedging and deer fencing leads you back into woods and eventually on to a private road and footpath leading to the A47.

5. Turn right along the grass verge and over a bridge, until you reach the Wittering turning on the right. Cross the busy A47, and follow the track between Toll Bar Cottage and Kennels into Bedford Purlieus, a Forestry Commission woodland area. Keep straight on for 1.8km until you reach the Wansford – Kingcliffe road at a T-junction. Cross the Old Leicester road into Sulehay Road and continue for 1 km. At Old Sulehay Lodge continue ahead.

Short Walk rejoins

6. At sharp left-hand bend go straight on down a byway. Ignoring the first path to your left and a farm track, take the second turn to the left, which crosses a farm track into a field. Keeping a wire fence to your left, follow the path until you reach the disused railway. Cross the bridge into a field.

7. Keeping the church spire slightly to your right, cross two fields to a stile to Nassington village. Follow the grass track between the houses, at the road turn right and, at the junction with Apethorpe Road, turn left – back into the village and towards the church.

Points of Interest

Nassington – village dates from a Saxon settlement. Its name means the Farmstead (tun) of the people (inga) of the headland (naess). The Gothic style church is probably built on the site of an earlier Saxon church. It is notable for having a step down, from the nave to the chancel and its relics of the past. These include a Saxon cross, possibly the only one in the county that depicts the crucifixion.

Opposite the church on the corner of Woodnewton Road is a 15th-century house with an oriole window. To the south-west of the church is the Prebendal Manor, dating from the 13th century. It is open to the public at certain times during the summer. In mediaeval times, when the diocese of Lincoln stretched from the Humber to the Thames, Nassington merited a Prebendal (parish court) stall in Lincoln Cathedral. The first Prebendal was granted in the early 12th century and the association with Lincoln remained until 1840.

Yarwell – is an ancient and historic village, which sits half a mile above the banks of the River Nene. All around is evidence of old limestone quarries. Most of the houses are built of local stone and roofed with Collyweston (SW of Stamford) slates. The 13th-century Church of St Mary Magdalene, stands in the centre of the old village.

Wansford – its name derives from the Saxon word, for a spring or whirlpool (wielm). A spring still flows into the River Nene by the 16th-century stone bridge.

During the 18th and 19th centuries, Wansford was an important river port standing, as it does on the union of the Old Leicester and Great North roads. From the bridge, which replaces a 12th-century wooden one, you will see to your right the Haycock Inn, known until 1770 and the incident of 'Drunken Barnaby' as 'The Swan'. The present Inn dates from the early 17th century.

Thornhaugh – village's name means Thorn Enclosure in Anglo-Saxon. The dwellings are largely built of stone with roofs of thatch or Collystone slate. It was declared a conservation area in 1979. The 17th-century manor was originally a fortified house belonging to the St Medard family. William Russell, the Lord Deputy of Ireland, under Elizabeth I lived there until his death in 1613 and was buried in the parish church of St Andrew. Nicholas de St Medard, who died in 1327, is also believed to be buried there.

Wittering – The Church of All Saints' is largely Saxon with 14th-century additions. The village has, of course, strong RAF connections.

43: The Geddington Triangle and the Eleanor Cross

A circular walk in the Rockingham Forest area starting from the village of Geddington with its fine bridge over the River Ise, the beautiful Eleanor Cross and linking the villages of Brigstock and Stanion

Distance: 15km (9½ miles). No Short Walk.

Duration: 5 hours

Maps required: OS Explorer 224 Kettering, Corby and Wellingborough, OS Landranger 141 Kettering and Corby

Terrain: Field paths and tracks

Starting point: Geddington Eleanor Cross (SP894830)

Refreshments: Public Houses in Geddington, Brigstock and Stanion

Bus/Train link: Kettering/Corby

The Route

1. From the church walk away from the Eleanor Cross along West Street, then left into Wood Street. This deteriorates into a track after the last houses. Continue on this track as it turns right through a metal barrier at a smallholding (the walk returns through this barns complex). Follow the track for over 4.8km as it passes through woods and fields and follows the edge of a wood for a long distance. It can be muddy in places but still attractive. Pass Chase Farm on the right. The track soon becomes metalled as it curves right with good views over Brigstock village. Go ahead into Park Walk at a T-junction to an enclosed path to the left of Harper's Court into the Brigstock churchyard.

2. Pass the church porch and turn left up Church Street to pass the Market Cross. Turn left into High Street and second left into Bridge Street. After the surgery on the right turn right into the playing field. Go ahead to a stile then join the stream on the right. Cross it after the next stile through a gap, then go diagonally left over the hill to a gap in the hedge and continue forward to come alongside a hedge on the left. Go through a wide gap, then bear diagonally left aiming to the right of a tall tree. Walk towards Stanion church spire through a long field, then bear right over the stile to a footbridge. Go ahead to a hidden double stile, then bear left to clip the corner of a bank in the recreation ground, over stiles to a road. To reach the village centre go slightly left into St Peter's Close and take an enclosed path on the left before the first house, into the churchyard. Pass through the churchyard and turn right

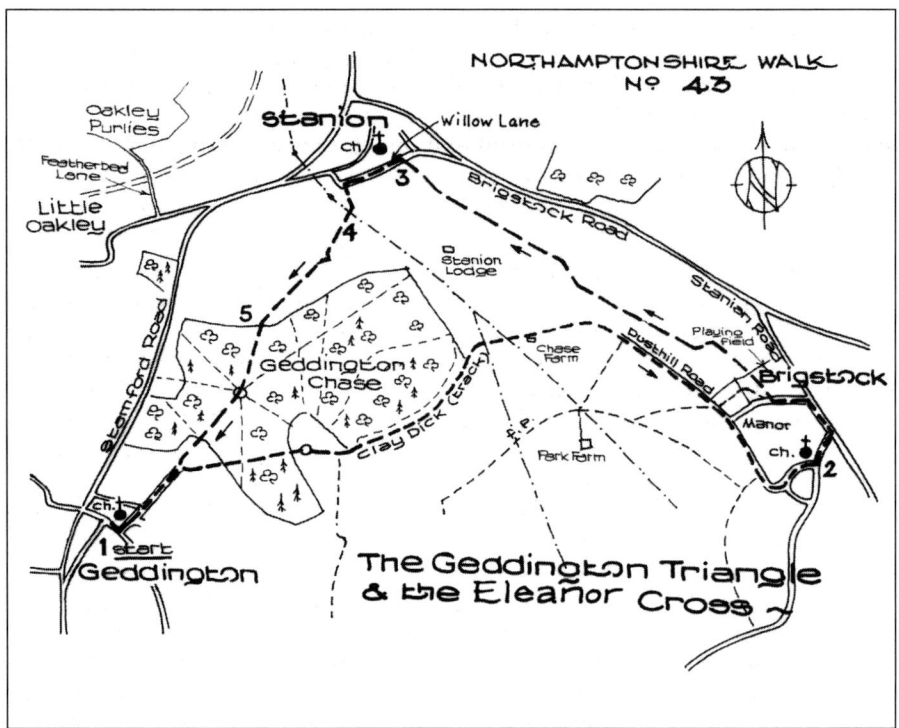

along Stanion village street (Cardigan Arms public house is to the right and Lord Nelson public house right at junction.)

3. Turn left into Willow Lane then left again where the road bends to the right onto a farm road and cross the brook to a footpath on the right.

4 Go diagonally left aiming for a hedge corner, then walk alongside a hedge on the left to a stile in the corner. Across this go diagonally right to join the hedge and continue along it to a wide gap. Go through this and follow the hedge in front. Keep to the right of it and go through two large fields to reach the wood.

5. Walk up the wide grassy drive to Chase Lodge, bearing to the right of the house as waymarked to go down a drive with a view of Geddington church straight ahead. Continue through the field with a hedge on the right to pass to the right of the barns and rejoin the outward route. Retrace your steps to the church.

Points of Interest

Geddington – Any description of the village must start with its most precious feature, the Eleanor Cross erected in 1294. The bereaved King Edward I stayed in a hunting lodge in the royal forest during his journey from Harby, in Nottighamshire, to London. The cross rises to a height of 40 feet and carries three images of the Queen under canopies. The surroundings retain their mediaeval character, with thatched cottages opposite, a bridge over the River Ise to the south which predates the cross itself and the church which has a Saxon core. The latter has a good 15th-century spire and tower, a fine east window of five lancets with excellent modern stained glass by Sir Ninian Comper, and some elegantly carved wooden screens and a magnificent 15th-century stone reredos.

Brigstock – One of Northamptonshire's famous Saxon churches. The chief pre-Conquest interest is the west tower, with its semi-circular western extension, similar to that at Brixworth. The tower arch to the nave impresses by its simplicity, but the original Saxon nave is now surrounded by later extensions from all mediaeval periods. Particularly fine are the decorated east window and the Perpendicular chancel arch. The contemporary screen to the north chapel is said to have come from Pipewell Abbey. The impressive Victorian marble tomb-chest is a memorial to the first Lord Lyveden, War Secretary at the time of the Crimean War. There are many attractive stone cottages in the village, a 16th-century manor house with recent sympathetic extensions and a mediaeval market cross. An interesting booklet on sale in the church gives more details.

Stanion – An attractive village in the heart of Rockingham Forest, with many thatched stone cottages. The church has a fine Perpendicular west tower and broach spire visible form afar, but much of the fabric dates from the late 13th century. Inside is an unusual 15th-century wall-painting depicting a stag and unicorn kneeling in homage, and some fine 18th century furnishings – a three-decker pulpit, two-decker reading desk and tiered box pews.

44: The Pitsford Figure-of-Eight

A bird watchers' delight! We start at the village of Moulton with its agricultural college and connections with William Carey, Baptist Minister and founder of the Missionary Society. Our walk also goes through the villages of Scaldwell, Old, Walgrave and Holcot returning to Moulton with the Pitsford Reservoir being the centrepiece of our walk.

Distance: Around Pitsford Reservoir 6.4km (4 miles), Long Walk 28km (17 miles); Short Walk 14km (8½ miles).

This walk can be shortened by starting from the car park at the Brixworth end of the causeway and either starting with a circuit of the southern part of the Reservoir or by walking directly to Scaldwell. Alternatively, either loop of the walk may be started from Holcot.

Duration: Long Walk 6½ hours; Short Walk 3¼ hours

Maps required: OS Explorer 223 Northampton and Market Harborough, OS Landranger 141 Kettering and Corby, OS Landranger 152 Northampton and Milton Keynes

Terrain: Easy walking farmland, and a hard surface path around reservoir.

Starting point: Moulton Parish church (SP783664)

Refreshments: There are public houses in all the villages mentioned except Scaldwell. Refreshments may be available at Moulton College Farm in the summer.

Bus/Train link: Northampton

The Route

1. From Moulton church go down Church Hill into West Street, past the College and turn right into Pitsford Road. Continue on this road until the College playing fields are reached. Take great care as part of the road is without a footpath.

2. Opposite the College drive go over stile. Keep the hedge to the right going round the field and along the edge of a narrow wood to Spectacle Lane.

3. Turn right to junction, cross this busy road with care into a large field. Follow the enclosed path around three sides of field, at field gate turn right (do not go through gate), go left along this hedgerow for 1½ sides, then go through opening (enclosed path). Be careful at this point because a 'conservation walk' continues along this hedgerow. At the end of the enclosed path cross stile to cottages, continue down the road to a road sign to 'Reservoir car park'.

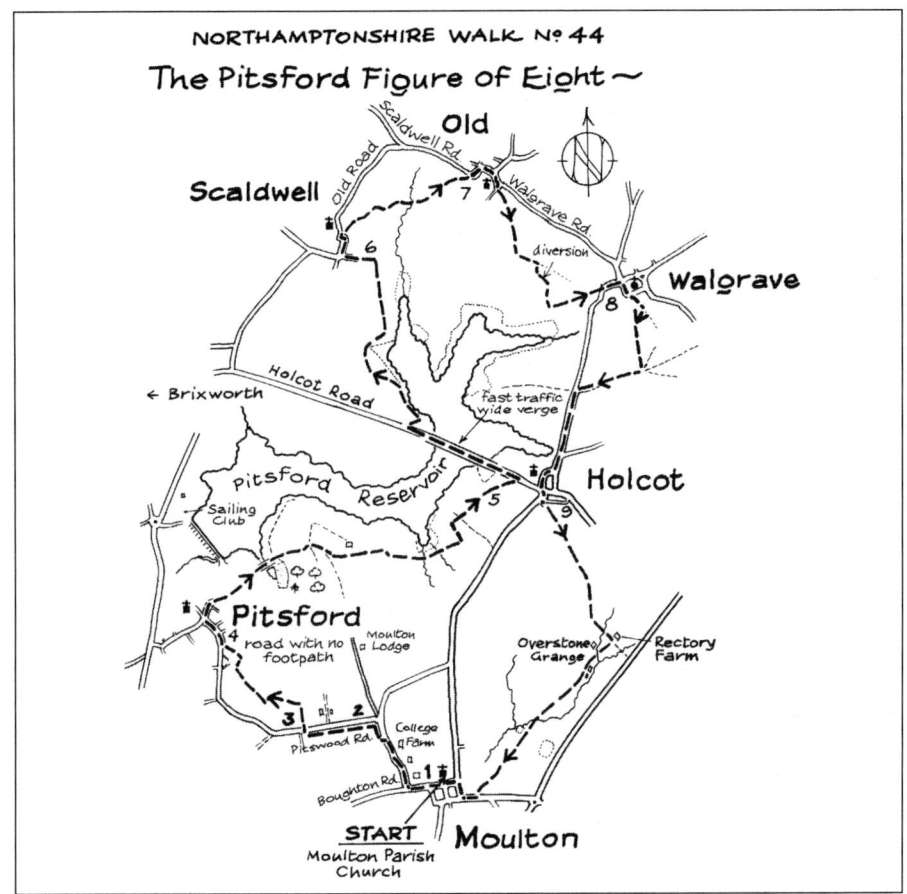

NORTHAMPTONSHIRE WALK № 44

The Pitsford Figure of Eight ~

4. Follow private road after a short distance, use footpath to right which runs
    parallel with road. At end of path continue along road to Moulton Grange
    entrance. A few metres left of the entrance, there are waymarks. Turn right
    and continue with hedge on right, over a footbridge and through several
    gates. At second footbridge go diagonally across field to a single electricity
    pole, go through hedge, keeping row of electricity poles on right. Cross the
    stream, again keeping hedge on right until the footpath (at waymark post)
    turn left crossing the field to a stile. After stile turn right, follow wide grass
    verge (gallops) for about 400 metres, at the bottom of the field, go right and
    immediately left up alongside hedgerow to top of field to stile cross field to
    stile on opposite side. You are now on the Brixworth to Holcot road.

5. Turn left and follow road until you come to the causeway (across Pitsford
    Reservoir) at the far end the entrance to a car park. Here, cross this very busy

road and walk on the grass verge keeping hedge on right until you come to an old road off to the right. Walk down this road to a stile and finger post on left. Cross stile keeping hedge on the left continue through two gateways, at the next go diagonally right downhill to a stile in corner of the field, cross then continue straight ahead to the brow of the hill to the end of a track. Continue on this bridleway to the village of Scaldwell.

6. At the road, turn right, continue to village green, keeping right and down School Lane. Pass over stile and diagonally right down the hill to footbridge. After a few metres cross a stile on the right and go diagonally up field to a stile leading onto a lane, turn right towards a stile (by a gate) entering farmyard, cross the yard to a stile in the fence. Turn left to the second opening in the hedge, here turn right keeping the hedgerow on the right down to footbridge. Continue diagonally left up the field to a field gate, go straight ahead to another gate, keeping hedge on right you will come to a double stile, cross then diagonally left to a stile in the hedge. Here go diagonally right to a stile (to where there is a depression in the ground), here you join the road at Old (30mph sign).

7. Continue to follow road through village round the front of the White Horse public house and turn right into Bridle Lane. After the houses turn left at a fingerpost, follow direction across the field to a stile in a wire fence and go over an old metal gate. Cross this field, keeping slightly right to a stile to a track where you turn right. At entrance to the field go at a slight left angle to a gate in the far hedge, cross the stile, then turn left to the end of the hedge. Here there has been a diversion, turn right and follow wide field edge for quite a distance to track off to the left, this track takes you to the road at Mill Farm, Walgrave.

8. Follow the road direct through the village to Church Road, turn right here and take an internal enclosed village footpath which brings you out opposite a stile/fingerpost. Cross the stile keeping the hedge on left down the field to a footbridge, take the footpath to the right heading for a stile at the top corner of the field. Turn left diagonally across this field to the hedge; go through, then cross the next field towards a point left of a group of trees, where you turn right and follow this byway to where it meets the road. Turn left (be careful this road can be very busy at certain times) follow it into Holcot.

9. Follow the road through the village to the War Memorial, and turn left in Back Lane. Almost immediately take a footpath to the right (at rear of some new properties) cross stile and follow the hedge to the left of farm building for quite a distance over a stile keeping a pond to your right. After leaving a spinney there is a gateway ahead of you, here go directly across the field keeping an enclosed pond on your right. At the stile go ahead to next stile alongside a field gate, cross stile and footbridge continue keeping farm buildings on left.

At the end of buildings turn immediately right and go alongside a wire fence to a stile. Drop down grass field a short distance to a small bridge across a stream (horses usually in this field). From bridge go diagonally left up to the corner of a farm building, go through animal pen to farmyard, turn left after farm building then immediate right to a track, here take field gate to the left of the track. Go quite a distance, keeping hedgerow on right over stiles. At second stile, go slightly right to field gate and stile. Cross this and aim to the right of a row of trees. Here, go ahead to the right-hand side of a row of houses, keeping hedge to your left. This takes you into Moulton. At the road, turn right for village centre and church.

Points of Interest

Moulton – was included in the Domesday Book as Moltone, but its history goes back to pre-Roman times. The Parish church of St Peter and St Paul is mostly late 13th century. William Carey, the founder of the Baptist Missionary Society in 1792, was pastor of the Baptist church, which dates from the middle of the 17th century. Lacemaking was a thriving cottage industry in the 19th century.

Pitsford – The original village was completely destroyed by fire in 1691. A mound, known as Longmans or Laymans Hill, beside the High Street, is thought to be a Saxon long barrow. All Saints Church, restored in 1866, has a 13th-century tower and a Norman doorway. The reservoir was opened in 1956 by the Queen Mother.

Scaldwell – meaning shallow wells, once had a healing well and the pond on the village green was the original source of water for the village pumps. H.E. Bates, the author, was a frequent visitor and is said to have set his novel, 'Love for Lydia' here. The local ironstone quarries were worked until the 1950s. Scaldwell is reputed to have several ghosts – all of them friendly.

Old – occasionally still called **Wold** by the older residents, first appeared in the Domesday Book as Wala. The Church of St Andrew, partially 13th century, has a two-day flower festival each July. Close by the one village pub, the White Horse, is a lime tree planted in 1887 to commemorate the Golden Jubilee of Queen Victoria.

Holcot – stands in an area of natural beauty containing an abundance of wild life. The Church of St Mary and All Saints, in the middle of the village, has a 15th-century limestone cross in its churchyard. The Town Well, situated in Main Street, provided fresh water for the village. The Wash Pit in Holcot was used by the village shepherd for dipping the sheep and has been cleaned and restored and is now a village pond.

45: Gunpowder, Treason and Plot

A circular walk on the Northamptonshire/Warwickshire border. You can see the Grand Union Canal bustling with life, explore a marina and view interesting churches and villages at Braunston, Welton and Ashby St Ledgers, famous location for the Gunpowder Plot.

Distance: 15km (9 miles). No Short Walk.

Duration: 4½ hours

Maps required: OS Explorer 222 Rugby and Daventry, Southam and Lutterworth, OS Landranger 152 Northampton and Milton Keynes

Terrain: Towpaths, footpaths, meadows and fields. Very slight inclines. Some walking through villages.

Starting point: The Green, Braunston (SP544663)

Refreshments: Public Houses at Braunston, Welton and Ashby St Ledgers, The Boat Shop, Bottom Lock, Braunston

Bus/Train link: Daventry/Northampton

The Route

1. From The Green, Braunston (just by the Village Hall, formerly the school) take the marked footpath by No.29 down to the canal. Cross the canal bridge and turn left along the towpath. Continue past the Admiral Nelson public house and Top Lock towards the tunnel. Just before you reach the tunnel, take the steps up and follow the green track to the main road (A361). Note Drayton Reservoir to your right, which supplies water to the canal. Also, circular brick ventilators for the canal tunnel seen below your feet.

2. Cross the road and follow the concrete road. When you reach the conifers, leave the road and continue straight along grass track, coming to the canal bank on your left (the other end of the tunnel). Take the steps up on your right and follow the path left to the road.

3. To reach Welton village, turn left for 800m then left again at the edge of Welton into Churchill Road, which leads into the High Street. After passing the White Horse public house on your right, you will see some steps on your left leading into the recreation ground. Take these steps and cross right to a gate into Ashby Road. Turn left along Ashby Road and you will see a footpath on your right (by No.28). Follow this path across the field.

4. Continue ahead through a gap in the hedge and look out for 'lollipop' discs on posts at several places. Cross a wooden plank bridge over a small stream and then bear slightly left, uphill. Go through another gap in the hedge and

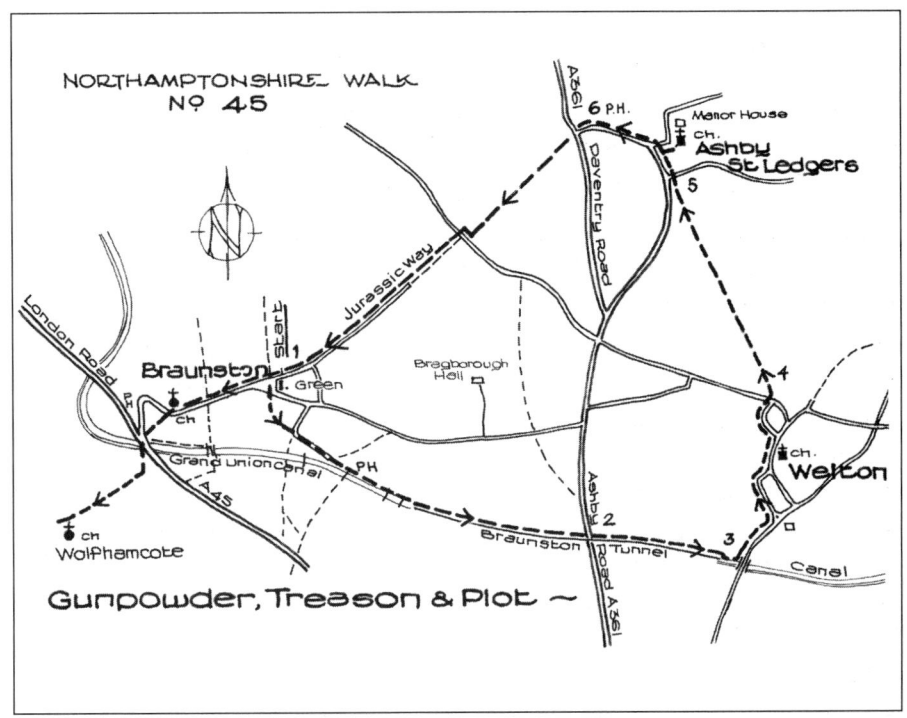

straight ahead to join the Watford/Ashby St Ledgers road at a gate. Immediately ahead is a road junction.

5. Follow the road to Ashby St Ledgers and turn left (signposted Kilsby) to reach the village. Take time to wander round (see the Elizabethan Mansion and Church by turning right and return). Turn back past the Coach and Horse public house to reach the A361 again. Cross over (you are now on the Jurassic Way Walk).

6. Follow the Jurassic Way (crossing one road only and looking for the signpost opposite and to your right) and you will arrive back in Braunston. Walk through the village and cross the A45 keeping the Mill House pub to our right. A private road leads to Wolfhampcote. When you have seen the church, retrace your steps and visit Braunston Marina (clearly marked off the A45) before returning to your starting point.

Points of Interest

Braunston – is an attractive canal-side village at the junction of the Grand Union and Oxford Canals. The magnificent spire of the 19th-century church, built in the 14th-century style, can be seen for miles around. Behind the church is a round windmill, in front of which is a cenotaph in memory of the local men killed in the 1914-18 War.

Welton – is a hill-top village, its name deriving from the springs and wells in the area. The Church of St Martin has a Saxon tub-shaped font, a beautifully carved pulpit and an alms box in the shape of an open hand. Many Roman urns and coins have been found in the area during building work.

Ashby St Ledgers – St Ledgers is a corruption of the name of St Leodegarius, patron saint of the church at the east end of the village. This is next to the manor house, the family home of the Catesbys from 1375 for 250 years. Robert Catesby was a leading figure in the Gunpowder Plot. He and his fellow conspirators are said to have met in the half-timbered gatehouse next to the church. Some fine brasses and monuments can be seen in the church and some recently uncovered wall paintings.

The Grand Union Canal – engineered by William Jessop, The Grand Junction Canal connected the River Thames at Brentford with the Oxford Canal at Braunston, thus giving a much shorter route to Birmingham. The original distance had been 269½ miles. This was reduced as more canals opened and was finally reduced to 138½ miles, when the Grand Junction was completed in 1805. In 1894, it acquired The Leicester & Northampton Canal and the old Union Canal (now known as the Leicester Section). In 1929, it amalgamated with three other canal companies to form the Grand Union Canal system of over 270 miles.

Braunston Tunnel – the tunnel is 2048 yards long. The builders began digging at each end on a slightly different bearing, which resulted in a kink in the tunnel.

46: The Royal Forest Walk

A circular walk starting from the village of Cogenhoe overlooking the Nene Valley to one of Northamptonshire's stately homes, Castle Ashby, ancestral home of the Marquis of Northampton, and then across a once Royal Hunting Forest.

Distance: Long Walk 21km (13 miles); Short Walk 8km (5 miles)

Duration: Long Walk 6½ hours; Short Walk 2½ hours

Maps required: OS Explorer 207 Newport Pagnell and Northampton South, OS Landranger 152 Northampton and Milton Keynes

Terrain: Farmland (mainly sheep pasture), farm tracks

Starting point: Brafield-on-the-Green Parish church (SP821590)

Refreshments: There are public houses in all villages except Horton

Bus/Train link: Northampton

The Route

1. From the church walk through the churchyard, taking the path downhill. Head for the large farm buildings. The path to Cogenhoe follows the left-hand side of the buildings following the stream. Just before reaching a dense thicket, take the stile seen ahead at the top of the slope. Turn right and walk to the next stile to head towards Cogenhoe village seen ahead. Aim for a row of silver birch trees and pass these to the right. The path is then well-marked to the road. Turn right and walk to the Royal Oak public house.

2. Continue along Whiston Road, and at the bottom of the hill and take the footpath to the right marked Jerusalem Steps. Walk uphill, under the power lines to the top of the field. Keep to the edge of the woods, following the headland, to the top of the field, to go up steps and to turn left. The path goes briefly into the wood and on emerging walk at right angles across the field to cross a stream and a road before picking up the bridleway to Chadstone. At the farm, take the farm road towards Chadstone village.

Long Walk

3. Walk straight through Chadstone to the T-junction, pass over a stile opposite and head across the field. This leads to the Main Ride in front of Castle Ashby House. On entering the Ride turn obliquely right and cross it at a shallow angle to reach the far side just beyond the brow of the hill. The gates on the main Bedford road (A428) should be well in sight. The path continues from here to Yardley Hastings.

Short Walk

3a. Take the footpath on the right just before Chadstone village towards Denton on the right. Start from pond and follow stream across fields on a clear path. At Denton, turn right along road and take the path on the left where road bends right. Keep on this path back to Brafield-on-the-Green and church.

Long Walk

4. Head towards the church and turn right at the main street. Walk up and cross the A428 into Chase Park Road. Follow this road until it ends, turn right to Chase Park Farm and then left on the well marked farm track. After the second disused railway track, walk straight across the field and pick up another track leading right to Manor Farm and the road to Horton village.

5. Walk through the village to Brafield (pronounced *Brayfield*) Road where you turn right. Follow this road and, about 200m beyond the houses, take the bridleway to the left. Head first for the end point of a hedge, just to the right of a clump of fir trees in the middle distance. Enter the field where the firs are, head for the clearly visible lone fir tree. Under that, take the gate/stile to the left and cross the field on a meandering path to the far-left corner.

6. Turn right into the lane at the edge of Hackleton village. Near the top of the lane, turn right through a gap in the hedge and go diagonally left to pick up a path along the right-hand side of the hedge. At the junction of paths turn right (towards Brafield Stadium) to cross the disused railway line. Turn left with the railway on your left. Your path crosses several fields and the railway eventually veers away to the left. Look for a hedge line pointing to Brafield-on-the-Green church on your right. **Do not** follow the first hedge but take the next right, to the old highway near Brafield-on-the-Green. Turn right to the A428 and continue past the filling station, Red Lion public house and after the Working Men's Club turn left (signed – village only). Follow this road round to the left and return to the church.

Points of Interest

Cogenhoe – may be derived from two old English words 'cucken' (to spy) and 'hoe' (hill). More likely, it simply means 'cugga's spur of land'. The present church, built between 1225 and 1280, by Nicholas de Cogenhoe, houses an effigy of a crusader, believed to be the aforementioned Nicholas de Cogenhoe, as well as many other interesting features.

Castle Ashby – is a classic estate village. Castle Ashley House is the seat of the Marquis of Northampton. Many dwellings in the village are roofed with tiles made at the estate between 1880 and 1930 and are unique in design.

Yardley Hastings – The congregational church in the village has a superb font. It is now in the National Resource Centre for the United Reformed Church. Next to the parish church are the remains of a Norman manor house. This is private property.

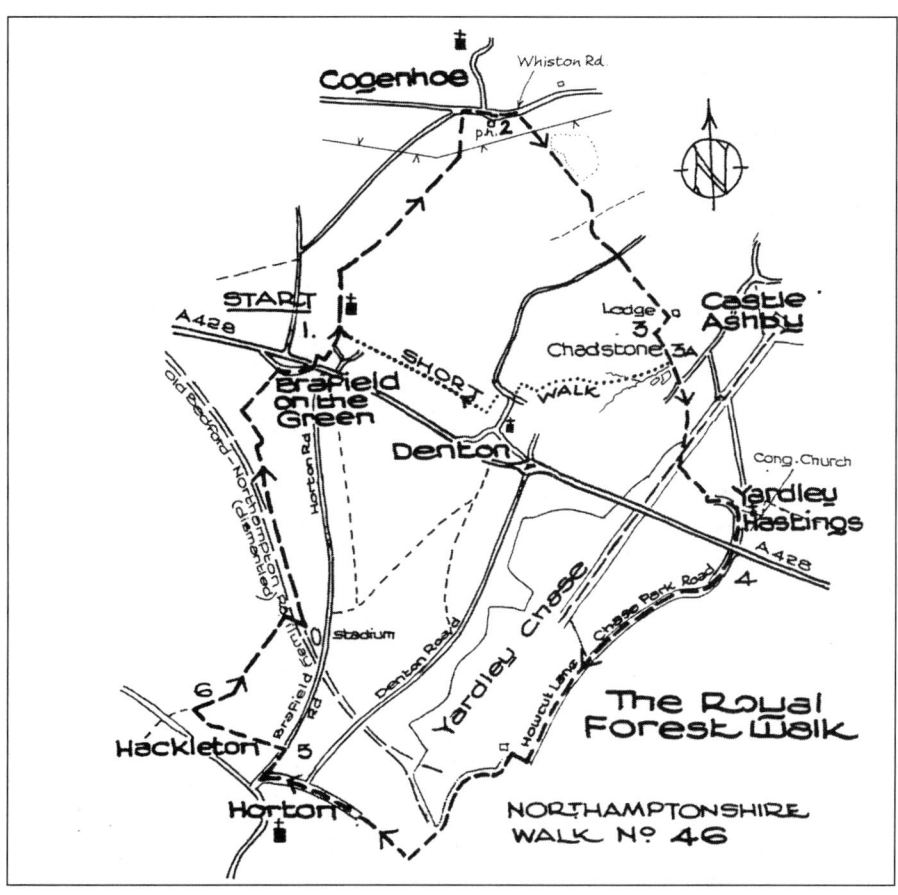

Yardley Chase – as the name suggests was a Royal hunting ground and part of Salcey Forest.

Horton – as you come into the village, there are some fine houses on your left. One of these is named The Arches. Viewing from the roadway it appears nothing special, but on the field side of the house it has a large arch built on it. This was a point of focus for the residents of Horton Hall, now demolished. The church contains the tomb of Sir William Parr and his wife Mary, whose niece, Catherine Parr, was the sixth wife of Henry VIII. Horton is also known as the birthplace of Charles Montague first Earl of Halifax, who in 1694 established the Bank of England.

Brafield-on-the-Green – is a village of many thatched cottages, one dating from the time of Cromwell. The church has many gargoyles, stone faces and a fine modern screen set in the massive tower arch.

47: Locked Up in Harrold

Starting at Bozeat (a former boot and shoe village) we cross Harrold Country Park, reclaimed from gravel workings but now an attractive area, into the village of Harrold with its ancient lock-up. Harrold was a former lace making town.

Distance: Long Walk 16km (10 miles); Short Walk 6.5km (4 miles)

Duration: Long Walk 5 hours; Short Walk 2 hours

Maps required: OS Explorer 207 Newport Pagnell and Northampton South, OS Explorer 208 Bedford & St Neots, Sandy & Biggleswade, OS Landranger 152 Northampton and Milton Keynes, OS Landranger 153 Bedford and Huntingdon

Terrain: Woods, farmland and lake-side paths

Starting point: Harrold Road, Bozeat (SP908592)

Refreshments: Public houses in Harrold, picnic tables and toilets at Country Park

Bus/Train link: Northampton/Wellingborough

The Route

1. The walk starts from the field next to the school on Harrold Road, Bozeat. Follow the footpath across the field to the far corner. Cross the road and follow the way-markers into the next field. Cross the stream to your right, then cross this field diagonally to the far corner. Go through the gate and follow the footpath, keeping the hedge on your left. At the end of this field, go through the gap in the hedge and across the next field, as indicated by the way-marker.

Long Walk

2. At the next hedge the footpath crosses the Three Shires Way and becomes a bridleway. (Note: excellent views from the trig point.) Follow the marked path towards a large barn. After passing the barn, cross the track and follow the bridleway along the edge of Park Wood.
    At the corner of the wood, follow the bridleway and go into the wood. On emerging at the other side, turn left and follow the edge of the wood again. After passing through the next hedge turn right and follow the bridleway, keeping the hedge on your right.

Short Walk

2a. Turn right at the trig point and follow the well-marked Three Shires Way

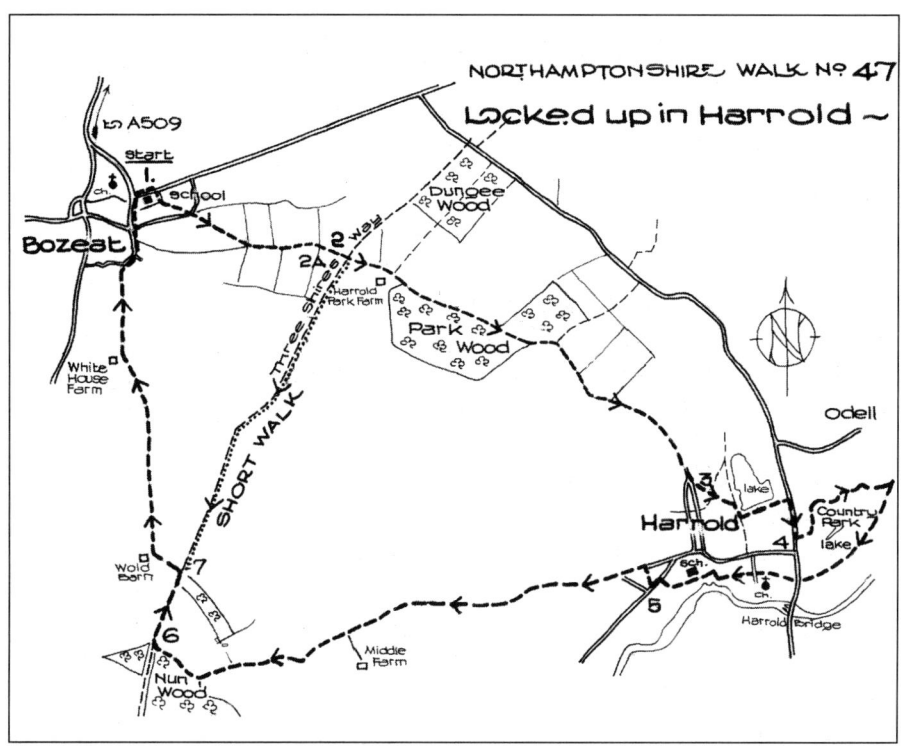

turning right to rejoin the Long Walk at the edge of The Slipe wood. (Go to point 7)

Long Walk

3. As you enter the village of Harrold the bridleway becomes a track and then a made-up road. After about 100m on the road turn left onto a footpath. About 20m after crossing the stream, take the footpath to the left into a field. The path crosses this field diagonally to the far corner. At the next stile, follow the signpost to Dove Lane. At the corner of the next field, follow the way-markers into a green lane; veer left after crossing a culvert to follow a path with wire fencing on the left. (Note the lake on the other side of the fence.)

4. Where the path leads out to the road, turn right. Just before a right junction indicating village centre, take the path on the left into Harrold Country Park. Once in the park turn left at the lake and follow the footpath to its junction with a bridleway. Turn right and follow it round to the visitor centre. Leave the park by the main entrance near the visitor centre. Cross the road and follow the footpath through a small cemetery, be sure to take the enclosed path adjacent to a private drive. Eventually to reach the village green. Note specially the village pound.

5. At the green turn left, cross the road and follow the private road passing a school. This leads out to the main road; turn left here. After about 50m on the road, turn right along footpath between the houses and into a field. Continue forward with a hedge on the right and at the corner turn left in the same field (Do **not** cross the stile in the corner.) Leave the field via a gate and follow the way-markers onto a private road. Follow this in the same direction as you have just left the path. After about 3km this private road becomes a footpath. Follow the way-markers around the edge of Nun Wood.

6. After passing through the next hedge, turn right and follow the bridleway (Three Shires Way) up the hill, keeping the hedge on your right. Turn left at waymarks at the crest of the rise.

Short Walk rejoins

7. Follow the well-marked footpath towards two derelict barns and follow the way-markers round them. After passing a small pond on the right, aim almost directly ahead (leaving hedge on right) to a gap in the hedge. Follow the waymarked route across two more fields to White House Farm, then along the edge of a field with the hedge on your right. Continue on the marked path across the next field and out into a housing estate. This is Fir Tree Grove, at the end of which turn right along St Mary's Road to Camden Square. Turn right and where the road bends sharply left go over the stile on your left and you are back in the field next to the school.

Points of Interest

Bozeat – it was once assumed that the name 'Bozeat' was a corruption of 'beaujet', good spring, but there is little evidence to support this. It is more likely that the name comes from 'Bosa's geat' (gate), a gateway controlled by a local tribal leader. In 1729, part of the village was destroyed by a fire that began at a place later known as Burnt Close. Dungee Wood, to the east of the village was once infamous for its connection with highwaymen.

Harrold – developed a flourishing lace industry during the 17th and early 18th century, which declined with the onset of machine lace in Nottingham. Buildings of note are the 13th-century Church of St Peter and on the village green the 18th-century market house and circular design lock-up built in 1824.

Odell & Harrold Country Park – covering 144 acres, has two main lakes created by gravel extraction. The riverbanks and water meadows that make up the rest of the park provide support for a wide range of wildlife. There is a Visitor Centre, with picnic tables and toilets.

48: The Lofty Heights of Northamptonshire

We visit Shuckburgh Park (where deer are often seen) and walk through the village of Hellidon, one of the loveliest villages in the county. Nearby are the sources of three of Northamptonshire's rivers, the Leam, Cherwell and Nene. We also visit Priors Marsham, crossing the county boundary into Warwickshire and also go to Marston Doles on the Oxford Canal.

Distance: 18km (11 miles). No Short walk.

Duration: 5 hours

Maps required: OS Explorer 206 Edge Hill and Fenny Compton, Badby, OS Explorer 222 Rugby & Daventry, Southam & Lutterworth, OS Landranger 151 Stratford-upon-Avon, OS Landranger 152 Northampton and Milton Keynes

Terrain: Parkland and good tracks

Starting point: Shuckburgh church (SP 491628)

Refreshments: Public houses at Hellidon and Priors Marston

Bus/Train link: Daventry/Northampton

The Route

1. Park in a lay-by past Shuckburgh church by the canal bridge, on a road signed to Flecknoe. Return to the church and cross the main road to find a stile on the left of a stone cottage that is facing you.

2. Set off half-left across the field to two metal gates. Continue in the same direction to pass the right-hand edge of a farmhouse. Continue up the hill in line with the telegraph poles to arrive at the gate into a deer park. (Look back from the brow of the hill for lovely views of Warwickshire.)

3. Once in the park, follow the well-defined grassy track. The church and Hall will come into view on your left – alas there is no access to the pretty church. Continue on the track to pass red brick farm buildings. After the buildings, go through a gate out of the park.

4. Through the gate, turn right on a track and follow it to a farm. Continue in the same direction to pass through a gate on the left of Park Farm and cross a field to another gate. Go through this gate and follow the fence on your left to a corner of the field. Go through another gate and turn sharp right, then follow the hedge to a gate in the corner of this field. Follow the hedge to another gate. Pass through this to join a wide grass track called Gypsy Lane.

5. Turn left on this green lane and continue to the village of Hellidon.

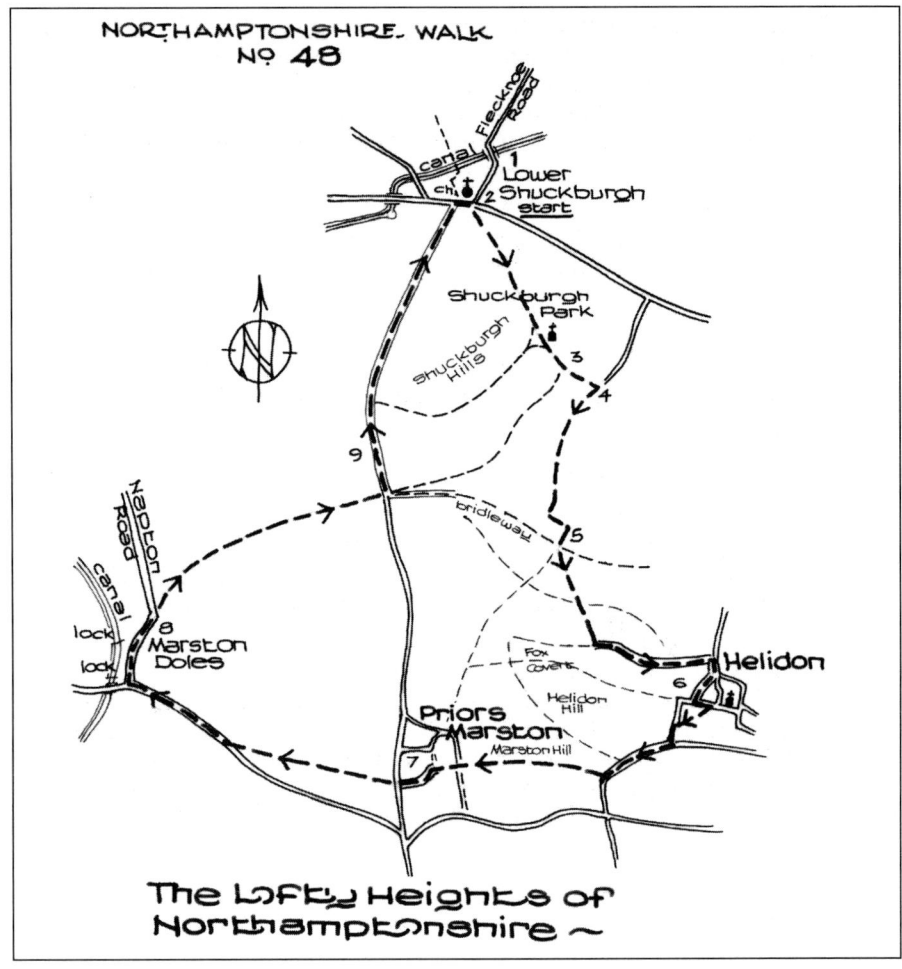

NORTHAMPTONSHIRE WALK
Nº 48

The Lofty Heights of
Northamptonshire ~

6. Arriving at Hellidon, bear right, pass the Post Office on Berry Lane and continue up the hill to a T-junction. Turn right and follow the lane, past a left-hand bend to a further T-junction. Turn right and continue past a golf course, soon you will see a house of the left "Fir Tree House". Opposite the house and on the right-hand side, there is a way-marked path. Take this, passing Hillcrest Farm (riding stables) and continue to Hill Farm. Pass through a gate to the left of Hill Farm to join a lane, with Priors Marston in view. Take the path opposite downhill towards the church, just before the school go left over a stile onto the road. Take the path to the left of the school and left again to meet School Lane on the right to cross Shuckburgh Road to the path opposite.

7. Take this path into the fields bearing slightly right. Follow the well-marked path to a farmhouse (The Meadows). Continue in the same direction passing the farm and several fields to join a road. At the road, turn right, shortly you will see the hamlet of Marston Doles. Just as you approach the first houses and canal bridge there is a right turn to Napton. (you need to take this right turn but it makes a pleasant break to continue to the canal bridge and watch the canal boats at the lock for a few minutes)

8. Follow the Napton road for about 300m to a point where the road turns left, continue ahead onto a track called Sow Meadow Lane. Follow this track until it joins a road (about 2.5km).

9. At the road turn left and soon, where the road turns left again, continue straight ahead on a lane signposted "Lower Shuckburgh". Follow this delightful tree-lined lane back to the start at Shuckburgh church.

Points of Interest

Hellidon – is one of the highest villages in Northamptonshire. The sources of the Rivers Leam, Cherwell and Nene are to be found in or around the village. The Church of St John the Baptist, dates from 1591, although the tower is said to have been built as early as 1350. The once productive ironstone quarries, situated at the southern boundary of the parish, were closed in 1961, but there is still some evidence of them to be seen.

Oxford Canal – Completed in 1790, it was another of James Brindley's canals although he died during its construction in 1772. The work was completed by his assistant and brother-in-law, Samuel Simcock. The canal connects the Thames at Oxford with the Coventry Canal at Hawksbury Junction – a distance of 78 miles and 43 locks. It was part of the original route from London to the Midlands but lost out when the more direct Grand Junction Canal was opened in 1805.

49: The Fawsley Walk

A circular walk taking in the large estate of the Knightley family and linking the villages of Everdon (connection with Thomas Gray, the poet),
Preston Capes (current home of Norman St John Stevas, the present
Lord Fawsley) and Woodford Halse, which sprang to life with the
coming of the Great Central Railway.

Distance: Long Walk 19km (12 miles); Short Walk 8.5km (5½ miles)

Duration: Long Walk 6 hours; Short Walk 2½ hours

Maps required: OS Explorer 206 Edge Hill and Fenny Compton, Badby,
OS Landranger 152 Northampton and Milton Keynes

Terrain: Rolling agricultural land, much given to sheep farming

Starting point: Everdon Parish church (SP595574)

Refreshments: There are public houses in Everdon and Woodford Halse

Bus/Train link: Daventry/Northampton

The Route

1. The path runs by the west side of the church. Go over the stile, turn sharp
    right and cross two fields. In the next field, go diagonally left, heading to the
    left of the slate and brick farm building. The path then goes alongside a
    hedge, left over a stile then through a wooded paddock to reach and go along
    a farm track. Carry straight on across the fields turning left after the drainage
    ditch to a gate. In the next field, turn right and cross to the middle of the far
    boundary (to the left of the willows). Go over a footbridge to follow the path
    with the wood on your right. Having gone through a small gate and a hedge,
    go diagonally left across the next field towards a shed. The path goes to the
    top corner of the next field to the road into Preston Capes.

Long Walk

2. Turn left and walk straight through the village across the crossroads. After
    220m, take the footpath to your right. It follows the very large first field's
    boundary. Cross the farm track at the bottom and continue with the wood on
    your right until it ends, whereupon go diagonally left across the field and
    straight on to the road. Turn right and walk along the road following the
    signs for Woodford Halse.

Short Walk

2a. Turn right along road and just after bend, take footpath on the left following
    the Knightley Way, heading towards Fawsley Park and Hall. Ignore path off

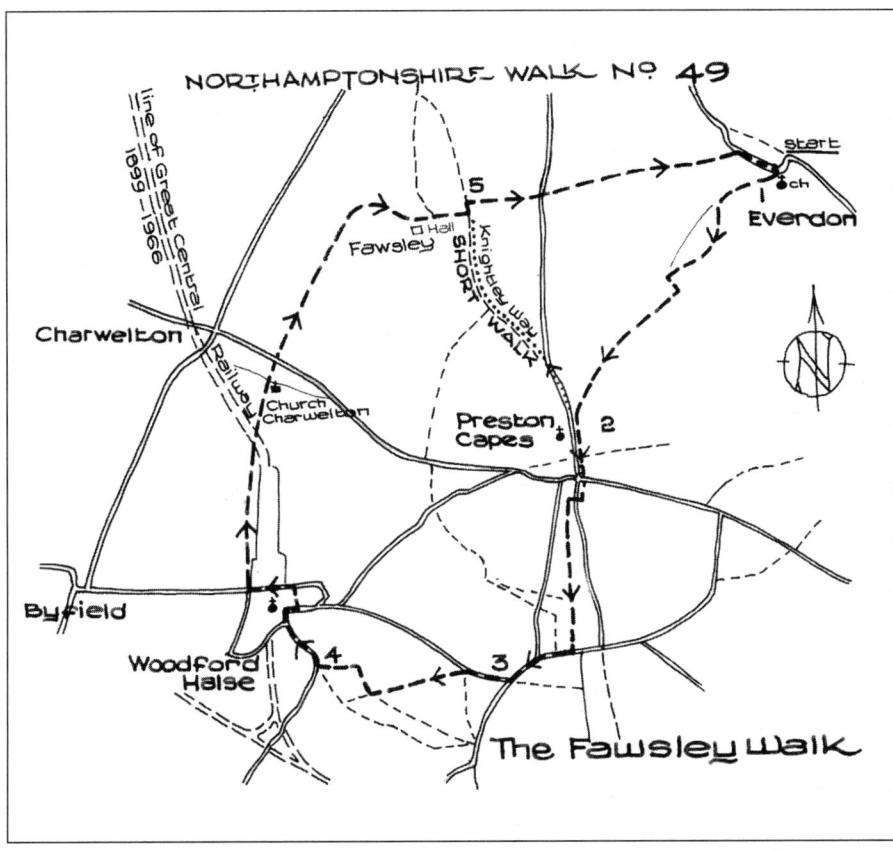

NORTHAMPTONSHIRE WALK No 49

line of Great Central Railway 1899 - 1966

Charwelton

Fawsley

Church Charwelton

Preston Capes

Byfield

Woodford Halse

Knightley Way

SHORT WALK

start

ch

Everdon

2

4

3

The Fawsley Walk

N

to left at edge of park and continue ahead towards the church. When path meets road turn right. (Go to point 5)

3. After the second junction look for the path going obliquely left to pass in front of some farm buildings. Follow this to the left of a house until it becomes an avenue, then turn sharp right with the hedge on your right. Walk to and over the brow of a hill and through a gap in the hedge. Go diagonally left to another gap in a hedge. Then follow the hedge on your right to a kissing gate onto the road to Woodford Halse.

4. Turn right, and right again into High Street. Turn left to pass in front of the church and then right into Castle Street. Take the path across the stream and turn right to the main road. Turn left and after about 130m right to a farm track. This is part of the Jurassic Way. Follow it for about 2km until it goes left to Church Charwelton and Fawsley Farm. Go straight ahead past Fawsley Farm buildings and the house. Cross minor road and continue forward. Keep in same direction until reaching a T-junction with the road leading past Fawsley Hall. Turn right passing Hall.

Short Walk rejoins

5. Immediately after the sign for the Knightley Way, the road loops round and the path for Everdon leaves the road on the left just behind a large oak tree. The path continues straight to Everdon, crossing one minor road. It is well signed and currently well maintained and affords many fine views. You enter Everdon at the top of the village. Walk down the street to the church.

Points of Interest

Everdon – its history can be traced back as far as AD944 and at the time of the Domesday Book (1086) it belonged to the Bishop of Bayeaux. The poet, Thomas Gray, whose uncle, the Rev. William Antrobus, was rector here from 1729-1744, frequently stayed in the village. Many believe that Everdon churchyard inspired his "Elegy" and not Stoke Poges. St Mary's Church is built partly of local iron-stone, which weathers badly; it has been extensively restored since the 1970s.

Preston Capes – was originally a village of thatch-roofed cottages, few of which remain today and formed part of the Fawsley estate until 1932. Saxon remains have been found near the manor house. Many interesting old buildings are still standing, including the Church of St Peter and St Paul, which dates from the 13th century.

Woodford Halse – was in the 19th century a major railway village, with the Great Central Line passing through. In the 1960s it was a victim of Dr Beeching, and reverted back to its rural life. It still has a Railway Club where enthusiasts meet to reminisce about the "golden days of steam".

Church Charwelton – is at the almost deserted end of Charwelton, the source of the River Cherwell, which joins the Thames at Oxford. Its church stands lonely and beautiful.

Fawsley Hall – was for centuries the home of the Knightley family. They cleared the land so it could be used for sheep farming, hence the lost village and lonely church.

50: Waterways and Woodlands

A circular walk taking in a substantial section of Salcey Forest (part of the mediaeval Rockingham Forest) and a short section of the Grand Union Canal, including the flight of locks at Stoke Bruerne and the south portal of the Blisworth tunnel.

Distance: Long Walk 23km (14 miles); Short Walk 9km (5½ miles) Nearly all within Salcey Forest

Duration: Long Walk 7 hours; Short Walk 2½ hours.

Maps required: OS Explorer 207 Newport Pagnell and Northampton South, OS Landranger 152 Northampton and Milton Keynes

Terrain: Forest, rolling agricultural land, canal towpath

Starting point: Car park and picnic site, north side of Salcey Forest on Wootton-Hanslope road (SP795517)

Refreshments: Public houses at Ashton, Stoke Bruerne and Roade; café at Stoke Bruerne (Old Chapel Tearooms) near car park

Bus/Train link: Northampton

The Route

N.B. Many of the forest bridleways are permissive and indicated as being for permit holders only – walkers do not need a permit.

1. Leave the car park at the north end by a short dog walking path at a notice "Start of Dog Loop. Links with Forest track in 200m". Turn left at junction with track (note post marked '2' bearing green, red and white stripes). At road, turn right for 75m and right again at a fingerpost (Bridleway to Piddington). The path goes in an almost straight line north-east through the forest for about 1.2km and is well-defined. (Note the commemorative mile-stone just inside the forest on your left.) Where the path emerges from the forest, follow the bridleway right along the outside edge to a T-junction.

2. Turn sharp right along an open track going south-east through the forest for almost 3km. Ignore all turnings. On reaching the Eakley Lanes/Hartwell road, continue ahead through a small car park. Follow a wide track signed as The Midshires Way, Woodpecker Trail and, later, Swan's Way. When the main track bears right at a Permit Holders Only sign, continue ahead for a few metres to a Y-junction.

Long Walk

3. Continue ahead on path. In a few metres fork right at a 'No Riding Please'

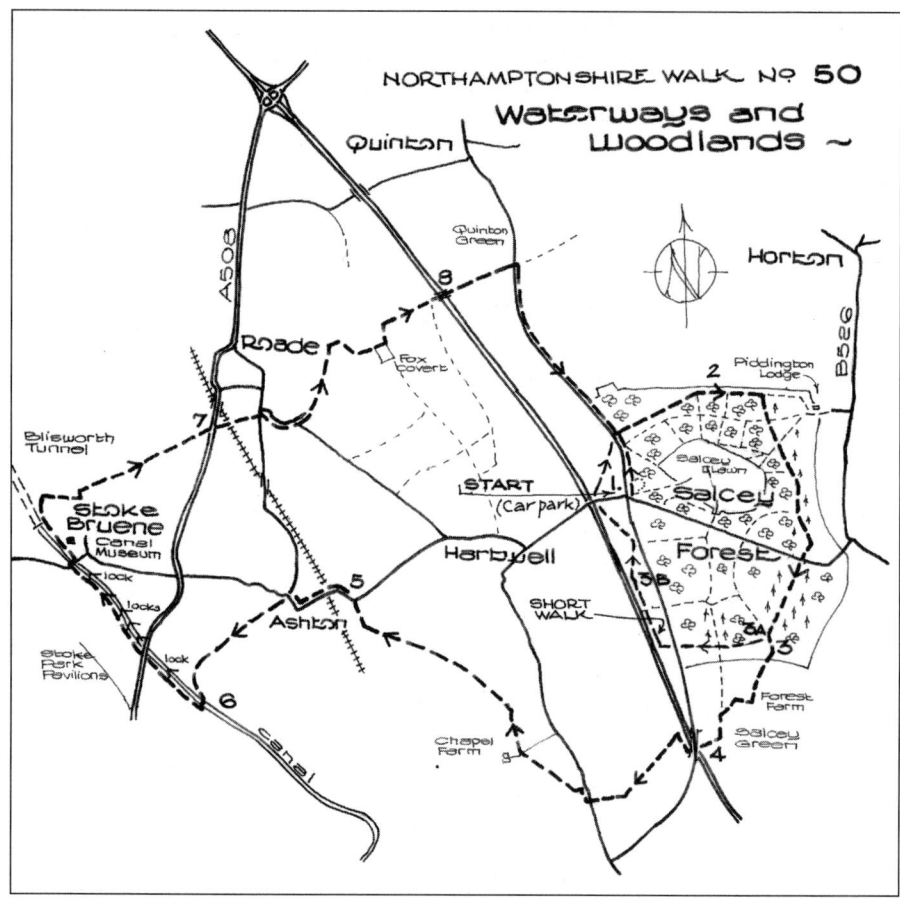

notice and straight out of the forest and across a large field to cross a foot-bridge over a ditch. Turn right along hedge towards Forest Farm. Bear left, keeping farm buildings to your right and go straight ahead along an avenue of trees on a good track. When the avenue veers right, veer left to pass farm buildings and a farmhouse to the right. Follow ranch fencing and turn sharp right when fencing does the same. Follow this to join road.

Short Walk

3a. Bear right and in a few metres, veer left to follow another fairly narrow and sometimes muddy 'Woodpecker Trail', clearly marked. This is quite a tortu-ous route, crossing numerous plank footbridges over streams through the forest; early on, there is a set of stepping-stones. In about 800m, at a cross-road of tracks, turn sharp left (Woodpecker Trail turns right) and soon left again to follow a public bridleway. When the bridleway veers left out of the forest, continue ahead inside forest and just before fencing at a road, take a right track. At a T-junction, turn sharp left. Continue ahead and cross a road (Quinton/Hanslope road) on a public footpath. Follow path until you can see (and hear!) the M1 in front of you on an embankment.

3b. Turn right along a crumbling tarmac track and at a T-junction bear left between old wooden gate posts. Continue forward along a good track and pass between two concrete blocks and a gate to join the Hartwell/Eakley Lanes road just east of a bridge over the M1. Turn right along the road and in 50m left at a metal gate with the sign "Walkers are welcome in this wood". Follow good path as it veers slightly left and soon sharply right to end on the Quinton/Hanslope road exactly opposite the dog walking route to the parking area at the end of the walk.

Long Walk

4. Turn left, cross bridge over the M1 and immediately right to follow bridleway. This hugs the west side of the motorway for one field and, at the first hedgerow joining from the left, turn left along it. Keep the hedge on your right, towards Roselane Farm. Shortly the path follows the right side of the same hedge (good views to the north); continue forward to join the Hartwell/Hanslope road. Turn right along it for 150m and when the road bends right, turn left at bridleway sign through a large metal gate. Follow the left side of the hedge, round a corner and then pass through a gap in the first hedge line. Walk straight ahead across the field towards a clump of conifers. Turn right along a metalled track (to Chapel Farm) and continue forward for a short way until it bears right. Go through metal bridle gate in fence on left and continue in same direction to cross a stream and pass through another bridle gate and then three metal field gates. Leave bridleway after third gate and take an undefined path bearing slightly left across a large open field, aiming for a lone tree. Go through gate to the left of the tree, on to a track then almost immediately turn left into the next field. Continue in same direction as before to cross a field to a gap in the wide hedge ahead. Go ahead with a hedge on the left crossing a stream via a culvert to a gap with a footbridge in the roadside hedge.

5. Cross the road into the next field and veer slightly right towards the right-hand side of a tree and cross a stile. Bear left through two small grass fields to a stile on left side of a field gate. Turn left along road and walk under railway bridge. Shortly, turn right into Cooks Close, at the end of which is a short metalled path to the road. Go ahead towards the Old Crown Inn. Beyond the inn, turn left into Stoke Road and in about 200m, at the Gate House, take a path between houses on your left. Veer slightly right to cross two paddocks to a gate in the left corner of the second. Proceed through two gates and walk ahead to a gate then a stile into the stable yard keeping close to the fence an your right. Cross the access drive to a metal gate and pass through aiming ahead to a bank of trees. Cross stile, go through the tree belt, cross the track then through a gap into a field and aim to the left of a derelict brick building in the valley. Veer right behind the building to a brook and a hedge. Turn left and continue ahead along field edge and go through small wooded area. Cross stile and continue to follow brook/hedge to a stile into a meadow. Walk along edge of meadow keeping brook to right, then cross another stile onto a short track to the Grand Union Canal.

6.   Turn right along canal and cross bridge to the other side at Bottom Lock No.20. Follow towpath (west bank), ascending locks to reach Stoke Bruerne in about 800m. Recross the canal immediately beyond the twin-arch stone bridge and follow towpath (now east side) towards the south portal of the Blisworth tunnel. The towpath climbs steadily from the canal through a wooded area. Look for a flight of wooden steps to right of towpath. Go up steps and follow path alongside hedge, over a stile and then through a kissing gate. After gate go left over stile. Pass between the remains of a former railway bridge then bear right up through rough grazing to a stile in left corner. Cross field aiming for a tree at left end of hedge. Go through gap and follow line of trees with ditch to the left. Go through another gap and cross a field aiming for large white disc in hedge adjacent to stile. Cross stile and veer left to poplar trees in valley. Cross footbridge and stile, then go right inside fence. Follow fence until you see a small waymark, then veering left across corner of school playing field, join the A508 over a stile in hedge.

7.   Turn left towards Roade. In a short distance, cross road at the garage (note footpath sign on road edge). Now follow excellent path through Chaplins Lorry Park, keeping hedge on your left. Cross railway bridge, then through a factory area to a gravel path to the road. Turn left, then right at an island (Memorial Green) towards Hartwell. When road turns right, keep ahead on Bretts Lane. Ignore path to left and continue along wide bridleway across middle of field at hedgerow. Veer left to follow right side of hedge and ditch. At the point where the bridleway enters a wide track (fingerpost in hedge) turn right and follow the hedge on the left at second hedgerow. Cross stile into corner of spinney (Fox Covert), then follow path to a metal gate at other side (joining Midshires Way). Turn left and immediately through another metal gate and follow hedge boundary on your right. Then turn sharp right through another metal gate to follow edge of field with thick hedge on right. Go through gap/gate and keep ahead to bridlegates. Turn left after second gate and pass through another handgate near the radio mast to cross the M1 motorway by a bridge.

8.   Follow granite chippings track to Quinton Green Farm. Pass through two gates and, in a few metres, join the Quinton/Hanslope road. Turn right, it is 2km back to the car park in Salcey Forest. Take great care as this can be a very busy road. It is possible to shorten the road walk slightly by turning left on to the dog walking route through the forest.

Points of Interest

Salcey Forest – Chapel Farm is a remnant of the mediaeval village of Hartwell, a hamlet in a clearing of the ancient Salcey Forest. The Norman church 1½ miles south of the village was sadly demolished in 1851. A fine Norman arcade from the old church as incorporated into its successor, dedicated to St John the Baptist.

Roade – a small village whose church, St Mary's, was built in 1830 but from the date on a stone – 1619 – it would seem that materials from an older building were utilised. The manor house, now Hyde Farm, has a 15th-century circular dovecote.

Grand Union Canal – Engineered by William Jessop, The Grand Junction Canal connected the River Thames at Brentford with the Oxford Canal at Braunston thus giving a much shorter route to Birmingham. The original distance had been 269½ miles, this was reduced as more canals opened and was finally reduced to 138½ miles when the Grand Junction was completed in 1805. In 1894, it acquired The Leicester & Northampton Canal ant the old Union Canal (now known as the Leicester Section). In 1929, it amalgamated with three other canal companies to form the Grand Union Canal system of over 270 miles.

Stoke Bruerne – one of the most famous canal villages on the British system. A flight of seven locks climbs from the River Tove. The main street in the village houses on one side the British Waterways Museum, open throughout the year, and on the other side, the Boat Inn.

Bisworth Tunnel – The tunnel is 3056 yards long. Started in 1796 but because of engineering problems work was abandoned on the first tunnel and another was dug. The tunnel was not opened until 1805. Meanwhile in 1797 a toll-road was built over the hill and was replaced in 1800 by a double-track horse tramroad. The present footpath follows the line of this tramroad.

ABOUT THE RAMBLERS

The Ramblers' Association helps you make the most of walking and your local environment. A registered charity, the Ramblers' Association was founded in 1935 to protect rights of way, encourage walking, to campaign for public access to open country and to defend the beauty of the countryside.

The Ramblers' Association is an active and effective organisation. We make ourselves heard at all levels, from parish council to national government – and the more people add their voice to ours, the better for the countryside and everyone who loves it.

The heart of our mission is to enable everyone to discover and enjoy the beauty of their local environment on foot, whilst protecting it for future generations. By joining the Ramblers, you help turn that mission into action – and enjoy yourself while you do so. It's inexpensive to join and is a great way to make new friends, get fit and discover your local surroundings.

As a member, you'll also have the opportunity to involve yourself with practical conservation activities in your area. Whether you're a serious hiker pushing yourself to the limit, an occasional walker blowing away the cobwebs, or you simply want to support the leading charity working to encourage walking and protect the countryside ...the Ramblers' Association is for you.

For further information please contact:

The Ramblers' Association
2nd Floor, Camelford House
87-90 Albert Embankment
London SE1 7TW

Telephone: 020 7339 8500; Fax: 020 7339 8501

Visit the Ramblers' website at www.ramblers.org.uk

Or email at ramblers@london.ramblers.org.uk

If, when using this book, you find any public rights of way obstructed or unusable, please report them both to the Ramblers and to the local authority in which the right of way is situated – see contact information for each section in this book. When phoning, ask for the Rights of Way Section – usually in the highways department. If possible try to indicate exactly where the obstruction is located and when it was encountered.